Constellations of Value

edited by

Christoph Jedan

Theorizing the Postsecular

International Studies in Religion, Politics and Society

edited by

Christoph Jedan, Arie Molendijk
and Justin Beaumont

Volume 1

LIT

Constellations of Value

European Perspectives on the Intersections of Religion, Politics and Society

edited by

Christoph Jedan

LIT

Gedruckt auf alterungsbeständigem Werkdruckpapier entsprechend
ANSI Z3948 DIN ISO 9706

Bibliographic information published by the Deutsche Nationalbibliothek
The Deutsche Nationalbibliothek lists this publication in the Deutsche Nationalbibliografie; detailed bibliographic data are available in the Internet at http://dnb.d-nb.de.

ISBN 978-3-643-90083-8

A catalogue record for this book is available from the British Library

Klosbachstr. 107
CH-8032 Zürich
Tel. +41 (0) 44-251 75 05
Fax +41 (0) 44-251 75 06
E-Mail: zuerich@lit-verlag.ch
http://www.lit-verlag.ch

LIT VERLAG Dr. W. Hopf
Berlin 2013
Fresnostr. 2
D-48159 Münster
Tel. +49 (0) 2 51-62 03 20
Fax +49 (0) 2 51-23 19 72
E-Mail: lit@lit-verlag.de
http://www.lit-verlag.de

Distribution:
In Germany: LIT Verlag Fresnostr. 2, D-48159 Münster
Tel. +49 (0) 2 51-620 32 22, Fax +49 (0) 2 51-922 60 99, E-mail: vertrieb@lit-verlag.de
In Austria: Medienlogistik Pichler-ÖBZ, e-mail: mlo@medien-logistik.at
In Switzerland: B + M Buch- und Medienvertrieb, e-mail: order@buch-medien.ch
In the UK: Global Book Marketing, e-mail: mo@centralbooks.com
In North America: International Specialized Book Services, e-mail: orders@isbs.com

CONTENTS

FOREWORD BY THE SERIES EDITORS

In recent years, the concept of the postsecular has received increasing attention. At its heart is the realization that sweeping statements about a unilateral secularization process, with their tendency to make religion more and more irrelevant to modern societies, have proved to be mistaken. Instead, we find a renewed confidence among religious communities and an increasing acceptance that they have an important role to play in the public domain. Nevertheless, to our minds, this finding does not call for sweeping delegitimizations of the modern world, such as have been pronounced in the theological context of a 'Radical Orthodoxy'.

What is needed instead is careful multidisciplinary scholarship to highlight the *ambiguities of modernity*. We live at a time when the contributions made by faith-based organizations to the functioning of society are gratefully acknowledged, especially where the modern welfare state's resources are being restructured and, it is claimed, rationalized. At the same time, many theorists welcome the contemporary role of religion in formulating and maintaining values that are fundamental to Western society. Indeed, we live at a time in which the contribution to public debate made from a religious perspective is increasingly accepted as legitimate. And all of this is happening *within* Western democracies as we have come to know them, and it is happening within a public culture that functions predominantly along non-religious lines. Among the processes of change, the signs of a religious revival have been eyed with suspicion by scholars and journalists looking to defend a secularist disjunction between religion and the public domain.

All in all, the concept of the postsecular offers a challenging focal concept to organize some of the best research into the role of religion in the public domain in contemporary society.

The series *Theorizing the Postsecular* aims to be the principal forum for scholars who want to analyse, refine, or even question, the concept of the postsecular. It aspires to encourage cross-disciplinary engagement by bringing into contact scholarship based on the conceptual and historical methods of the humanities (e.g. history, philosophy, religious studies and theology) and scholarship employing the methods of social science (e.g. sociology and urban studies). As series editors, we look forward to contributions that discuss the role of religion in contemporary society as well as tracing the historical antecedents of contemporary debates about the role of religion in the public domain—contributions asking, for instance, in what ways the paradigm of justificatory liberalism has been challenged in order to make space in public life for religion. We also look forward to empirical, conceptual and discourse analyses of the diverse manifestations of religion and religious organizations in the public domain, not only among European democracies but also beyond the continent of Europe.

C. Jedan / A.L. Molendijk / J. Beaumont (Groningen)

ACKNOWLEDGEMENTS

The present volume is the result of a collaboration that began several years ago. Soon after I began working as a lecturer in ethics at Groningen in the autumn of 2003, I started to prepare an application for an Erasmus Intensive Programme on the intersection of religion and politics in Europe. On this occasion, as on many others, I profited immensely from the generous help of Patrick Vandermeersch and his student assistant Peter Broekema.

It soon became clear to us that such an initiative should not only include the 'old' member states of the European Union, but that it ought to reach out to embrace perspectives from Poland and Turkey as well. In the event, I was able to submit the application with the cooperation of the theological faculties of Uludag University Bursa, the Catholic University of Leuven, the Catholic University of Lublin, Philipp University of Marburg, the Faculty of Protestant Theology in Montpellier, Uppsala University, and the Aristotle University of Thessaloniki. I want to express my thanks to the faculty staff who made the application possible.

The European Commission funded the Intensive Programme under the title 'The Janus Faces of Religion: A European Perspective on the Religion-State Relationship' (with the acronym Jafare) for two years (29015-IC-1-2003-1-NL-ERASMUS-IPUC-2 and 29015-IC-2-2004-1-NL-ERASMUS-IPUC-2). Many thanks are due to the referees and staff of the Commission for their cooperation and support. The funding enabled us to hold two summer schools, in Montpellier (2005) and in Groningen (2006).

The problems posed by the interaction of religious and secular values have remained high on the political and academic agenda since then. Indeed, they are of such a scale that it is more urgent than ever to take different perspectives into account. It was simply a logical step to ask colleagues from the Jafare project to contribute to this volume, not to re-iterate the papers that they gave a few years ago, but rather to articulate their characteristically different perspectives in order to inform the present debate. And so this volume includes perspectives from Northern as well as from Southern Europe, from theology as well as from political theory, in discussions of literature and phenomena ranging from the Old Testament to Swedish Environmentalism and the recent resurgence of religion regularly referred to as 'the postsecular'.

A book representing such different perspectives will, I hope, be a promising inauguration of a new series aiming to investigate the new visibility of religion in the public domain.

I end with my thanks to the contributors to this volume and to Michael Rice for anglicizing our very different takes on the lingua franca of our times.

Without their generous support, this whole initiative would have been impossible.

Christoph Jedan
Groningen, September 2012

LIST OF CONTRIBUTORS

Gerlinde Baumann is Adjunct Professor of Old Testament Studies in the Faculty of Protestant Theology at Philipps-University Marburg, and she also works as a freelance author and translator of theological books (www.gerlinde-baumann.de). She received her Ph.D. from the Heidelberg Faculty of Protestant Theology (1997) and her Habilitation from Philipps-University Marburg (2004). Her research has focused on the Wisdom Figure in biblical wisdom literature and on the topic of divine violence in the Old Testament. She is currently working on questions of Old Testament hermeneutics and on New Testament interpretations of Jesus's death. Her publications include *Gottesbilder der Gewalt im Alten Testament verstehen*, Darmstadt 2006 (also published in Portuguese in São Paulo/Brazil); and *Fundament des Glaubens oder Kulturdenkmal? Vom Umgang mit der Bibel heute*, Leipzig 2007. She edited (with Elisabeth Hartlieb) *Ewiges Leben. Hoffnung über den Tod hinaus*, Freiburg 2010; and (with Maria Häusl, Dirk Human and Susanne Gillmayr-Bucher) *Zugänge zum Fremden. Methodisch-hermeneutische Perspektiven zu einem biblischen Thema*, Frankfurt/M. 2012.

Marc Boss is University Lecturer in Systematic Theology and Philosophy in the Faculty of Protestant Theology at Montpellier. He received his doctorate in theology from the University of Laval, with a thesis on *Le principe de l'autonomie chez Paul Tillich: ses sources kantiennes et postkantiennes* (The Principle of Autonomy in Paul Tillich). He is the editor of many books, including (in collaboration with G. Émery et P. Gisel) *Postlibéralisme? La théologie de George Lindbeck et sa réception*, Geneva, 2004; and (with D. Lax et J. Richard) *Éthique sociale et socialisme religieux*, Münster 2005.

Carl Reinhold Bråkenhielm received his doctorate in theology at the University of Lund with a dissertation on *How Philosophy Shapes Theories of Religion,* Lund 1975. Since 1990 he has been Professor for the Empirical Study of Worldviews in the Faculty of Theology at Uppsala University. His publications include *Problems of Religious Experience*; Uppsala 1985 and *Forgiveness*, Minneapolis 1993. He has edited many books on the empirical study of worldviews, including *Världsbild och mening. En empirisk studie av livsåskådningar i dagens Sverige* (Worldview and meaning: an empirical study of worldviews in Sweden today), Nora 2001.

Evert-Jan Brouwer has an MA degree in political philosophy. He has specialised in minority rights issues. From 1998 to 2007 he was political advisor to the Reformed Political Party (Staatkundig Gereformeerde Partij, SGP) in the Dutch House of Representatives. For the SGP he has published extensively on religion and politics, the integration of minorities, the political aspects of Islam and other topics. He is currently Advocacy Coordinator for Woord en Daad, a Protestant foundation which supports programmes for sustainable development in Asia, Africa, Latin America and the Caribbean.

Elian Cuvillier is Professor of New Testament studies in the Faculty of Protestant Theology in Montpellier. He obtained his Ph.D. from the Montpellier Faculty of Protestant Theology (1993) and his Habilitation from the University of Strasburg (1999). His career began with research into the Gospel of St Mark and the Book of Revelation. Currently, he is working on a commentary on the Gospel of St Matthew and on the Epistle of James. He is also interested in biblical anthropology and psychoanalysis. His publications include *Divine violence. Approche exégétique et anthropologique*, Paris 2011 (with Jean-Daniel Causse and André Wénin); *De Jésus à Jean de Patmos: l'annonce de l'Évangile dans le Nouveau Testament*, Lyon 2010 (with Emmanulle Steffek); *Mythes grecs, mythes bibliques. L'humain face à ses dieux*, Paris 2007 (edited with Jean-Daniel Causse); *Naissance et enfance d'un Dieu. Jésus Christ dans l'Evangile de Matthieu*, Paris 2005; and *L'Évangile de Marc. Traduction et lecture*, Paris/Genève 2002.

Christoph Jedan is Associate Professor of Ethics in the Faculty of Theology and Religious Studies at the University of Groningen. He received his Ph.D. in philosophy at the University of Bonn (1999) and was awarded a Habilitation at the Humboldt University of Berlin (2006). His research interests focus on ancient practical philosophy and the intersections of religion and contemporary practical philosophy. His publications include *Willensfreiheit bei Aristoteles?*, Göttingen 2000; *Modalities by Perspective: Aristotle, the Stoics and a Modern Reconstruction* (2002, with N. Strobach); *Stoic Virtues: Chrysippus and the Religious Character of Stoic Ethics* (2009); *Exploring the Postsecular: The Religious, the Political and the Urban* (2010, co-editor, with A.L. Molendijk and J. Beaumont); and *Philosophische Anthropologie in der Antike* (2010, co-editor, with L. Jansen).

Kasim Küçükalp is Professor of History of Philosophy in Uludag University Faculty of Theology at Bursa (Turkey). He obtained his Ph.D. from the Uludag University Institute of Social Sciences (2008). His research career commenced with doctoral research on Nietzsche's influence upon postmodern philosophy. In his academic career he has also studied Husserlian phenomenology and post-structuralist and postmodern philosophies, particularly Heidegger's critiques of the tradition of Western metaphysics, Derridean deconstruction, Levinas' ethical philosophy and Deleuze's philosophy of difference. His publications include: *Nietzsche and Postmodernizm* (Nietzsche and Postmodernism),

Istanbul 2003; *Husserl*, Istanbul 2006; *Batı Metafiziğinin Dekonstrüksiyonu: Heidegger ve Derrida* (The Deconstruction of Western Metaphysics: Heidegger and Derrida), İstanbul 2008; and (with Ahmet Cevizci) *Batı Düşüncesi* (Western Thought), İstanbul 2009.

Paul Lucardie obtained his PhD at Queen's University (Kingston, Canada). After 1979 he was Researcher in the Documentation Centre on Dutch Political Parties (DNPP) at the University of Groningen. Although he has been officially retired since 2012, he continues to work part-time on a voluntary basis. His research interests focus on political ideologies and new parties in the Netherlands, Canada and Germany. On these topics he has published articles in *Party Politics*, the *European Journal of Political Research*, *Acta Politica* and the *American Review of Canadian Studies*, as well as chapters in several edited volumes. In 2011, he and Gerrit Voerman published *Populisten in de polder*, a history of populism in the Netherlands.

Patrick Vandermeersch is Professor Emeritus of the Psychology of Religion in the Faculty of Theology and Religious Studies at the University of Groningen. In 1972 he received his Ph.D. at the University of Leuven with a thesis on the unconscious in the work of Freud and Jung, and he was trained in psychoanalysis at the Belgian School for Psychoanalysis. He has published extensively on the intersection of psychology of religion, psychoanalysis and ethics. His publications include: *Het gekke verlangen: psychotherapie en ethiek*, Antwerp/Nijmegen 1978; *Ethiek tussen wetenschap en ideologie*, Leuven 1987; *Passie en beschouwing: de christelijke invloed op het westerse mensbeeld*; *La chair de la Passion. Une histoire de foi: la flagellation*, Paris 2002; and (with Herman Westerink) *Godsdienstpsychologie in cultuurhistorisch perspectief*, Amsterdam 2007.

Erin K. Wilson is the Director of the Centre for Religion, Conflict and the Public Domain, in the Faculty of Theology and Religious Studies at the University of Groningen. She previously worked at the Globalism Research Centre, RMIT University, Melbourne, Australia, and she received her PhD from the University of Queensland in 2008. Her research focuses on the relationship of religion with various dimensions of politics and public life, including globalization, political ideologies, migration, global justice, human rights and the post-secular turn. Her first book, *After Secularism: Rethinking Religion in Global Politics*, was published by Palgrave Macmillan in 2012.

Henk E.S. Woldring studied sociology and philosophy at Groningen, Amsterdam and Frankfurt. He received his Ph.D. from the Free University in Amsterdam. He has been a Professor of Political Philosophy at the Free University (1986-2008) and a member of the First Chamber (Senate) of the

Netherlands Parliament (1999-2007). He is the author of several books, including *Karl Mannheim. The Development of his Thought.*

Jean-Francois Zorn is Professor Emeritus of the History of (contemporary) Christianity in the Faculty of Protestant Theology at Montpellier. He is a specialist in mission studies and has published extensively in this field. His publications include *La missiologie. Émergence d'une discipline théologique*, Geneva 2004; and Le grand siècle d'une mission protestante: La Mission de Paris de 1822 à 1914, new, revised and augmented edition, Paris 2012. He has also edited many volumes on mission studies, including (in collaboration with Jan Borm et Bernard Cottret) *Convertir/Se convertir. Regards croisés sur l'histoire des missions chrétiennes*, Paris 2006 and (with Salvador Eyezo'o) *Concurrences en mission. Propagandes, conflits, coexistences (XVIe-XXIe siècle)*, Paris 2012.

OVERCOMING THE DIVIDE BETWEEN RELIGIOUS AND SECULAR VALUES: INTRODUCTORY ESSAY

Christoph Jedan

The present volume, entitled 'Constellations of Value', inaugurates a new series: 'Theorizing the Postsecular: International Studies in Religion, Politics, and Society'. In contemporary scholarship the notion of the postsecular is frequently used to indicate a rapprochement between religious and non-religious modes of thinking. In this vein, I attempt to show how much of the prior theorizing about a clash between religious and secular values proves to be misguided and how a more fruitful description of the interaction between religious and secular values can be conceptualized. I conclude by indicating how the contributions to this volume advance scholarly debate on the postsecular.

1. Beyond the Religious-Secular Divide

My attempt to overcome the exaggerated opposition of religious and secular values begins with a discussion of definitions. I argue that a closer look at the supposed meanings of 'secular values' versus 'religious values' reveals that there is no convincing way of separating them. I take my cue from *The New Shorter Oxford English Dictionary*, which defines 'values' (in the sense relevant to our enquiry) as follows: values are 'the principles or moral standards of a person or social group; the generally accepted or personally held judgement of what is valuable and important in life'. As far as it goes, the definition appears unproblematic: its emphasis on individual or collective moral standards and judgements of what is important in life is consistent with the public discourse on values.[1]

We seem more or less agreed as to what 'values' are. The problems begin once we attempt to characterize 'religious values', and what 'religious values' might be in opposition to 'secular values'. I propose to begin unravelling this problem from a definition of religious values, which might be defined as 'values that are (at least in part) dependent on religious texts, beliefs or traditions'. I am fully aware that I am opening a can of worms with this proposed definition, since it is irremediably vague in crucial respects. Scholars of religion will focus

[1] In the Netherlands, for instance, the past decade has seen a frequent invocation of 'norms and values', precisely in a time when such moral standards and shared values have become more and more problematic and subject to pressure from a far-reaching economization of public life.

primarily on the notion of religion and point out the breadth of the cultural phenomena we can call religious. It is important to realize that it does not matter so much which particular *strategy* one adopts in defining religion. The larger trend in scholarly definitions of religion points in the direction of inclusive definitions covering a broad range of phenomena. Thus, it will make no difference whether one offers definitions of religion that focus on the *function of religion* in the life of believers or in society at large; or, alternatively, whether one offers definitions in terms of the *contents of religious beliefs*. Take the following two examples of 'function definitions'. In one, Clifford Geertz (1993: 90) famously defined religion as:

> (1) a system of symbols which acts to (2) establish powerful, pervasive, and long-lasting moods and motivations in men by (3) formulating conceptions of a general order of existence and (4) clothing these conceptions with such an aura of factuality that (5) the moods and motivations seem uniquely realistic.

In the other, John Milton Yinger defined religion as:

> A system of beliefs and practices by means of which a group of people struggles with the (...) ultimate problems of human life. It expresses their refusal to capitulate to death, to give up in the face of frustration, to allow hostility to tear apart their human aspirations. (quoted in Clack and Clack 1998: 4)

Compare those with content-focused definitions of religion. A well-known definition was proposed by William James (2008: 31): 'the feelings, acts, and experiences of individual men in their solitude, so far as they apprehend themselves to stand in relation to whatever they may consider the divine'. Note that James's idea of whatever human beings may 'consider the divine' is quite broad, embracing 'concrete deities' (2008: 34) as well as other things divine. In effect, James's idea of the divine may be congruent with what Paul Tillich (1951) famously referred to as the Ultimate Reality at which, as an attitude of 'ultimate concern', religious faith is directed. Tillich's characterization stands, directly or indirectly, behind many of the attempts at defining religion that we find in today's philosophy of religion. See, for instance, the following definition in a standard textbook:

> [R]eligion is constituted by a set of beliefs, actions, and experiences, both personal and corporate, organized around a concept of an Ultimate Reality (Peterson et al. 2003: 7).

There are two ways of dealing with such a variety of definitions. We can either view them microscopically and wonder about differences of nuance between them, and whether or not they really denote the same concept. Instead, I propose that we look at the overall trend in these definitions, a trend covering a plurality of phenomena labelled 'religion'. All of the definitions seem to allow for, say, Roman Catholicism, different currents of Islam as well as esotericism and the 'new Spirituality' of today; they might also allow for the house shrines that have recently become fashionable. The definitions are thus set apart from any preconceived, or parochial, idea of what religion is 'about'. We find a sublime and deservedly famous caricature of the parochial idea in Henry Fielding's (1749) novel *Tom Jones*. The Reverend Mr Thwackum remarks: 'When I mention religion I mean the Christian religion; and not only the Christian religion, but the Protestant religion; and not only the Protestant religion, but the Church of England'.[2] Beverley and Brian Clack (1998: 1) refer to this idea as the 'Parson Thwackum Fallacy', and in what follows I shall employ this label.

It is probably not unfair to state that the roles are now reversed. Where to Fielding's satirical eye this eighteenth-century parson embodied a ridiculous parochialism as far as religion is concerned, we now see a similar parochialism in the general public. There are preconceived ideas about religion; one knows already, precisely and in advance, what religion is, pointing (at best) to some atypical set of phenomena, or to an outright caricature. Today's representation of Islam in the political debate in the Netherlands provides a good example of this, as well as the representation in one secularist outlook after another of religion as an opponent.[3] The most significant area of contention lies not within the scholarly field but rather in the clash between scholarly work on religion on the one hand, and beliefs about religion maintained by the general public on the other.

A similar clash is observable when we turn to the notion of dependency in the definition. What does it mean for a value to depend on religious texts, beliefs or traditions? Does it mean that a statement of the values in question will contain explicit references to religious texts, beliefs or traditions? Religious values frequently seem to be understood in this vein, in particularly whenever religion is criticized. Religious values are then identified with value-statements in which a holy text or tradition is invoked directly, often to demand behaviour at odds with the norms embraced by the secular majority. The endorsement of ritual slaughter or male circumcision, for instance, is considered to work simply along the lines of 'my holy text (or my tradition) commands it'.

However, religion often plays a less visible role in value judgements, when religion is invoked, as it were, remotely. Such 'remote invocations' of religion include situations when, if we wish to give a more complete account of why we affirm certain values, we will *at some point* come up with a story in which religious texts, beliefs or traditions are mentioned. In our present context, it is significant that in the dominant public discourse such 'remote invocations' of religion are not taken very seriously. A good example are contributions by

---

[2] Quoted by Clack and Clack (1998:1).

[3] See, e.g., Cliteur (2010a; 2010b).

Dutch academics of a type frequently encountered at conferences. They assert first that they are neither religious believers nor pursuing a research interest in religion, and thereafter they come up with stories about how some of their value judgements—concerning, for instance, punctuality—are attributed by foreign friends or partners to Dutch Calvinism. All this is told with a certain good-humoured air of amusement, to convey how much it is innocent folklore, to underpin a value judgement that could probably also be justified without it.

In the dominant public discourse, religion is thus caught between two (mis)representations. Either it contributes to public debates with value statements containing direct ('fundamentalist') references to religious texts, beliefs or traditions; or, alternatively, it contributes with remote invocations which are not taken seriously—in fact, they are typically seen as harmless folklore. The possibility, however, that such remote invocations deal with something central to the lives of many citizens and something that believers see as resisting prevailing modes of secular thought, does not surface in the dominant public discourse. This possibility, however, is central working ground for those scholars in the field of religion who study the intersections of religion and culture. Here again we find a clash, not among scholars of religion but between scholars of religion and the dominant public representations of religion.

How could we overcome the opposition between religious and that underpins many of our present difficulties? One feasible strategy might include an analysis of prevalent concepts of the secular.[4] Another such strategy might focus on an evaluation of stories aiming to explain why religion ought to be kept out of the public domain.[5] However, in this essay I want to explore a different strategy. I propose to trace key ideas that have led to today's suspicion of religious values. In the European context, these suspicions have built up in response to Christianity. Over more than seven hundred years we have found such suspicions expressed in attacks—often vitriolic—upon Christian values.

A good starting point for a *tour de force* of such attacks is *trecento* Florence, with Boccaccio's *Decameron*. The *Decameron* is set against the background of a Black Death epidemic in Florence in 1348. Boccaccio notes that all sorts of precautions proved to be futile. He notes that prayers proved to be in vain and he dwells on the destructive forces of the Black Death, which corrupted every aspect of social harmony and human allegiance. In this situation, religion proved ineffective: it did not prevent the outbreak; it did not protect the faithful; and it could not prevent the complete disintegration of social structure. Boccaccio notes the widespread disillusion with religion, e.g. by referring repeatedly to the inefficacy of prayer and devotion.[6] In this situation a group of young people decides, like so many others, to leave Florence and weather the

---

[4] See Lübbe 2003.

[5] See Cavanaugh 1999 and Wilson's contribution to this volume.

[6] 1994: 10: *Ed in quella non valendo alcun senno né umano provvedimento (...) n'e ancora umili supplicazioni non una volta ma molte ed in processioni ordinate ed in altre guise a Dio fatte dalle divote persone.*

storm on a country estate on the hill of Fiesole, just outside the city. Once there, they occupy themselves by telling stories, choosing a different theme for each day's topic. The story I shall analyse here is the first story of the third day, which tells of people who 'by dint of their own efforts have achieved an object they greatly desired, or recovered a thing previously lost'.[7] The story is framed by a general comment to the effect that it would be foolish to believe that either secular occupation or entry into a religious order could ever change human nature.

The story that Boccaccio tells to underscore this message goes as follows: Masetto, a young farm labourer from Lamporecchio meets a fellow Lamporecchian who has just quit his job as gardener in a small convent, where the young nuns require too much work for too little pay. This information arouses sexual desire in Masetto. In order to gain employment in the convent in spite of his personal physical attractiveness, he pretends to be deaf and dumb. He is taken on as a gardener, and is able to provoke sexual desire among the nuns. After a while, his erotic services are in so much demand that an exhausted Masetto thinks it wise to 'regain' his speech. He is allowed to stay on, fathering 'many a young monk' in the course of time, and he eventually returns to his native Lamporecchio a wealthy man. There he tells everyone who will hear him that 'Christ treats thus whoever cuckolds him'.[8]

This short story repeatedly brings home Boccaccio's general lesson. Masetto's sexual desire violates sacred space, only to find out that the sacred space shelters the same human drives that he himself is driven by. The nuns want to experience 'what sort of beast man is' (*provare che bestia fosse l'uomo* [1994: 190]). One nun brushes aside any concern about the vow of virginity: 'So many promises are made to God all the while without being kept; if we have promised virginity to God, there will be someone else to keep the promise' (1994: 189). Finally, as Masetto's success demonstrates, religion is ineffective at either explaining or ordering the distribution of worldly rewards.

Religious values and religious observance, in short, are depicted as a façade, concealing a uniform human nature in which desires that are repressed or denied by Christianity are the motivating force. Religion is thus ineffective at defining a space within which a different moral reality might prevail.

The next line of attack on Christian values that I want to examine is directed at the political implications of Christian values. Are Christian values dangerous once they structure political reality? The most powerful exponent of this critique also comes from Tuscany: he is Niccolò Machiavelli (1469–1527). The exact relationship between his two major works, *The Prince* and the *Discourses on Livy*, is the subject of scholarly debate but this need not concern us here, since both works offer the same assessment of the political dangers of Christian values. In *The Prince*, Machiavelli famously recommends that a ruler who

[7] 1994: 181. The English version above (unlike the translation of other passages) follows MacWilliam's translation.

[8] 1994: 192: *così tratava Cristo chi gli poneva le corna sopra il cappello.*

wants to maintain his position, will have to learn 'to be able not to be good' (*imparare a potere essere non buono*: XV 6 [1995: 103]), where, as the rest of the chapter shows, the standard of goodness is defined by Christian values. Machiavelli cautions against the danger of trying to realize Christian values in the political realm. While *The Prince* analyses codes of conduct for a political ruler, the *Discourses* focus on the sustainability of a republican political order and thus enquire into the virtues necessary for the citizenry under such a regime. In the latter work, the warning against the adoption of Christian values receives more extensive treatment. Here is a central passage (II 2):

> Our religion has glorified humble and contemplative men, rather than men of action. It has assigned, as man's highest good, humility, abnegation, and contempt for mundane things, whereas the other identified it with magnanimity, bodily strength, and everything else that conduces to make men very bold. And, if our religion demands that in you there be strength, what it asks for is strength to suffer rather than strength to do bold things.
> This pattern of life, therefore, appears to have made the world weak, and to have handed it over as a prey to the wicked, who run it successfully and securely since they are well aware that the generality of men, with paradise for their goal, consider how best to bear, rather than how best to avenge, their injuries. But though it looks as if the world were become effeminate and as if heaven were powerless, this undoubtedly is due rather to the pusillanimity of those who have interpreted our religion in terms of *laissez faire*, not in terms of *virtù*. For, had they borne in mind that religion permits us to exalt and defend the fatherland, they would have seen that it also wishes us to love and honour it, and to train ourselves to be such that we may defend it.
> This kind of education, then, and these grave misinterpretations account for the fact that we see in the world fewer republics than there used to be of old, and that, consequently, in peoples we do not find the same love of liberty as there then was. (2003: 278–9)

Machiavelli suggests that the Christian outlook on values may be malleable once reinterpreted from the perspective of patriotism, which even Christianity allows. However, his critique is scathing. To implement Christian values as commonly understood would be dangerous at the political level. It is precisely this message which is taken over by Jean-Jacques Rousseau in the *Social Contract*. Like Machiavelli, he castigates the spirit of meekness and passiveness instilled by Christianity:

> Christianity is an entirely spiritual religion, only occupied by things of Heaven; the fatherland of the Christian is not of this world. He does his duty, it is true, but he does it with a profound indifference to the good or bad outcome of his cares. Provided he has nothing for which to reproach himself,

> it is of little import to him whether all fares well or poorly here below. If the State is flourishing, he hardly dares to enjoy the public felicity, for he fears to take selfish pride in the glory of his country; if the State declines, he blesses the hand of God that weighs down heavily on his people.
> In order that the society be peaceable and harmony be maintained, all Citizens without exception would have to be equally good Christians. But if unfortunately there is found in it a single ambitious man, a single hypocrite, a Catiline, for example, a Cromwell, such a man very certainly would have an advantage over his pious compatriots. The Christian charity does not easily permit one to think ill of one's neighbor.[9]

The next step in my selection of attacks upon Christian values is taken by Immanuel Kant (1724–1804). It is often claimed that Kant views Christianity as a clear expression of his ideal of an autonomous morality, i.e. a morality based on reason, which exerts motivational power through reason alone without being confounded by heteronomous, empirical drives. However, while there is some room for ambivalence in Kant's thought, the main thrust of his discussion of Christianity is highly critical of the historical rootedness of religion, its narrative shape, and the idea that religion, including the Christian religion, circumscribes a separate realm of values. This line of thinking has proved particularly fertile with later revivals of Enlightenment critiques of religion.[10] Kant sets out from an understanding of morality as a matter of general rules or universal application. This understanding is compounded in his account of the categorical imperative, the test criterion for maxims (i.e. subjective rules of conduct): 'Act only in accordance with that maxim through which you can at the same time will that it become a universal law.'[11]

In Kant's opinion, reason rather than the long history of religious narratives is the true source of morality. Religion can play a role in the acquisition of values, but it cannot add any content of its own. In his book *Religion within the Boundaries of Mere Reason* Kant defines religion as follows: 'Religion is (subjectively considered) the recognition of all our duties as divine commands' (1996: 177; AA 6.153), and this is clearly a universal morality based on reason. It is therefore the case that religious values must be measured by reason-based morality, not vice versa. In this sense, Kant writes that:

> We shall also find that this is how all types of faith—ancient and new, some written down in holy books—have always been treated, and that rational and thoughtful teachers of the people have kept on interpreting them until, gradually, they brought them, as regards their essential content, in agreement with the universal principles of moral faith (den allgemeinen moralischen

[9] Rousseau 1964: 466 (Du contrat social IV.8, here in the translation by Charles M. Sherover, quoted from Cahn 2005: 318.

[10] See, e.g. Cliteur 2010a and b.

[11] Kant 2002: 37 (AA 4.421).

> Glaubenssätzen). (6:110-1, di Giovanni).

He thus rejects the historical situatedness and narrative structure of biblical texts. A prime example of this is his treatment of the story of Abraham, in *The Conflict of the Faculties:*

> For if God should really speak to a human being, the latter could still never *know* that it was God speaking. It is quite impossible for a human being to apprehend the infinite by his senses, distinguish it from sensible beings, and *be acquainted with* it as such.—But in some cases the human being can be sure that the voice he hears is *not* God's; for if the voice commands him to do something contrary to the moral law, then no matter how majestic the apparition may be, and no matter how it may seem to surpass the whole of nature, he must consider it an illusion. [The discussion continues in a footnote as follows:] We can use, as an example, the myth of the sacrifice that Abraham was going to make by butchering and burning his only son at God's command (the poor child without knowing it, even brought the wood for the fire). Abraham should have replied to this supposedly divine voice: 'That I ought not to kill my good son is quite certain. But that you, this apparition, are God—of that I am not certain, and never can be, not even if this voice rings down to me from (visible) heaven.' (1996: 283; AA 7.63)

While Kant critiques religious values from the viewpoint of universal morality, the last of the detractors of religious values whom I present here, Friedrich Nietzsche, shuns such pretensions of universality. To Nietzsche, morality is always formulated from a specific position. The problem with Christian values is that they are formulated from an inappropriate position and are thus the wrong kind of values. Originally, value judgements such as 'good' or 'virtuous' expressed the evaluations and preferences of the strong. It is with the rise of Judaeo-Christian religiosity that the weak and the meek have started a revolution in values by favouring weakness and discouraging the strong. This subversive creation of values is driven by resentment, as Nietzsche does not cease from repeating (e.g. *On the Genealogy of Morals* I.14 [1988: 5.281–3]). Following the realization that we have to assume the vacant role of a divine law-giver, the path is free for a new creation of values beyond Christianity.[12]

The above critiques of religious (Christian) values are highly diverse. Nonetheless, they are each surprisingly decisive in identifying what religious (Christian) values are. This is the Parson Thwackum Fallacy all over again, but this time from the opponents of Christian values. It would be possible, of course, to opt for a defensive strategy of pointing out the complexity of religion—in this case Christianity—against essentializing Parson Thwackum tendencies. While being perfectly feasible, such an essentially negative strategy

---

[12] See also *The Gay Science* 125 (1988: 3.480–2).

would be hard-pressed to suggest the outlines of a more positive view of the interaction of religious and secular values, without itself defaulting to a strategy of essentialization. If we want to renegotiate the boundaries between religion and secularism, this will inevitably involve generalizations of sorts. What I propose here, therefore, is to tackle the assumption underlying the different critical perspectives. This assumption is what I propose to call 'ideological monism'. For a society to be feasible, we all have to think alike; a true plurality of different fundamentally irreconcilable worldviews is somehow dangerous. John Rawls famously castigated the monism which undergirded earlier political philosophy, and suggested the theory of a political liberalism that was meant to be proof against pluralism. However, the way in which he developed his idea fell short of his intentions. With the model of a unitary public reason to be endorsed by all citizens, Rawls reintroduced through the back door the monism he wanted to exclude.[13] From the perspective of this ideological monism, it becomes compelling to perceive disunity in terms of threat. A fight for domination begins, and a cultural climate is produced in which religious values are either sharply distinguished from secular values in order to be attacked to attack them, or in which the admissible space for religion and religious values is narrowly defined by a standard of (supposedly universal) reason.

In order to leave behind the struggle for domination and enter a more cooperative model of interaction between religious and secular values, we need to theorize a radical pluralization of the public sphere. We need not all think alike in order to maintain civic bonds. What we require are clearly and minimally circumscribed procedural rules to which we must adhere (e.g. Rescher 1993). In this context, I cannot enumerate the changes to political structure that the proposal would entail. What I want briefly to explore is how the realization of such pluralism can free religious communities from the urge to respond to the pretensions of ideological monism.

Religious communities can drop their claim that there is an identity of religious and secular values, and likewise they can avoid any stubborn claim about the radical alterity of religious values. Instead, they are free to explore a more sensible option: 'religious values' do overlap with 'secular values'—quite unsurprisingly so, since such secular values will very often turn out on closer inspection to be 'religious values' in the sense that they rely on long-range invocations of religion. Moreover, the concept of long-range invocations of religion allows for a far-reaching fertilization of religious values by values held outside a core domain of religious believers. In short, the need to conceptualize religious and secular values as two separate domains and thus to create the need to theorize their relationship in terms of dominance will disappear. The effort of religious groups to help preserving our biosphere would be a good case study of the 'overlap' and the need to reject a clear separation between the religious and secular domains.

---

[13] See Stout 2004; Jedan 2006; Jedan 2010; and Jedan's contribution to the present volume.

However, it is prudent to accept that within religious communities there are values which challenge received opinion. The exhortations of the Sermon on the Mount, which point towards a time or place where new values are redeemed, would be a good example of this distinctness. Clearly, religious communities can function as laboratories of new values, challenging mainstream society to redirect its attention.

Realizing pluralism would also free religious communities to admit that their worldview relies crucially upon stories. Religions have *narrative, community-based, and particularistic origins*. They need not conceal these characteristics for the sake of conforming to universal reason.[14] At the same time, religions consistently maintain a *universal calling*. To honour this calling, religions ought not to replicate the universalist pretensions of Enlightenment ethics, as if religious ethics could do no better than inculcate the universal duties envisaged by Kant (or for that matter, the republican engagement demanded by Machiavelli and Rousseau). To realize the universal calling means making others—and, ideally, all others—see the attractions of the religious outlook so that they then modify their worldview. However, while this object can be achieved by demonstrating the distinctiveness of the religious outlook, it is also important to avoid overstating the differences between the religious and the secular. Bridges between them must remain.

2. The Contributions to this Volume

Europe is a highly interesting laboratory of the future. It is a cultural realm in which religious communities increasingly perceive, whether as certain or as probable, that they will be placed in a minority position in which they will have to embrace ideational pluralism. The contributions to this volume try to make sense of this European experience.

The first part, *Religious Traditions, Old and New*, analyses the contributions of religious traditions to today's analysis of the religious-secular divide. Gerlinde Baumann deals with hermeneutical issues surrounding political perspectives derived from the Bible. While the dominant public perception is that there has been a history of craven alliances between religion and secular power, and that monarchies and all kinds of oppressive government were unquestioningly legitimized by Christianity, Baumann warns against such easy reconstructions. She shows how crucial passages in the Old Testament display a deeply-held ambivalence concerning the political power of kingship. Those passages show understanding for the urge to have a king, while at the same time warning against the abuses of power implicit in human kingship. In short,

[14] It was important that Stanley Hauerwas (1983) pointed out the particularism and narrative structure of Christian virtue ethics. However, his theory remains inward-looking; he makes insufficient allowance for the outward-looking universal calling and the consequences that this will have for any public theology.

Baumann indicates the need to carefully contextualize notions such as 'kingship' or 'religion' and to realize how differently they were understood in the context of the Ancient Near East. Baumann concludes that a critique of politics based on biblical motifs, and on Old Testament texts in particular, can still be fruitful today.

The topic of ambivalence concerning political power is continued in Elian Cuvillier's contribution. In 'Submission and Resistance: Christian Communities and Imperial Power in the First Century AD', Cuvillier analyses attitudes found in New Testament authors towards the authority of the Roman empire. These attitudes are best appreciated for their dissident quality, once we recognize the intellectual dominance of the imperial ideology. In the first century AD, there was an almost universal consensus that there was no alternative to the efficient and successful imperial administration. Against this background, the ambivalence found in the New Testament is particularly salient. We find, in addition to an attitude we could describe as 'submission' as found in Paul and the epistolary traditions, a clear call to resistance in the Apocalypse of John. Cuvillier goes on to ask whether, for all their apparent antagonism, these two attitudes share a common basis in an 'anarchist' attitude on the part of the New Testament authors. Political authority is accepted only insofar is it permits people to live together in the free realization of their faith, but this free submission turns into resistance wherever political rulers overstep this boundary.

The discussion of religious 'anarchism' is continued in the contribution of Kasim Kücücalp, who compares Emmanuel Lévinas' philosophy with Islamic mysticism. Lévinas famously critiques the main current of Western philosophy for its ontological imperialism. As a philosophy of power, it assimilates the Other to the self, thus denying the irreducible otherness of the Other. A philosophy which takes its cue from the radical otherness of the Other will result in an ethical relationship that is anarchical, in the sense that it does not strive for domination of the Other but puts the Other first and leads to an attitude of self-sacrifice for the Other. Küçücalp argues that this attitude of self-sacrifice is also the goal of *tasawwuf*, the discipline of spiritual development found in Sufism. The philosophy of Lévinas and Islamic mysticism suggest that religious thought might provide a better foundation for the protection of the Other than can be found in secular Western talk about rights.

Carl Reinhold Bråkenhielm takes his cue from the observation that the distinction between the secular and the religious is far from clear-cut. Environmentalism is a prime example of a broad and deep belief system that increasingly legitimates identities for political power. In effect, environmentalism is taking on the function of a civil religion, and with his analysis of the political and cultural developments in Sweden Bråkenhielm presents a fascinating case study.

The first part ends with a contribution by Jean François Zorn, who describes how Christian missionaries were co-opted into a French colonial enterprise proposed and theorized by Utopians, Liberals and Republicans. Christian missionaries were mentioned in the same breath as scientists and explorers with respect to their crucial role in advancing the civilizing initiatives of the colonial powers. Zorn points to the fact that the period of colonization has fixed the boundaries of religious blocks rather than allow religions to make major inroads into 'foreign' territory.

The second part, *Religious versus Secular Values*, examines the intersections and possible conflicts between religious and secular values. Patrick Vandermeersch shows how the European religious (and, more broadly, cultural) heritage revolves around the recognition that religion does not belong to the religious communities alone, and that the state and the state universities play a crucial role in promoting knowledge about religion. The research provided by universities can contribute, so Vandermeersch explains, to fostering 'moderate', non-extremist religion. From this perspective, Vandermeersch questions the liberal distinction between public and private with the concomitant attribution of religion to the private realm.

While the heritage of liberalism is deeply problematic, not every attack on liberalism and liberal democracy will meet its target. Liberal democracy has a crucial promise to offer, as Marc Boss shows in his discussion of one of the most prominent contemporary critics of liberal democracy, Alasdair MacIntyre. Boss suggests that MacIntyre's philosophy is less incompatible with liberalism than might appear from the radical rhetoric of delegitimization that we find in his writings. What is at work behind MacIntyre's critique of liberal democracy, Boss suggests, is rather the radicalization of a key tenet of liberal democracies: the deliberative practice of rational investigation. In MacIntyre, so much stress is put on this concept that existing liberal democracies simply fail to meet his highly-demanding standard.

While there is reason to shun sweeping delegitimizations of liberal democracy, as Boss's contribution shows, Christoph Jedan's contribution 'Towards the Postsecular' asks how both the renewed visibility of religion in the public domain and also the attempts to theorize a rapprochement between religious and secular modes of thinking could be conceptualized in political philosophy. Jedan begins with a discussion of Rawls's project of a justificatory political liberalism, since Rawls's theory has defined the map of subsequent discussions. Jedan argues that Rawls's theory is often misunderstood, because his commentators have failed to take into account the concrete experience of US constitutional history that undergirds his theorizing. Against the backdrop of the history of the US constitution, one better understands the specific profile of Rawls's theory and why it fails to take into account sensibilities that have developed in Europe. Jedan points to the Dutch constitution as a point of comparison. In addition, Jedan takes issue with the unrealistically narrow, all-or-nothing concept of political legitimacy that underlies many of Rawls's more questionable proposals. Jedan ends by outlining five points that will be pivotal for theorizing a political postsecularity. Most importantly, perhaps, Jedan calls for the symbolic presence of religion in the public forum, where politicians should attempt to show how the values and coercive laws that they promote can be derived from one or more religious traditions. This will be particularly valuable whenever such attempts are undertaken by politicians who do not themselves belong to the religious tradition(s) in question.

Erin Wilson's contribution also takes issue with calls to keep religion out of the public domain. Such calls are underpinned by a secularist narrative that presupposes three dichotomies: institutional versus ideational, individual versus communal, and irrational versus rational. Religion in Europe is regularly characterized by the first elements of the dichotomies, in that social scientists have focused on an institutional phenomenon that exerts influence over the individual lives of believers and should above all be interpreted as irrational. This representation becomes compounded in the recommendation to maintain religion as an essentially private affair outside politics and the public realm. Wilson calls for a reconceptualization of religion. Taking her cue from Julia Kristeva and Raia Prokhovnik, she calls for a 'relational dialogism' that highlights the fluidity of the notions involved in the three dichotomies and the connections that exist within the dichotomous pairings. Such a relational dialogism allows us to question the separation of religion and politics.

In the third part, *Religious Political Parties—Dutch Perspectives*, the book offers three chapters on Dutch religious political parties. The Netherlands are an interesting case study, since we find what can be described, in Paul Lucardie's words, as an apparent 'paradox: religious parties seem to flourish in a secularized society'. No fewer than three Christian parties are represented in parliament at the national level: the Christian Democratic party (CDA), the Christian Union (CU) and the Calvinist or Reformed Party (SGP). Lucardie explains, through an historical reconstruction, the success of these parties and he delineates their theological and political profiles. He relates how in the nineteenth-century 'school struggle' (the Dutch variant of the *Kulturkampf* that took place in neighbouring countries), the Conservative party lost its appeal and many of its voters switched to denominational parties. In spite of the undeniable strength of religious parties in the Netherlands, certainly when compared to other countries, Lucardie is convinced that this strength must be theorized against the background of an ongoing secularization. He explains it by the religious parties' ability to adapt to secularization and to accept liberal reforms. Nonetheless, he considers the future of the three parties to be insecure. Indeed, considering the long-term trends of the electoral share of religious parties in the Netherlands, theorizing postsecularity should carefully disentangle cultural notions of a rapprochement of religious and secular modes of thinking from political theories concerning the existence and the political success of religious political parties.

The last two contributions each focus on one of the religious parties represented in the Dutch parliament. Evert-Jan Brouwer deals with the oldest party in the Netherlands, the SGP, which is a small orthodox Calvinist party, with (as at September 2012) three seats in the Second Chamber of the Dutch parliament. Crucial to the SGP's view of politics is the standpoint that government is ordained by God and has the function to protect the true (Christian, and more specifically Calvinist) religion. The SGP thus rejects liberal ideas about the religious neutrality of government. The SGP's position is called 'theocracy' but, unlike other political structures referred to as theocratic, it favours an institutional separation of church and state. SGP-style theocracy means the 'recognition by the rulers of the reality that God is King of the whole world and that He is entitled to our obedience'.

Brouwer explains that the SGP favours representative democracy as the best strategy to achieve legitimate political decisions, and he goes on to discuss hotly-debated issues such as the party's exclusion of women from political office.

Henk Woldring's contribution focuses on the largest religious party in the Netherlands, the CDA. His contribution turns on the concept of civil society. He analyses how the Roman Catholic concept of subsidiarity and the (Neo) Calvinist idea of 'sphere sovereignty' feed into the Christian democratic ideal of civil society, and he contrasts the Christian democratic emphasis on the multivarious responsibilities which actors in civil society ought to have with liberal and centralistic ideas of society. In emphasizing that although 'liberalism aims to revitalize economic activities, in the long run the application of the capitalist model and the operation of the market will seriously impair the quality of society', Woldring underscores a historical characteristic of the Dutch Christian democratic party which is also analysed in Lucardie's contribution. Lucardie describes how tendencies within the Dutch Christian democratic party keep religious ideas on the foreground and attempt to steer clear of right-wing politics as exemplified by the German CDU. By Lucardie's reckoning, Dutch Christian democrats 'tend to be more egalitarian and less nationalistic than secular conservative parties in Britain, Germany or France'. Yet, he hastens to add, 'the differences between them seem to be diminishing'. It appears to be precisely this movement and the engagement with liberal politics which has contributed to a fragmentation of the CDA's voter base in recent years. It is highly significant that at the same time as a new visibility of religion in the public sphere is much talked of, the largest religious party in the Netherlands is shifting towards a more 'secular' right-wing political outlook.

References

Boccaccio, G. (1994): *Decameron*. Edited by M. Marti. Eleventh edition. Milan. [English translation by G. H. MacWilliam, Second edition, Harmondsworth 1995.]

Cahn, St. M. (ed.)(2005): *Political Philosophy: The Essential Texts*. Oxford.

Cavanaugh, W. T. (1999): 'The City: Beyond Secular Parodies'. In Milbank, J., Pickstock, C. and Ward, G. (eds) *Radical Orthodoxy: A New Theology*. London/ New York.

Cliteur, P. (2010a): *Het monotheïstisch dilemma.* Amsterdam/Antwerp.

——— (2010b): *A Secular outlook: In Defense of Moral and Political Secularism.* Oxford.

Clack, B. and Clack, R. (1998): *The Philosophy of Religion: A Critical Introduction.* Cambridge.

Geertz, C. (1993): 'Religion as a Cultural System'. In: *The Interpretation of Cultures: Selected Essays*, London, pp. 87-125.

Hauerwas, S. (1983): *The Peaceable Kingdom: A Primer in Christian Ethics.* Notre Dame.

James, W. (1902/2008): *The Varieties of Religious Experience: A Study in Human Nature.* Reformatted edition. Rockville MD.

Jedan, C. (2006): 'Das Recht zu reden: Eine sozialethische Theorie über die Präsenz von kulturell-religiösen Minderheiten im öffentlichen Diskurs', in: *Nederlands Theologisch Tijdschrift* 60, 235–53.

——— (2010): Beyond the Secular? Public Reason and the Search for a Concept of Postsecular Legitimacy, in: A. L. Molendijk / J. Beaumont / C. Jedan (eds) *Exploring the Postsecular: The Religious, the Political and the Urban.* Leiden/ Boston, 311–27.

Kant, I. (1996): *Religion and Rational Theology.* Translated and edited by A. W. Wood and G. di Giovanni. Cambridge.

——— (2002) *Groundwork for the Metaphysics of Morals.* Edited by Allen W. Wood. New Haven CT.

Lübbe, H. (2003): *Säkularisierung: Geschichte eines ideenpolitischen Begriffs.* Third edition. Freiburg/Munich.

Machiavelli, N. (1995): *Il Principe.* New edition by G. Inglese. Turin.

——— (2003) *The Discourses.* Edited by Bernard Crick. Reprinted edition. London.

Nietzsche, F. (1988): *Sämtliche Werke.* Fifteen volumes. Edited by G. Colli and M. Montinari. Second edition. Munich/Berlin/New York.

Peterson, M. et. al. (2003): *Reason and Religious Belief: An Introduction to the Philosophy of Religion.* Third edition. Oxford.

Rousseau, J.-J. (1964): *Oeuvres complètes, III: Du contrat social. Écrits politiques.* Paris 1964.

Stout, J. (2004): *Democracy and Tradition.* Princeton.

Tillich, P. (1951): *Systematic Theology.* Vol. I. Chicago.

PART I

RELIGIOUS TRADITIONS, OLD AND NEW

CRITICISMS OF KINGSHIP IN ANCIENT ISRAEL

Gerlinde Baumann

Monarchies in Europe were perceived for a long time as both rooted in and also legitimized by Christianity. Close alliances between European kings and the Pope as head of the Roman Catholic church served to stabilize both institutions. In consequence of various developments, this situation changed. An account of it might begin, albeit controversially, with the developments leading to the schism between Rome and Byzantium in the eleventh century, and it would continue with the Reformation that began in Germany in the early sixteenth century. It would probably end with the far-reaching separation between church and state that originated in the Enlightenment and now characterizes most European countries in the twenty-first century.

These developments make it possible, nowadays, to read Biblical texts from a different perspective. The texts no longer serve to legitimize any particular government or form of monarchy but can now support a more critical stance. Indeed, historical-critical scholarship has discovered a large number of Old Testament texts that argue against kingship. They not only outnumber the texts in favour of monarchy but they also offer detailed theological explanations of their critical standpoint. The purpose of this chapter is to give an overview of those texts (3), and to draw some conclusions (4) for the discussion of the relationship between church and state in Europe today. First of all, though, it would be helpful to embark on some hermeneutical reflections (1) and to review the main periods of Israelite history (2).

1. Hermeneutical Considerations

The Old Testament is a literary document rooted in ancient Israel. It was written and re-written over a long period. Ancient Israelite culture and religion are highly dependent on the cultural and religious concepts of the ancient Near East.[1] In the ANE, kingship is the central institution of the state. This is the main reason why the question of the relationship between 'state' and 'religion' in ancient Israel can best be discussed by reference to the Old Testament texts concerning kingship.

---

[1] In what follows I shall use the abbreviation 'ANE' for 'ancient Near East' and its adjectival form 'ancient Near Eastern'. ANE includes not only Mesopotamian, but also the Egyptian and Western Semitic territories, cultures and religions.

When discussing 'state' and 'religion' in the ANE and in present-day Europe, we need to bear in mind that there are considerable differences between our current concepts and the political and religious realities of the ANE. To begin with the 'state': modern states in Europe are (mostly) democracies. They are legitimized through elections—that is to say, through the people. In most cases they are secular states, which means that political power must be separated from religion and religious institutions. Normally, the state and its institutions care for social security, the infrastructure, education, the economy, and so on. By contrast, an ANE 'state' was in most cases a monarchy, ruled by a king (or, less frequently, by a queen). Often there was dynastic kingship. The king or queen was legitimized by the deities; he or she could have cultic functions as well. Thus, religion and the state or monarch were much more closely connected than they are nowadays. The economic and political interests of the royal family and the state were closely bound together, in addition. As the representative of the deities, the monarch cared both for peace and justice and also for the poor and needy.

In the same way, we can look at the difference between the present-day and ANE concepts of 'religion'. Today, attitudes towards religion depend mostly on personal choice. We often find that we can choose between different religions and denominations. Religion is practised in places or institutions such as synagogues, churches, or mosques. The separation between state and religion is thought of, in most states at least, as an attainable ideal. In the ANE, however, the entire population of a nation or city worshipped the deities of the national or local pantheon. This devotion was not normally secured by force; it was self-evident in those cultures that the people worshipped the local deities. There was no religious freedom. Institutions such as temples were under the control of the economic and political power. The connection between religion and the state or monarch was very close.

2. Periods of Ancient Israelite History

The history of Ancient Israel begins around 1200 BCE. At that time, we can speak only of the families or clans that began to form what later becomes 'Israel'. About 1016 BCE, first Saul and later, in about 1000 BCE, David became the founders of Israel as a kingdom. The period when Israel had a single dynasty came to an end in 922 BCE, when the Northern, Israelite kingdom separated from the Southern kingdom of Judah. In 722 BCE, the Northern kingdom ceased to be an independent state and became part of the Assyrian empire. The same fate befell Judah in 587 BCE. As successors to the Assyrians, the Babylonians conquered the country and its capital Jerusalem. Some of the people of Judah were deported to Babylon but, after the breakdown of the Babylonian empire in 539 BCE, they were allowed to return. In the subsequent 'post-exilic' period, Judah became part of the Persian empire and its successors, until Hellenistic rulers took over in 333 BCE.

As this brief overview makes clear, we can speak about Israel and Judah as a 'monarchy' only for a limited period, from the time of Saul in about 1016 BCE to the fall of the Judean monarchy in 587 BCE. Bearing in mind that—according to historical-critical scholarship—most of the Old Testament texts were probably written or revised in post-exilic times, during the Persian era, we realize that Israel wrote or edited texts about monarchy mostly from a post-monarchic perspective. This might help us to explain why we find so many texts that are critical of monarchy. However, as I shall argue, it cannot be the only explanation of the criticisms of kingship in ancient Israel. For a more detailed analysis, we need to examine the relevant biblical texts.

3. Relevant Texts about the Religion-State Relationship in Ancient Israel

Several Old Testament texts criticize the institution of kingship in ancient Israel. There are also texts, mostly in the Old Testament prophets, that criticize Israelite kings on account of their social, cultic or foreign politics. However, I shall not examine these texts in the present chapter. Instead, I propose to look at three texts which are in my view the most important sources for a reconstruction of the critical perspective on kingship in the Old Testament. I shall examine these texts in the order in which they were most probably written: first Judges 9:8–15, then 1 Samuel 8:10–18, and lastly Deuteronomy 17:14–20.[2]

3.1. Judges 9:8–15: 'Jotham's Fable'

Judges 9 is found in the main part of the book of Judges. This book can be divided into three parts: the introduction (Judg 1:1–2:10), with a look back to the age of Joshua followed by the main part containing narratives about several 'judges', who were charismatic leaders, inspired and empowered by the spirit of the Lord (Judg 2:11–16:36). In the closing part (Judg 17–21), we find accounts of serious criminal acts. The fact that such crimes can happen is seen as the result of a lack of institutional order in Israel. So much is obvious from the 'motto verse' of this part: 'In those days there was no king in Israel; all the people did what was right in their own eyes' (Judg 17:6; 21:25).

The Book of Judges was probably written and re-written over a lengthy period of time (from the ninth to the fourth century BCE). The setting, part-chronicle and part-legend, is the time before Israel installed its monarchy, that is to say before 1000 BCE. The purpose of writing or conserving such a text is to imagine a society without its own kingship, as became the reality in post-exilic Israel. The question as to when exactly Jotham's fable was written is still a

---

[2] As the purpose of this article is to present some of the texts more briefly, it does not focus on their diachronic examination.

matter of scholarly debate.[3] Thus it seems possible not only that the critique of kingship was a reason for transmitting the story but also that its purpose was to interpret Israel's kingless state in a theological context.

In the literary context of Jotham's fable, Abimelech makes himself king. Directly before that episode, the highly-popular 'judge' Gideon has been asked by the people to be a king himself or to permit one of his sons to become king. Gideon refuses with the words: 'I will not rule over you; and my son will not rule over you; the Lord will rule over you' (Judg 8:23). After Abimelech has made himself a king, he murders his brothers (Judg 9:1–6). Then the people from the city of Shechem acclaim him as their king. Only the youngest son of one of Abimelech's brothers survives, and this is Jotham. He is the one who sings our fable (Judg 9:8–15):[4]

> (8) The trees once went out to anoint a king over themselves. So they said to the olive tree: 'Reign over us.'
> (9) The olive tree answered them, 'Shall I stop producing my rich oil by which gods and mortals are honoured, and go to sway over the trees?'
> (10) Then the trees said to the fig tree, 'You come and reign over us.'
> (11) But the fig tree answered them, 'Shall I stop producing my sweetness and my delicious fruit, and go to sway over the trees?'
> (12) Then the trees said to the vine, 'You come and reign over us.'
> (13) But the vine said to them, 'Shall I stop producing my wine that cheers gods and mortals, and go to sway over the trees?'
> (14) So all the trees said to the bramble, 'You come and reign over us.'
> (15) And the bramble said to the trees, 'If in good faith you are anointing me king over you, then come and take refuge in my shade; but if not, let fire come out of the bramble and devour the cedars of Lebanon.'

In the literary context, the fable is followed by an allegorical interpretation (9:16–20).[5] In this interpretation, the fable is connected with Abimelech's kingship. It ends with a curse, the outcome of which is related in Judges 9:52–57.

What picture of kingship is offered by this fable? At first, it does not seem to be an attractive proposition. The three fruit trees all deny the offer. This might have been reason enough for the other trees to end the search for a useful candidate—after three refusals, the chances of finding another competent

---

[3] A very complex model for the diachronic development of Judg 8:22–9:57 and other texts is given by Moenikes (1995: 151–73). The problem has been discussed more recently by Müller (2004: 31–4).

[4] NRSV 1989. The other translations of Biblical passages are also taken from NRSV 1989.

[5] If one follows the theoretical framework of *Literarkritik*, the fable ends in v. 15a. V. 15b already counts as interpretation. See, e.g., Becker 1990: 190–97 and Ruprecht 2003: 11.

candidate would be very poor.[6] This is demonstrated by the qualities of the bramble (Hebrew: *'atad*). It is a thorny bush with fruits that cause diarrhoea when they are eaten. Moreover, the bramble's promise to shade the other trees is wholly unrealistic, so we must interpret it as ironic.[7] From this perspective, the chosen candidate is hardly capable to fulfil the duties of the king, and he threatens the 'people' with burning if they do not obey him. Although the metaphor of the king as shelter has some ideological import,[8] kingship is not theologically legitimized in this text.

Readers might assume that the book of Judges is a royalist manifesto because it emphasizes the need to have some kind of government with legal institutions (Judg 17:6; 21:25; see above). This text, however, shows that the book's message is more complex. At almost certainly a late stage in its compilation, the text containing the fable of Abimelech and Jotham was inserted as a critical commentary in opposition to kingship or against unrealistic expectations of the personal qualities, and especially of the personal integrity, of a king. This is also emphasized by the irony in our text: The fruit trees refuse to be king, because they have better things to do and do not acknowledge kingship as something worthwhile. In short, Judges 8:9–15 is an unequivocally anti-royalist tract (Becker 1990: 193).

3.2. 1 Samuel 8:10–18: The 'Rights of the King'

It can be assumed that this story detailing the 'rights of the king' was written some hundred years after the inauguration of kingship in Israel—probably in the seventh century BCE, when Israelite kingship and the Davidic dynasty underwent a severe crisis. In the scholarly debate, it remains an open question as to exactly when this text was written.[9]

At the time the events in the first book of Samuel are set, Israel was not yet a monarchy; it was still governed by judges. The surrounding countries, however, all had kings and they threatened Israel with their military force. This is the reason given for the people to turn to the outstanding judge and prophet,

---

[6] Becker (1990: 192) refers to this as a critique of this specific procedure of choosing a king.

[7] Crüsemann (1978: 22) points to the irony of the text.

[8] The ANE background of the text is highlighted by, among others, Crüsemann (1978: 22) and Ruprecht (2003: 17–25): In the ANE it is one of the characteristics of the king to shelter his people. It might thus be said that Jotham's fable aims at the heart of the ANE royalist ideology (Ruprecht 2003: 19).

[9] Stoebe (1973: 187) emphasizes that the text details monarchal rights in Israel's neighbouring territories and is therefore probably quite old. Donner (1987: 175–6), however, points to the fact that the text already knows the 'outcome' of Israelite kingship. This is clearly a deuteronomistic perspective, but it remains an open question whether it is post-exilic. Dietrich and Naumann (1995: 23–4) emphasize that the text is undateable ('zeitlos').

Samuel. Samuel is already old, but his sons are not eligible to become his successors because they are incompetent (1 Sam 8:2–3). And so the people ask Samuel to give them a king. 'We are determined to have a king over us, so that we also may be like other nations, and that our king may govern us and go out before us and fight our battles' (1 Sam 8:21f.). So Israelite kingship was legitimated both by the people and by the Lord, and the reason for instituting it was the need for national defence. In the literary context, the beginnings of Israelite kingship are narrated from 1 Sam 9 onwards.

Samuel dislikes the people's demand: the Lord feels neglected by the people, because *he* is supposed to be their king (1 Sam 8:7). But the Lord respects the will of the people and tells Samuel to explain the rights of a king to them, as he does in this passage. The translation goes as follows (NRSV):

> Samuel reported all the words of the Lord to the people … (11) [and] said: 'These will be the ways of the king who will reign over you: he will take your sons and appoint them to his chariots and to be his horsemen, and to run before his chariots; (12) and he will appoint for himself commanders of thousands and commanders of fifties, and some to plough his ground and to reap his harvest, and to make his implements of war and the equipment of his chariots. (13) He will take your daughters to be perfumers and cooks and bakers. (14) He will take the best of your fields and vineyards and olive orchards and give them to his courtiers. (15) He will take one-tenth of your grain and of your vineyards and give it to his officers and his courtiers. (16) He will take your male and female slaves, and the best of your cattle and donkeys, and put them into his work. (17) He will take one-tenth of your flocks, and you shall be his slaves. (18) And in that day you will cry out because of your king, whom you have chosen for yourselves; but the Lord will not answer you in that day.'

1 Sam 8 creates a scenario in which the people are warned that there will be negative consequences if they install a king in Israel. In effect, this is what is being told in so many stories in the first and second books of Kings. These stories adopt the deuteronomistic view that human kingship is not a positive institution. Human kingship is perceived as in conflict with the kingship of God. However, in spite of the depravity of human kingship, it is understood as ultimately bestowed by the Lord. Therefore, in this text we find some kind of moderate religious legitimization of Israelite kingship.[10]

From the text, we come to know some of the king's duties. He is the ruler of the people and their leader in warfare. What is emphasized are the king's rights, and these rights are many in number. What becomes obvious is that human kingship is highly ambivalent: although no positive consequences can be

[10] Stolz (1981: 61) describes human kingship in this text as part of the Lord's 'Notordnung' for Israel—not something ideal, but rather an emergency arrangement to avert further damage.

predicted with certainty, the negative consequences will inevitably come to pass. Divine kingship would be ideal, but in the given circumstances (namely the military threat and the popular demand for a human king) human kingship is acceptable—even to the Lord.

3.3. Deuteronomy 17:14–20: The Deuteronomic 'Law of the King'

Unlike the other major bodies of law in the Old Testament, Deuteronomy 17:14–20 is the only one in which we find rules dealing with kingship.[11] The book of Deuteronomy was probably written and rewritten over a protracted period (from the sixth to the fourth century BCE). The book in its entirety is presented as a speech made by Moses when inspired by the Lord. The setting—whether historical or legendary—is the time before Israel inaugurated its kingship, at about 1000 BCE.

The 'law of the king' (Deut 12–26) is part of the Deuteronomic law, which forms the central part of the book of Deuteronomy. This corpus of legal texts is framed by a prologue (Deut 5–11) and an epilogue (Deut 28); another frame is provided by narratives, retrospects and admonitions (Deut 1–4), the stories of the covenant, the installation of Joshua as the successor of Moses, the song of Moses, Moses' final blessing conferred upon Israel, and the story of the death of Moses (Deut 29–34).

The 'law of the king' is also part of a smaller body of legal writing, which is sometimes presented as an outline of Israel's constitution; it consists of laws regulating official leadership: the powers and obligations of judges, the king, priests, and prophets (Deut 16:18–18:22). There are several noteworthy features: the separation of powers, the attempt to avoid the leader's hierarchical separation from the people, and the *tora*—the guideline for life given to Israel by the Lord—as leading principle for society. The translation of the 'law of the king' is as follows (NRSV):

> (14) When you have come into the land that the Lord your God is giving you, and you have taken possession of it and settled in it, and you say: 'I will set a king over me, like all the nations that are around me', (15) you may indeed set over you a king whom the Lord your God will choose. One of your own community you may set as a king over you; you are not permitted to put a foreigner over you, who is not of your own community. (16) Even so, he must not acquire many horses for himself, or return to the people of Egypt to acquire more horses, since the Lord has said to you, 'You must never return that way again.' (17) And he must not acquire many wives for himself, or else his heart will turn away; also silver and gold he must not

[11] Müller (2004: 197): 'Im Unterschied zu den anderen großen Rechtscorpora des Alten Testaments enthält das deuteronomische Gesetz einen Passus, der sich mit dem Königtum befaßt'.

> acquire in great quantity for himself. (18) When he has taken the throne of his kingdom, he shall have a copy of this law [*tora*] written for him in the presence of the levitical priests. (19) It shall remain with him and he shall read in it all the days of his life, so that he may learn to fear the Lord his God, diligently observing all the words of this law [*tora*] and these statutes, (20) neither exalting himself above other members of the community nor turning aside from the commandment, either to the right or to the left, so that he and his descendants may reign long over his kingdom in Israel.

The law of the king takes a critical stance towards certain forms of kingship as, for instance, practised by Solomon: a luxurious life, many wives, and many horses (1 Kings 10:14–11:8). Such a life can only be led by oppressing and exploiting the people. Another king with a negative image is Manasseh (2 Kings 21), who worshipped other deities and therefore does not fit into the frame of Deut 17:18–20 which points, *inter alia*, to the first commandment of the decalogue (Exod 20:2–17; Deut 5:6–17). Furthermore, we find an egalitarian concept of Israelite kingship in this text: with regard to his lifestyle, the king is an ordinary Israelite (v. 20). We do not hear of any special rights accorded to the king, as in 1 Sam 8. The king's only privilege is that he shall have his own copy of the *tora* (v. 19).[12] The king is here the prototype of a pious Israelite.[13]

This text mirrors the reality of post-exilic Israel, at the time when the book of Deuteronomy is likely to have been re-written. Kingship had existed at some earlier period of Israelite history. In the post-exilic time, this institution existed no longer. Most of what the king was obliged to do was already being done by other leaders. The specific tasks which are the reason for kingship in Judges 9 or 1 Samuel 8—giving shelter to the people, being the leader in warfare—are not mentioned here. Others are mentioned only to be denied: The king is no longer a 'judge', because this is an institution separated from kingship (Deut 16:18–20).[14] The duties and the specific life of a king are described only in negative terms. We learn much about what a king should not do or be. What remains is that, instead of being a person of high authority or power, he now is one among other Israelites.

Yet kingship is legitimated by religion. Verses 14–15 speak of the people's urge for a king, much as in 1 Samuel 8, and they speak of the Lord as the one who chooses the king. This can be interpreted as an allusion to the Davidic dynasty, which the Lord had established forever (2 Sam 7,13.16 par 1 Chr 17,12.14).[15] Even though there was no king at present, the promise of a king was still valid—until the Messiah as a successor of David came and established

[12] Braulik (1986–92: 129).

[13] Braulik (1986–92: 129): 'Der König ist deshalb vor allem Musterisraelit.'

[14] See Müller (2004: 207).

[15] See Müller (2004: 213).

his reign of peace (Isa 11:1–10); and then the gulf between human and divine kingship would be bridged.[16]

4. Conclusions

Much of what we find in the way of criticism of kingship in the Old Testament probably dates back to post-exilic Israel, a time by which Israelite kingship had ceased to exist. Yet the Lord had promised an eternal Davidic kingship to His people. The reason for the loss is, in the view of the Old Testament, Israel's own fault: It worshipped other deities than the Lord. The kings did not follow the *tora* and they made political mistakes by entering into pacts with the wrong allies.

What aspects of the Old Testament view of kingship are relevant when we look at the relationship between church and state in Europe at the present time? Nowadays (see above, part 1), we do not (normally) face the risk that a government will seek to legitimize its activities by reference to religion. The power of the church(es) is limited by constitutions. In Europe, we have more-or-less secular states with a more-or-less strict separation of church and state.

It is still possible to criticize governments from a religious or, more specifically, from a Biblical perspective, in a constructive manner and for the public good. There are, even so, some moral provisos for such criticisms. With democracy, the separation of powers, and the separation of religion and state as key factors, their aim must not be to destabilize a government or to contest the state's constitutional framework. Within the mainstream currents of Christianity in Europe at least, the broader constitutional framework is usually uncontroversial. However, within this framework, religion can and should be a critical voice speaking out against problematic forms of government, always with the intention of making government better.

Against this background, the Old Testament criticism of kingship can become a fruitful element of today's debate. I mention only a few ideas inspired by the discussion earlier in this chapter of three central Old Testament texts:

- Following Judges 9, one can question a government's competence. This might be most useful during election campaigns. Are the candidates really qualified to shoulder the burdens of the office they seek to hold? This question should, of course, be understood to focus on the

[16] Müller (2004: 213): 'Die durch das Monarchiestatut [Deut 17:14–20] angebahnte Synthese liefert damit eine wichtige Voraussetzung für die Herausbildung des Messianismus im Gewand der Theokratie: Die Israel gemäße Herrschaftsform ist das Königtum des paradigmatisch frommen David … [hier] erlebt die alte Vorstellung der Komplementarität von göttlichem und menschlichem Königtum in stark gewandelter Form eine Wiederkehr.'

qualifications of a candidate for the exercise of power (Judg 9:15: giving shelter), but should not focus on their attitude towards religion.

- According to Judges 9 and 1 Samuel 8, the people themselves can be challenged—in case of a call for a 'strong government' in times of crisis. Is such a call legitimate, or are other solutions possible?
- Pursuing the line of reasoning in 1 Samuel 8 we might ask: What about the government's administrative competence? What about its budget management? Are there signs of abuse of authority?
- To recapitulate the ideas in Deuteronomy 17: Does the government maintain the opinion that its members are part of society and are also subject to the law—even though they enact the law? '*Tora*' in this respect has to be seen not as a body of religious law, but as a body of law which also contains basic social or economic provisions (Segbers 2002).

In most of the cases mentioned, the church will probably not be the only voice to pose a specific question about a government's competence. It can support other voices, such as those of a civil rights movement. Nevertheless, its contribution to (inter)national debates should not be restricted to 'religious affairs' in the narrow sense of the term. This would be to ignore an important part of the European religious and cultural heritage.

References

Becker, U. (1990): *Richterzeit und Königtum: Redaktionsgeschichtliche Studien zum Richterbuch*. Berlin and New York.

Braulik, G. (1986–92): *Deuteronomium.* 2 vols. (Die neue Echter-Bibel: Kommentar zum Alten Testament mit der Einheitsübersetzung.) Würzburg. 1986–92.

Crüsemann, F. (1978): *Der Widerstand gegen das Königtum. Die antiköniglichen Texte des Alten Testaments und der Kampf um den frühen israelitischen Staat.* Neukirchen-Vluyn.

Dietrich, W., and Naumann, Th. (1995): *Die Samuelbücher.* Darmstadt.

Donner, H. (1987): *Geschichte des Volkes Israel und seiner Nachbarn in Grundzügen.* Göttingen.

Moenikes, A. (1995): *Die grundsätzliche Ablehnung des Königtums in der Hebräischen Bibel: Ein Beitrag zur Religionsgeschichte des Alten Israel.* Weinheim.

Müller, R. (2004): *Königtum und Gottesherrschaft: Untersuchungen zur alttestamentlichen Monarchiekritik.* Tübingen.

NRSV (1989): *The Holy Bible Containing the Old and New Testaments. New Revised Standard Version.* Anglicized Edition. Oxford.

Ruprecht, E. (2003): *Die Jothamfabel und außerisraelitische Parallelen.* Göttingen.

Segbers, F. (2002): *Die Hausordnung der Tora: Biblische Impulse für eine theologische Wirtschaftsethik.* Third edition. Luzern.

Stoebe, H.J. (1973): *Das erste Buch Samuelis.* Gütersloh.

Stolz, F. (1981): *Das erste und zweite Buch Samuel.* Zürich.

SUBMISSION AND RESISTANCE: CHRISTIAN COMMUNITIES AND IMPERIAL POWER IN THE FIRST CENTURY A.D.

Elian Cuvillier

This chapter is divided in four parts. In the first part, I argue that the situation found in the first century AD as a consequence of Rome's uncontested hegemony over the entire Mediterranean world was politically without precedent. In the second part, I attempt to analyse the apparently irreconcilable attitudes towards the authority of the Roman empire—on one hand an attitude of submission, on the other hand one of resistance—taken by the writers of the New Testament. In the third part, I review explanations for the coexistence in the New Testament of these two attitudes and I seek their respective theological foundations. Finally, I venture some ideas about the situation at the present day.

1. The Political Situation in the First Century AD

The first century AD, the age of the *pax romana*, despite local and occasional variations that deserve our attention, was a period that we can think of as a new era. It was characterized by political stability and economic growth that were unparalleled in the history of the world. Rome had subscribed to Alexander the Great's universalist ideal and shouldered its burden, as was characteristic of an imperial power. The development of lines of communication, of economic prosperity, of the Roman citizen's way of life that was offered to the elites of conquered cities, and the development of the *cult of the emperor* as a political concept: all of this constitutes the outcome, in its Roman form, of Alexander's ideal of universalism and cosmopolitanism. This particular stage in the development of the Roman Empire is the first period in world history about which we can speak of a 'single-track' system of thought: there was no alternative to the imperial administration, which coordinated with great efficiency not only political and military power but also economic growth and culture, thereby winning admiration from many people.

With respect to this point, which has been substantiated by historians, we can demonstrate that the authors of the New Testament adopted two attitudes which seem at first glance to be diametrically opposed, and that at least one of these attitudes represented a clean break with the consensus. In the epistolary tradition, we find repeated exhortations to the early Christians to submit to the representatives of imperial authority, while in the Revelation of St John the

Divine we have an urgent call to resist imperial authority without compromise. I next examine each of those attitudes.

2. Exhortation to Submission in the Epistolary Tradition

The New Testament epistles repeatedly exhort people to submit to political authority. Chapter 13 of Paul's Epistle to the Romans is of greatest interest in this respect. 'Let every person be subject to the governing authorities; for there is no authority except from God, and those authorities that exist have been instituted by God.' (Rom. 13:1, NRSV).

A few remarks about this passage (see Käsemann 1969 and Cuvillier 1992): Let us remember that this exhortation to submit to secular authorities on the ground that they were instituted by God is not central to Paul's argument in the Epistle to the Romans. We do not find with Paul, either here or elsewhere in his epistles, any profound discussion of this point that might have led to the development of a Christian Doctrine of the State. Paul is heir to the concept of political power found in Hellenistic Judaism as is shown by Flavius Josephus, who states that 'No ruler attains his office but by the will of God' (*Bellum Judaicum* 2.140). It was this tradition that Paul was to reinterpret in the light of his faith in Jesus as the Messiah.

From his Jewish heritage, Paul retained the idea that the divine institution of power works as a critical element in human justice and that it facilitates an essential transition for the believer: obedience to political authority entails submission not to the men who are empowered by it but to God who is the source of their power. This attitude of submission is therefore not guided by any preoccupation with ingratiating or showing servility towards those in power. It is based on the recognition of God's authority over creation and over mankind, over the governors and the governed, over free men and slaves, and over the weak and the powerful.

For Paul, those who hold power have no particular qualities that differentiate them from common men. It follows that he shows not the slightest allegiance towards those who exercise political power, as is clearly attested in 1 Cor. 2:8, where he asserts that 'None of the rulers of this age understood this; for if they had, they would not have crucified the Lord of glory.' For Paul, these rulers have, like everyone else, a fundamental inability to know and to adore the true God from whom, notwithstanding, they draw their authority. As neither beast nor angel, the holders of political office accomplish, in Paul's opinion, a particular task: they ensure that life on earth carries on according to the divine ordinance. Submission to authority is therefore to obey God's will, which has permitted something rather than nothing at all to regulate life in society. By submitting to this authority, believers do no more than the non-believers do. And having done their duty, they are then free to accomplish their special mission—namely, to live in the world as witnesses to Christ.

This is where we discover the particular point that marks Paul's intentions. From his perspective, the Christians in Rome are called on to have no 'debt' (Greek: *opheilê*) towards the authorities. We touch here upon the paradox of submission, as Paul understands it: for him it means, by strict observance of prescribed rules, nothing less than freeing oneself from any dependence upon political authorities. As an inhabitant of a worldly city, whether a free citizen or a slave, a Jew or a Greek, man or woman, the Roman believers accomplish the duties associated with their secular status in such a way as not to be indebted to anyone. They are indebted to no-one, except for the things due to their specific vocations. We must reread closely the text of verses 7–8: 'Pay to all what is due to them—taxes to whom taxes are due, revenue to whom revenue is due, respect to whom respect is due, honour to whom honour is due. Owe no one anything, except to love one another ...' Therefore, far from either fulfilling itself, or even exhausting itself, by submission, the true Christian vocation finds its accomplishment in another reality—that of living out amongst men the communion of brothers of different conditions as a witness to Christ.

In the pastoral epistles (cf. 1 Tim. 2:1–8; Tit. 3:1–7), written a generation later than Paul, the secular authorities are no longer said to be instituted by God but they are not viewed negatively, either. In fact, the author concerns himself with those who occupy high functions in human government—'for kings and all who are in high positions'—yet are just like any other sinful people whom Christ calls to repentance. To pray for kings and governors and to obey them is simply to live a particular dimension of the Christian vocation that consists in witnessing in words and in acts: 'to be ready for every good work'. 2 Peter, in a Pauline manner, goes even a step further—it is as 'free people' that believers must submit. They are free in that they have been clearly freed by Christ, and therefore servants of God who know to make the difference: to 'honour everyone' and 'honour the emperor' on one hand, and to 'love the family of believers' and 'fear God' on the other hand.

The exhortation to submit to authorities, which can be found repeatedly in the epistolary tradition, takes root in a strong religious belief. The death and resurrection of Christ are interpreted as the advent of a new understanding of reality, according to which through Christ the new world had irrupted into the heart of the old world. This belief is expressed in relation to another belief, according to which the believer is the citizen of another fatherland, the celestial city ('But our citizenship is in heaven': Phil. 3:20), so that he is a stranger on earth. On this point, the author of 1 Peter expresses himself in an evocative passage: 'Beloved, I urge you as aliens (*paroikos*) and exiles (*parepidêmos*)' (1 Peter 2:11). In this temporary existence, it is important to put time to good use by preaching the Gospel without cease: 'so that I might by any means save some' (1 Cor. 9:22). It is within these limits that we must interpret the exhortation to submit to secular authority as a vital but unforced concession to the temporary world order. The 'instituted powers' belong, as does the world that these powers are supposed to govern, to secondary realities that are destined to disappear with the new Creation. Submission to their authority is intended to reap benefits for the missionary task. In no way did submission imply the endorsement of the status quo or the surrender of principle to the old world. It was rather the submission by those who knew themselves to have been emancipated from the power of this world, since Christ had made them free.

Such an attitude is signalled by a paradox that always surprised the early Christians' pagan contemporaries. On one hand, there was an infallible legitimacy, so long as this legitimacy was not contrary to the Gospel. However, at the same time there was a radical relativism in the idea of 'secular authorities': kings, princes and governors are nothing more than men who need to be saved. Hence, as soon as one felt that the essential was at stake in the form of the Gospel, it became necessary to obey God—and Christ—rather than to obey men and the emperor.

3. The Apocalypse of John as a Call to Resistance

The theme of resistance is found only within the framework of the Apocalypse of John.[1] It is constructed around what one could call the 'diabolization' of the imperial constitution (especially Apoc. 13 and 17–18). This diabolizing, however, does not find its origin in a paranoid delirium or in any uncontrolled apocalyptic speculations. On the contrary, it is born from a lucid theological analysis of the political situation as it was at the end of the first century AD: in fact, John of Patmos interprets the situation in which he grew up as a totalitarian and idolatrous claim to imperial power. This power is denounced as a religious system claiming to rule over every aspect of human life, whether political, cultural or economic. This claim is not so much a sign of men's arrogance, and especially of the arrogance of emperors, as it is of their submission to the powers of evil at work in Creation. At the centre of this protest was a belief in the entry of the 'new world' into the very heart of the old world with the event of the Resurrection. At the level of the believer's understanding of his place in the world order, this apocalyptic interpretation of reality finds its object not in a preoccupation with salvation but in a spiritual resistance towards idolatry and in the expectation of judgement that was ordained to befall a world at the hands of the powers of darkness. What is in question is not so much the promulgation of the gospel of salvation as the declaration of the imminence of the Last Judgement and the confirmation of the believer in opposition to the world and its secular power.

It is in the name of a key event, the crucifixion of Christ or 'a slaughtered lamb' (Apoc. 5:6), that the Book of Revelation develops what must be seen as a theological resistance to the secular establishment. St John rebels against the logic of the world and against the Caesar who claims to place restrictions on the

---

[1] On the political context of the Apocalypse of John, see Slater 1998, Thompson 1990 and Cuvillier 2001.

life of each human being. Here, therefore, the confession of faith is a political act, and it brings to each believer a truly hermeneutic approach, which is an understanding of their own existence and the world in which they live. Now to interpret reality is not to objectify it, neither is it to render reality transparent; instead, it is to reconstruct it from a given point of view. It is to understand the world while understanding oneself in the world, which consists in interpreting one's own existence. In a way, we can say that John of Patmos 'recreates' the world; that is to say, he interprets it, rebuilds it, and makes a re-reading from the standpoint of faith in Christ who was crucified, died and was resurrected. To that end, he needs a symbolic language because this language moves towards breaking-point and transports the reader to a different vision and a different understanding. Faith was for John, therefore, an interpretation of the world beginning with the death of Christ and in the conviction that He had been raised from the dead. But in what sense was that a political act? The Resurrection is seen by John as a call to rise up against the logic of the world in which he was living. It brings to life 'something other' than the world, with its belief-system and embedded knowledge. It challenges the status quo ante around which Roman society was organized, and it brings about another reality in which conventional logic is called into question.

For John, to be faithful to this event is to proclaim that the reality of this world is not the last word and that the slogan of power to which all are invited to subscribe is not the right one. But what is this slogan? It can be summarized as: 'There is what there is'. The things you see are the truth: imperial power, the imperial order, the *pax romana* and the hierarchical organization of the world. This is what there is. And this is good.

To have faith in the Resurrection is to proclaim precisely the opposite: 'There is what there is not'. This means that in spite of all appearances and in opposition to the world, Christ conquered death and the powers of evil. Consequently, present reality is only a deception and an illusion, which implies that Roman power and its wish to embrace the totality of human existence is a blasphemous fraud.

In the Roman world, an exaggerated claim to universality (*oikoumênê*, the inhabited earth as bounds of the Empire) coexisted with a no less exaggerated hierarchical partitioning of society: a human being exists only as defined by the place he or she occupies (free man versus slave, Jew versus pagan, Roman versus barbarian, and man versus woman). On the contrary, the Resurrection made manifest that before God and in Christ there were no longer any differences between persons. This means that all individuals, whoever they might be, are loved and recognized independently of their role, objective qualities, or heritage. This gives birth to a real universalism. The only mark that identifies the individual as a subject is not the 'mark of the Beast' (Apoc. 13:16), which indicates to each person the class to which they belong; rather, it is the invisible mark, the new name enrolled in the 'Book of Life', the name that is hidden from the powers of darkness, known only by that the one who receives it (Apoc.

2:17). In brief, the death of Christ and faith in His resurrection is for John the birth of a subject before God, as a unique subject who, with the men of all tongues, nations and tribes who worship the Lamb, makes up the new people of God: a people of priests (Apoc. 1:6). It is this conviction that can be considered revolutionary, in that it overturns the hierarchy that structured Roman society, rendering the believer a dissident in the midst of the world.

4. Submission and Resistance: the Reasons for 'Coexistence'

Submission and resistance. Resistance or submission? How then can we explain the presence at the heart of the New Testament, in the beginnings of Christianity, of two such different positions?

The first response, and the one most frequently made, is to argue historically from the evolution of the earliest Christian communities. Paul and the epistles bear witness to a period when the Roman Empire had not yet identified the Christian community as being distinct from Judaism, and the Jews were not yet subject to persecution—hence their legitimist attitude. The 'diabolization' at work in the Apocalypse would be due, on the contrary, to the first persecutions, especially those of Nero in 64 AD and, subsequently, those of Domitian at the end of the first century.

However, that response is unsatisfactory. Apart from turning the authors of the New Testament into merely 'reactive' theologians—who adapted their beliefs to the perils of the day—it is for the most part contradicted by the texts. In the epistles, Paul states on a number of occasions that he had suffered from the secular authorities. 1 Peter, particularly, discusses the question of submission as treated in Rom. 13, and it is clearly addressed to a community threatened by oppression from those authorities. Lastly, it is important to bear in mind that the Pastoral Epistles and the Apocalypse were in all likelihood written in the same geographical area, at the same time, and for similar communities.

As for the Apocalypse, rather than an encouragement to a persecuted community, it should be read as an exhortation to refuse to accept the logic of the world.[2] While inviting the reader to look critically upon Roman society and upon imperial power, John of Patmos castigates the life of these communities as it might have been reconstituted through the 'letters to the churches'. The Apocalypse of John is certainly an attempt to respond to pressures brought to bear on the Christian communities, but it was most of all a response to their wish to conform to the traditional social practices in the Roman provinces of Asia Minor.

In fact, for the whole of this period the situation of the Christian communities can be characterized as precarious. At any one moment these communities could be the targets of the hostility of the crowds and therefore, sooner or later, of the secular authorities. But it was often true, depending on the

[2] Cf. the author's stern warnings to the seven churches in Apoc. 2–3.

time and place, that they were able to survive for long periods in peace and tranquillity. We should therefore look for an explanation other than the direct influence of the contemporary historical situation upon these conflicting positions. In fact, it is the specific theological tenets of these two traditions, the epistolary and the apocalyptic, that we must question.

Their common foundation is the belief that the Christian subjects find their place outside the secular realities and power, namely in the eschatological intervention of God in the person of Jesus of Nazareth. However, the deployment of this belief takes two different directions, originating in two different conceptions of what is the heart of Christian faith, and they lead, finally, to two quite different ways of looking at the same political reality.

For the epistolary tradition, the event of the death and resurrection of Christ is principally interpreted as an aspect of of soteriology: the call made to all men so that they may receive and believe in the Good News while living in the world; this is the anthropocentric view.

For the Apocalypse of John, the Christological event is above all interpreted within the apocalyptic categories of the claim of God's right over creation and its creatures in the hands of the evil powers; this is the theocentric view.

In both cases, the Christological event reinterprets in depth the traditional attitudes of 'submission' and of 'resistance' that were elsewhere present in the secular or religious ideals of the age. For the epistolary tradition, submission is not understood as the fulfilment of the ideal of the Roman citizen, ideals which reached their apogee in the 'laudation' received by praiseworthy citizens on behalf of the authorities for services rendered to the city or the community. It consists rather in a genuine subversion of the established order and its hierarchies in the name of the call made upon all men by the Gospel of Christ—a call made in a missionary spirit.

For the apocalyptic tradition of John of Patmos, the resistance to the Roman Empire is quite different from the desire to propose a secular or nationalist alternative to it, as was the case with the Zealot movement and at Qumran. It is about spiritual resistance in the face of what is denounced as idolatry and the will to destroy mankind, and its perspective is that of a universalism founded in Christ before whom men and women of all tribes, tongues and nations gather in a prophetic spirit.

5. Conclusion: the Christian Condition as Resistance *and* Submission

To conclude, then. Whether they adopted an attitude of submission following Paul and the epistolary tradition or an attitude of resistance following John of Patmos, the issue for the early Christians was not to take flight but to live in the world on a day-to-day basis, as strangers simply passing through it. The believers of that time considered themselves to be citizens of a truly new fatherland with a different origin from those of this world. Theirs was a Kingdom which challenged the proud kingdoms of this earthly world and which, at the same time, welcomed each of its inhabitants irrespective of their personal attributes, wealth or nationality. Such was the belief of the early Christians.

And what about the people of today? When this question is posed by a commentator engaged in the pursuit of historical knowledge within a department of theology, it should be answered directly. I end by looking briefly at three possible extensions to the enquiry, for both personal and collective reflection.

First of all, I believe the authors of the New Testament remind us, during a careful reading of the Gospel, that the political situation of the day cannot be limited to a single interpretation. The same goes for the capacity of the Christian faith to maintain, when under pressure, two outlooks that are at same time radically critical and reassuringly calm about a political arena that hosts the economic, cultural and religious activities any society.

But we might take one further step and ask ourselves if submission and resistance do not make up two facets of the same reality, namely that of the believer's situation in the world. On one hand, there is a radical resistance in the face of worldly seductions, a resistance that simultaneously grants both faith and insight and which makes of a Christian an 'unrepentant dissident'. Alternatively, if we follow what Jacques Ellul said, the Christian is someone whose choice entails 'a questioning of everything that lays claim to a power or a domination' in the world order (Ellul 1984: 138). And I add this this power could be political, economic, mass media, judiciary, religious or of any other kind.

At the same time, at the core of this 'anarchist' attitude—literally anarchist, in the sense of a refusal to recognize any human power that establishes rights of restraint over the individual—there is a voluntary submission to secular institutions insofar as they permit people to live together as well as possible while allowing all individuals to live out their beliefs. Here is the option of freely submitting in the name of the Gospel, a submission by people who are themselves free.

This is not the alternative of resistance *or* submission but, in a more demanding manner, the uniting of both resistance *and* submission.

References

Cuvillier, E. (1992): 'Soumission aux autorités et liberté chrétienne: exégèse de Rm 13', *Hokhma* 50, 29-47.

——— (2001) 'Christ Ressuscité ou Bête immortelle? Proclamation pascale et propagande impériale dans l'Apocalypse de Jean' in D. Marguerat and O. Mainville (eds), *Résurrection: L'après-mort dans le monde ancien et le Nouveau Testament*. (Genève and Montréal, pp. 237–54.

Ellul, J. (1984): *La Subversion du Christianisme*. Paris.

Käsemann, E. (1969) : 'Principles of Interpretation of Romans 13'. In: *New Testament Questions Today*. London, pp. 196–216 .

Slater, T.B. (1998): 'On the Social Setting of the Revelation to John'. In: *NTS* 44, 232–56.

Thompson, L.L. (1990): *The Book of Revelation: Apocalypse and Empire*. New York and Oxford.

ON HUMAN RIGHTS AND OTHERNESS IN LÉVINAS AND ISLAMIC MYSTICISM

Kasim Küçükalp

In contemporary political philosophy and ethics, the concept of human rights is often discussed with reference to the concept of otherness. I shall argue that both in the writings of Emmanuel Lévinas, a Jewish philosopher with a good grasp of Jewish law, and also in Islamic mysticism we find despite their cultural apartness a philosophical perspective that allows us to re-establish—and to provide a better basis for—the concept of otherness than any one that we can find in mainstream political philosophy and ethics.

At first sight this might appear to be a problematic claim, since the starting points of Lévinas' philosophy and Islamic mysticism are markedly different. Lévinas' philosophy begins with a reflection on the ethical problems of the Western philosophy, whereas Islamic mysticism begins with a spiritual notion of love. However, the concepts of 'human rights', 'freedom of expression', 'freedom to criticize' and 'freedom of opposition', ultimately require an 'ethical I' rather than an 'ontological subject', and both Lévinas' philosophy and Islamic mysticism provide such an approach to the Other. Islamic spiritualism stipulates the 'ethical I', not the 'ontological subject', in its sacred book and tradition, while in Lévinas, one of the foremost representatives of Western philosophy, the necessity for an 'ethical I' is similarly emphasized.

In the present day the main theme of philosophy, and of ethics especially, is the concept of identity and difference. If we seek a reason for that, we need to turn to its philosophical and socio-cultural background and this, I think, can be elucidated by a discussion of Lévinas. According to him, Western philosophy has been from its inception an activity with a human (or subjective) focus. The centrality of the human (or the subjective) gave philosophers an opportunity to define everything from their own epistemological point of view. The ontological question posed by classical philosophy has traditionally been 'What is this?' By taking this perspective, the epistemological subject reduced its own research to the object and placed it in one of the available epistemological categories that eliminated its differences for the sake of identity or unity. Thus, the 'Other' that was conceptualized as the object of ethical philosophy lost its original identity and distinctness. This means that in classical Western philosophy, the foundation of core ethical concepts has been ontological, not truly ethical. However, if we want to fully realize concepts such as human rights, freedom of expression, and freedom to criticize, which are critically important for a healthy society and for good social relationships, we need to redefine the classical ontological perspective so that the otherness of the Other is not eliminated.

1. Lévinas versus the Ontological Imperialism of Western Philosophy

The investigation of the concept of transcendental Good was a lifelong commitment for Emmanuel Lévinas. As Roger Burggraeve remarked, Lévinas locates the idea of the Good in our relation to the Other. What is the idea of the Good? From Lévinas' perspective the answer to this question is that the idea of the Good can be found in us

> as the 'an-archic' fundamental condition in which we find ourselves as subject, and which we also discover through the ethical appeal to an unconditional responsibility that the face of the other awakens in us by its appearance as 'the poor, widow and the orphan': awakening of the I by the other. From this ethics of heteronomy which also forms this basis for a radical redefinition of human rights, there runs a metaphysical trace 'to-God' as a desire for the wholly Other, or the Infinite (Burggraeve 2002: 37–8).

The ethical I is a subject who recognizes the radical difference of the Other and does not strive to assimilate it. Likewize, the ethical I is a subject who esteems the value of difference in itself and does not fall into the temptation of an ontological imperialism of sameness.[1]

For Lévinas, the notion of the ontological subject is based on Western metaphysical thought, specifically the concept of *logos*, that is to say, the Greek concept of truth, in the realm of thinking and speaking. For this reason, Lévinas attempts first of all to elucidate the distinctive character of the Greek language of philosophy. Accordingly, if the essence of this language is taken into consideration, truth is a *present* or *co-present* entity in a totality that can be called 'world' or 'cosmos'. Thus, in the context of the Greek model, truth is a *presentable* and *re-presentable* entity in an eternal here and now. To associate truth with presence in that way means that truth and presence are equivalent and can be identified with one another. Being is reduced to presence (Lévinas 2002: 266–7). By means of this reduction, philosophy aims at establishing a first cause, an absolute beginning, an ontological foundation which renders everything comprehensible by dissolving the *explanandum* in a totality. It is obvious that this tendency of dissolving differences in the sameness of totality has grave

[1] In my opinion, both in Western and Eastern traditional thought, but especially in Islamic thought, the legality of others' human rights—in other words, the others' freedom of existence and the rights of existence, described or criticized in discussions about freedom of expression and freedom to criticize—is possible only if individuals are conceptualized as ethical subjects.

ethical implications. For Lévinas, Western philosophy is a philosophy that destroys the otherness of the Other by describing it as 'a being':

> Western philosophy coincides with the unveiling of the Other where the Other in showing itself as being, loses its otherness. From its infancy, philosophy has been filled with the horror of the Other which remains Other, an almost incurable allergy to it. It is because of this that it is essentially a philosophy of being, that the comprehension of being is its last word and the fundamental structure of man. It is for that reason also that it becomes a philosophy of immanence and autonomy, or atheism. The God of philosophers, from Aristotle on to Leibniz, is a God adequate to reason, a God who is understood, who will not trouble the autonomy of consciousness—this consciousness which find itself after all of its exploits, returning home like Ulysses who, through all his wanderings, was really only traveling to his native isle. The philosophy which has been transmitted to us leads to this starting point not only speculative thought, but all spontaneous movement of consciousness. It is not only the world understood by reason which ceases to be other because consciousness rediscovers itself there (Lévinas 1966: 35).

For Lévinas, Western philosophy—or, in other words, ontology—strives to dissolve meaning in totality and reduces the irreducible alterity of transcendence to an encompassing ontological ground. This becomes most apparent from the perspective of Greek ontology, which seeks to anchor truth in unity. According to the Greek ontology, the last word is a unity, a uniting truth that combines the plural appearances of beings in a synthesis. Lévinas, by contrast, argues that 'difference' is a more suitable word than 'totality' to interpret a human's ethical relationship with the Other (Lévinas 2002: 270–1).

From this starting point, Lévinas argues that the concept of totality has developed in Western philosophy as a consequence of the demand for unity, and that it has determined the dominant understanding of the Other in Western philosophy. In this philosophy, every attempt to understand the Other has in reality destroyed its radical difference by pressing it into the same mould as everything else. Accordingly, for Lévinas, ontological imperialism is the hallmark of Western philosophy. As a philosophy of power, it operates by transforming the Other into the Same. Lévinas states that this ontological imperialism is based on the notion of the ontological subject. The only way out of such ontological imperialism is to establish and take as a starting point a notion not of the ontological subject but of the ethical subject instead. As Madan Sarup has stated, there is a relationship between Lévinas' ethical subjects and the Other but, contrary to the main current of Western philosophy, this relationship respects the heterogeneity of the Other (Sarup 1996: 68). This ethical relationship is a relationship with a mortal being and consists both in not deserting the Other in his or her death and also in dying for the Other, or sacrificing oneself for the Other (Direk 2005: 32).

This, I think, is the point at which Lévinas and Sufic ethics break away from the main current of Western ethics. Western philosophy crosses out the otherness of the Other by defining him or her within the epistemological boundaries of the subject, and thus Western philosophy does not permit the Other to define him- or herself as he or she actually is. In opposition to this metaphysical comprehension of difference, Lévinas offers a kind of ethical thinking that depends on the principle of 'irreducibility of the Other'. This line of thought also has important consequences for theology. Lévinas rejects the well-worn arguments about the existence of God which seek to understand God according to a pattern of logical reasoning (Lévinas 2002: 265). He proposes that God is the absolute Other and that 'going to God' should not be understood in terms of classical ontology, which understands this going as turning to God who is the Beginning or End of temporal existence. 'Going to God' must be understood primarily in terms of going to the Other. For this reason, the criterion of 'going to God' is being worried about the Other and demonstrating ethical concern for him or her. Consequently, by being ethically responsible to or for the Other, one is freed from the bondage of the natural world and able to think about the Other in ways that do not reduce him or her to 'a being'; in this way, the political concepts based on reduction are undermined (Lévinas 2002: 272).

In Lévinas' perspective, the ground of the relationship with the Other is a love that demands suppression of the ego in favour of the Other so as to give priority to ethics. This relationship presupposes that an entity does not survive alone and does not find any meaning in the ontology of sameness. In Lévinas' ethics, the Other's right to exist takes priority over the rights of the self. By emphasizing the precedence of the Other over the self, Lévinas' ethics prohibits violence on the part of the self. It is only possible to actualize this prohibition if priority for the Other is activated by what goes beyond the natural. According to Lévinas, God is the Other who calls into question our striving for ontological domination. Put differently, this is precisely the call to an ethical conscience that we find in the Judeo-Christian tradition as well as in all other religions (Lévinas 2002: 273).

2. The Basis of Ethical Responsibility to or for the Other in Islamic Mysticism

Human self-realization is essential, both in Islamic moral philosophy in general and in one of its most special forms, namely *tasawwuf*, the discipline of spiritual development often associated with Sufism. The concept of self-realization, however, is an ethical one; it is not based on any epistemological or rational ground. Coming closer to the divine can be realized only through an ethical process.

From the perspective of *tasawwuf*, the Other plays a determining role in human self-realization. The individual's renunciation of his or her ambition and ego is essential for a meaningful relationship with the Other.[2] To remove the differences with the Other entails rebuilding the self in the other's ego, rather than assimilating the latter to the former. The concepts of *fanâ fi'l-ihvan* (obliteration of the self in one's companions), *fanâ fi'r-rasûl* (obliteration of the self in the Prophet) and *fanâ fi'llâh* (obliteration of the self in Allah) are ethical terms with a practical import that make it possible to achieve the ultimate goal of being at one with God (Kara 1995: 165).

The emphasis upon renunciation of oneself in favour of the Other is so strong in *tasawwuf* that it is deemed necessary for human beings to consider themselves as not only lower than their fellow-humans but also lower than all other creatures. In this respect, the story of Moses in the epic tradition of Sufism is telling. As the story goes, God asked Moses to bring to Him the vilest being on earth. Moses searched everywhere, and when at last he found a diseased dog he put its collar around his own neck and returned to God saying, 'O Lord, I could not find any being viler than me.' That is the point which constitutes the basis of the ethical relationship of the self with Others in *tasawwuf* and in Islamic moral philosophy in general.

In the tradition of *tasawwuf*, the ethical relationship with the Other is embodied in the concept of *isar*. This concept, in the general sense of the word, refers to the preferring of the Other to the self (al-Qushayrî 1986: 502). The Qur'an verse ([Al-Hashr] 59:9) '(They) give them preference over themselves, even though poverty was their (own lot)', and the famous Hadith 'He who sleeps with a full stomach when his neighbour is hungry does not belong to us', both illustrate the concept of *isar*. Accordingly, preferring the Other to the self in any situation where benefits are to be had, and volunteering oneself instead of the Other where discomforts must be endured, are essential for the ethical relationship between human beings.

This is illustrated by the following story. On a journey, Ebu Hüseyn el-Nuri and his friends were caught by brigands. The brigands decided to execute them. Despite the fact that Ebu Hüseyn el-Nuri was at the end of the line, he demanded that the killing begin with himself, so that his friends could live longer than he ('Attâr 1907: 46). This story shows that preferring the Other at the expense of one's own life was one of the most important principles in *tasawwuf*. Even the concept of 'faith' (*iman*) requires us to give preference to the Other. We find the same principle expressed in the following saying of the Prophet Muhammed, peace be upon him: 'None of you truly believes until he wishes for his brother what he wishes for himself' (Hadith 13 [Nawawi]) and in Abu Bekr's prayer: 'O my Lord! In Hell, enlarge my body until there remains no empty place for any human beings to come into it.'

In Sufism, all creatures are worthy of unrequited respect because of their divine status. In the Qur'an, the human connection to the Deity is expressed in

---

[2] The ultimate goal of *tasawwuf* is the experience of being at one with God—who is called 'the absolute Other' by Lévinas—removing all differences between God and mankind.

the idea that God created humanity by exhaling His soul. Accordingly, human beings are seen as having a divine 'essence' from the beginning of creation. It is essential for humans to protect and maintain this divine essence. The same idea is also found in Islamic mysticism, in the distinction between self and soul (*nefs-ruh*). While the 'self' characterizes the egoistic aspect of humanity that must be purified and refined, the 'soul' represents the divine aspect of humanity that must be enhanced and protected.

Moreover, the use of language, in which human beings resemble God, is the foundation of the ethical relationship with the Other. This is because the disclosure of truth, which is specific to human beings, is possible only through language. The Hadith 'Whoever believes in Allah and the Last Day should speak a good word or remain silent'[3] and the ethical imperative 'Do not make disparaging remarks about anybody' are therefore very important principles in Islamic ethics. It is necessary for human beings to take responsibility for the truth that is disclosed through language. If a human being expresses his or her relationship with the Other by referring to their negative features, it fixes the Other's identity in a negative framework. This means both the Other's losing his or her chance of becoming different from the self and also the Other's social exclusion. Contrary to this approach, *tasawwuf* implies that every human being has some good attributes. The enhancement of these attributes by revealing the Other's good qualities is important in minimising the destructive and unethical dimensions of language.

Furthermore, since social norms depend on the ego and serve to protect the continuity of the ego, *tasawwuf* argues that censure must be avoided if a truly ethical personality is to develop. Both praise and blame deny the difference of the Other and ultimately advance the development of a wholly selfish ego. To attach importance to society's assessments would be to give importance to the selfish ego (*nefs*). In Islamic mysticism, therefore, we find the idea that the development of a true ego is possible only by becoming indifferent to society's praise or blame (al-Sulamî 1942). At this point, there is a clear similarity between *tasawwuf* and Lévinas. Just as in the Sufi perspective, Lévinas calls attention to the threat of societal domination that is exerted through praise and blame.

In order to understand what kind of personality *tasawwuf* wants to establish, we can consider a central idea expressed in the concept of 'abandonment' (*terk*). In a famous couplet, Imam Rabbani takes up the concept of terk like this:

Der tarîk-i nakş-bendî azıma-mı çâr-i terk
Terk-i dünyâ, terk-i 'ukbâ, terk-i hestî, terk-i terk

---

[3] Abū Hurayrah relates that Allah's Messenger (peace be upon him) said: 'Whoever believes in Allah and the Last Day should speak a good word or remain silent. And whoever believes in Allah and the Last Day should show hospitality to his neighbour. And whoever believes in Allah and the Last Day should show hospitality to his guest' (*Sahīh al-Bukhārī* and *Sahīh Muslim).*

> In the way of Nakşibendî, four kinds of abandonment are necessary: Abandonment of the world, abandonment of the next world, abandonment of existence and abandonment of the abandonment (al-Sirhindî 1972).

A true Sufi must abandon what his ego (*nefs*) likes and must be open to rescue from his egoism and moral diseases. What is implied here is that some moral or spiritual diseases present themselves in a religious guise. At this point, the idea of abandonment helps human beings to struggle with these diseases. In the context of the idea of abandonment, we find the idea that nothing is worthy of being desired for itself except God (*Allah*).

In *tasawwuf*, ethics or morality necessitate a person's reflective thinking about his or her own existence. From the Sufic perspective, pondering one's own existence leads to important ethical and spiritual conclusions. First of all, a person must accept his or her limited and finite being as part of creation. Secondly, through honest reflection on their own existence, people become fully aware of their ethical diseases, deficiencies and weaknesses. And finally, they understand that they cannot attain every truth by means of human reason. They must abandon their reason and existence in order to attain the truth (al-Haravî 1962). From the viewpoint of Islamic mysticism, it is the person's own existence that impedes their contemplation of truth.

This corresponds closely to Lévinas' insistence that the radical alterity of God or the Other reveals the essential inadequacy of attempts to understand them. According to Lévinas, the 'un-known-ness' of the Other is essential, not accidental or coincidental. It is necessary to understand that the conceptualizing ego has no access to a state in which the Other is completely understood and 'grasped':

The 'un-known-ness' of the Other is not merely accidental or coincidental but essential and definitive. The conceptualizing ego will never be in a position to completely grasp and know the Other. The face is the site of what will forever remain 'ungiven'. It manifests itself paradoxically, as the 'great un-known', or better, the 'great unknowable'. It appears in disappearing; it shows itself by withdrawing (Burggraeve 2002: 92).

3. Conclusion

I have argued that the dominant current of Western ontology does not provide a comprehensive ethical position from which a truly ethical relationship with the 'Other' can be established. In European philosophy, one of the most interesting criticisms of this Western ontology has been elaborated by Emmanuel Lévinas, who sharply criticizes the Western (and European) perception of the other as metaphysical violence or ontological imperialism exerted over the Other. This is so, in his opinion, because the humanistic or epistemological perspectives of Western metaphysical thought had separated the human being or the epistemological subject from the Other, giving him or her secondary importance and eventually leading to the annihilation of the Other's otherness. Lévinas wants to distinguish ethics from ontology. His ethics is situated in an 'encounter' with the Other which cannot be reduced to a symmetrical 'relationship'. He believes that a pre-ontological ethics needs to be established in order to obtain a truly ethical philosophy. A relationship with a mortal being can be ethical if and only if it allows the Other to live and does not leave the Other alone to his or her death, but it also entails 'dying' for the sake of the Other, or sacrificing the self for the Other, or taking the Other's place in his or her death (Direk 2005: 32).

To conclude, I have shown that Lévinas suggests an alternative ethics, which he calls 'first philosophy' or a pre-ontological philosophy. I have also argued that Lévinas' ethical project presents a surprising and striking resemblance to the traditional Sufic perception of the ethical subject. Just as Lévinas does, the Sufic tradition makes us aware of the fact that it is not possible to create an ethical 'I' without giving priority to the Other over oneself. In Sufic discourse, this type of ethical 'I' can be reached through certain attempts at self-control and self-criticism. On the basis of this perspective drawn from Lévinas and Sufic ethics, I conclude that a truly ethical relationship with the Other requires us to establish an unconditional ethics that does not attempt to dominate the Other, that does not deny the differences of the Other, and that does not erase these differences in the unity of sameness.

In the light of this perspective, I believe that without establishing such an ethical philosophy there will be no recognition of the Other in his or her otherness. What we need, just as in Lévinas' and Sufic understanding, is an ethic that does not attempt to assimilate the Other to sameness.

References

'Attâr, Farîd al-Dîn-i (1907): *Tadhkirat al-awliyâ' ii*, Leiden.

Burggraeve, Roger (2002): *The Wisdom of Love in the Service of Love*. Transl. by J. Bloechl. Milwaukee.

Direk, Z. (2005): 'Sunuş', Emmanuel Lévinas, *Zaman ve Başka*. Transl. by Ö. Gözel. İstanbul.

al-Haravî, 'Abdallâh al-Ansârî (1962): *al-Manâzil al-Sâirîn*. Ed. by S.L. Beaurecueil. Cairo.

Kara, M. (1995): *Tasavvuf ve Tarikatlar Tarihi* (The History of Tasawwuf and Orders). Istanbul.

Lévinas, E. (1966): 'On the Trail of the Other'. Transl. by D. J. Hoy. In: *Philosophy Today*, 10:1 pp. 34–47.

——— (2002): 'Fenomenolojiden Etiğe'. Transl. by. Ö. Gözel. In: Z. Direk and E. Gökyaran (eds) *Sonsuza Tanıklık*. Istanbul.

al-Qushayrî, 'Abd al-Karîm (1986): *al-Risâla*, Cairo.

Sarup, M. (1996): *Identity, Culture and the Postmodern World.* Ed. by R. Tasneem. Edinburg.

al-Sirhindî, Ahmed (1972): *Maktubât-ı Imâm Rabbânî*, Karachi.

al-Sulamî, Abû 'Abd al-Rahmân Muhammad b. al-Husayn (1942) *al-Risâla al-Malâmiyya*. Ed. by Abû al-'Alâ 'Afîfî. In: *al-Majalla al-Kulliyya al-Âdâb*, Cairo.

ENVIRONMENTALISM AS A CIVIL RELIGION: THE CASE OF SWEDEN

Carl Reinhold Bråkenhielm

Although belief systems may be developed by influential philosophers, they may also be disseminated in a popular form. Environmentalism is such a belief system—a very broad one, embracing everything from the ordinary citizen's concerns about pollution and climate change to elaborate ecological credos. I shall not seek to define environmentalism more precisely than that, but towards the end of the chapter I shall return to the more theoretical question and make a few observations about it. My main thesis is that environmentalism can be interpreted as a civil religion, and I shall use Sweden as an example. The concept of civil religion was revived by Robert Bellah in the nineteen-sixties to designate the affirmations of a transcendent religious reality revealed through the experience of the American people and celebrated at various points in the life of the nation (Bellah and Hammond 1980). I propose that environmentalism (or ecologism) can perform a similar function. It is not my intention to misuse the concept of religion, but I would like to suggest that the distinction between the secular and the sacred is not so clear as is sometimes assumed in religious studies. In fact, environmentalism hovers somewhere between the secular and the sacred. That is one of the reasons why it is of special interest both to theology and to religious studies.

In the first part of the chapter, I shall seek to cast light on the complexity of the dominant forms of environmentalism. In the second part, I shall show how the main political actors on the Swedish stage have made use of common environmental concerns to support particular political objectives. After providing identities of resistance, environmentalism has been transformed in order to deliver legitimizing identities for political power. This process has an analogy in the development of the early church, from providing identities of resistance towards both Jewry and Roman power, through being turned gradually into a set of identities legitimating the imperial power, and ultimately to being transformed by Constantine into a state religion. Of course, Swedish environmentalism has not officially been declared a state religion, but it has come quite close to that in recent decades. That was especially true under the former Social Democratic government, succeeded in 2006 by the centre-right Alliance for Sweden (which continued as a minority government after the general election in September 2010). Initially, the Alliance had a more restrained approach to environmental issues, but this has changed and environmental issues are now high on the political agenda.

1. The Nature of Sweden

I make my point of departure the main Chamber of the Parliament Building in Stockholm. When Parliament reassembled for the first time after the building's renovation in 1983, its members found the Chamber decorated with a remarkable work of art. Above the podium now hangs a tapestry of 54 square meters by the Swedish artist Elisabet Hasselberg Olsson. It bears the title *Memory of a Landscape* and it represents a misty landscape, such as might be found almost anywhere in Sweden. No human beings are present; we are put in mind of nature, untouched by human hands.

In studies of Swedish culture, we are repeatedly reminded of the Swedish passion for nature. A recently-published book on the Swedish mentality, by Henrik Berggren and Lars Trägårdh (2009), opens with a review of similar observations made by twentieth-century scholars. Some would even argue that the love of nature is the obverse of a more detached attitude to other people. 'We Swedes are interested in nature, but not in other human beings', wrote Professor Gustaf Sundbärg in 1911. And the journalist Sanfrid Neander-Nilsson subsequently claimed that 'outside the big city, the major part of Swedish consciousness is dominated by the Swedish forests'.

These students of the Swedish national character were not, of course, detached and objective observers; they are part of a specific discourse fed by the *Blut und Boden* philosophy and later—in a different way—by the environmentalist agenda. But before focusing on that particular perspective, I cannot refrain from another quotation—this time from Astrid Lindgren. She was primarily a writer of children's books, and children all over the world know that Pippi Longstocking is the strongest girl in the world, and that Emil is mischievous but kind-hearted. To a large extent Astrid Lindgren drew inspiration from her native Näs, not far from Vimmerby in the province of Småland. In a picture-book (*Mitt Småland*, 1987) she pays tribute to her heritage and childhood.

> If somebody asks me what I remember from my childhood, then my first thought is not the people but *nature*, which embraced my days then and filled them so intensely that as adult one can hardly understand it. The strawberry patches, the anemone fields, the cowslip meadows, the bilberry thickets, the wood with the pink twinflower bells in the moss, the pastures around Näs, where we knew each track and each stone, the stream with water lilies, the ditches, the brooks and the trees; all this I remember more than I remember the people. Trees and stones, they were almost as close to us as living beings, and it was nature that protected and nurtured our playing and our dreams. (Lindgren, Strömstedt and Norman 1987: 20)

Whether or not these sentiments are unique to Swedish culture is open to question. It is easy to find parallels to these sentiments in other cultures, and many scholars have argued that the Swedish love affair with nature is nothing but a myth. Even so, tourist websites portray Sweden as a nature-loving country. We are told that Swedish poetry and its prose literature are filled with imagery from forests, mountains and lakes, and that reverence for nature is part of Swedish national identity. Americans of Swedish origin agree. One such person is the American theologian James M. Gustafson, who writes in one of his books about his parents, who came from Luleå, in the north of Sweden:

> While technology and industrial interests were penetrating what was almost wilderness, my father, like almost all Swedes I have known well, retained a deep respect for the natural environment and an almost mystical relation to waterfalls, birch trees, and other of its aspects.[1]

Are these attitudes representative of most Swedes—or are James Gustafson's friends in the minority? Gustafson's remarks do not correspond with the more general remarks about the industrial conquest and exploitation of nature. Many scholars would argue that pre-industrial and industrial attitudes to nature have been idealized and romanticized. Lars Kardell—a retired professor from the Swedish University of Agricultural Sciences—has studied Swedish attitudes to one particular aspect of nature, namely the forest. He argues that 'from medieval times onwards, we have numerous examples in written documents of a powerfully negative shared attitude to forests' (Kardell 1990). Modern urban attitudes are more positive, albeit romantic. Is the love story between Swedes and nature a modern myth?

Kardell's studies are consistent with the general idea that pre-industrial attitudes to the natural world were more hostile and that industrial sentiments were more exploitative than was later the case. There might be important exceptions to this idea in the nineteenth century, involving artists and cultural elites both in Sweden and in many other countries. For example in the USA, John Muir (1838–1914) and his supporters formed the Sierra Club 'to make the mountains glad'. The general impression is that these were indeed exceptions to the rule of nature-exploitation. But what about *post*industrial attitudes to nature in general—and more specifically—in contemporary Swedish society?

---

[1] Gustafson 1994: 2. Is this mystical feeling for nature a uniquely Swedish sentiment? We have insufficient data for a clear answer to the question. But it is noteworthy that, after analysing popular reactions to the Great Storm that hit Southern England on 15t October 1987, the English sociologist Peter Dickens claims that this material is evidence of a feeling of alienation from nature. After a great storm such a sentiment is not surprising, but Dickens argues that there are other data which make it clear those attitudes towards nature in England are different from those in Sweden. See further Peter Dickens (1991).

2. A New Environmental Paradigm

This question about postindustrial attitudes towards nature has been addressed by scholars working in different disciplines, such as historians, philosophers, and political and social scientists. Limiting the field to empirical surveys, there have been many international surveys of attitudes towards the environment and to environmental policies.[2] Many of these surveys have been carried out in the context of the World Value Survey led by the American social scientist Ronald Inglehart. Others have been inspired by Riley Dunlap and his ideas of an emerging 'New Ecological Paradigm' (NEP). Many of these studies were undertaken in the 1980s and 1990s, and they revealed a 'fundamental shift from a primarily technologically to a primarily ecologically inspired social value pattern' (Ester et al. 2003: 19).

These ecological attitudes have been interpreted by Paul C. Stern and others as values, and Stern has distinguished 'several stable and coherent value clusters that correlate strongly with environmental attitudes and behaviors'. Environmental concerns are rooted in a person's value system (Stern et al. 1995, Stern and Dietz 1994). Stern and others have argued that people's attitudes to environmental issues are based on the values that they place upon themselves, upon other people, and upon plants and animals. Each of these clusters of values provides a distinct basis for environmental concern, such that two people could express the same level of general concern (e.g., concern for air pollution) for fundamentally different reasons (e.g. polluted air is dangerous to my health, polluted air is dangerous to children's health, or polluted air is damaging to forests) (Ester 2003: ch. 1).

Subsequently—in collaboration with colleagues—Paul Stern has developed a value-belief-norm (VBN) theory. According to this theory, five variables explain environmentally significant behaviour and especially nonactivist environmentalism, that is to say 'support for or acceptance of public policies (for example, stated approval of environmental regulations, willingness to pay higher taxes for environmental protection)' (Stern 2000: 408, 417). This kind of *nonactivist* environmentalism could be contrasted with environmental *activism*, i.e. active involvement in environmental organizations and participation in demonstrations. Personal values are but one component in a cluster of factors that explain nonactivist environmentalism. There are, however, also a number of other factors such as (i) assent to the items of the *new environmental paradigm* (NEP), (ii) *beliefs* about major environmental threats and what actions might avert those threats and, most importantly, (iii) *personal norms* (about pro-environmental actions), that are activated by those beliefs.

---

[2] Inglehart (1997), Inglehart and Welzel (2005), Ray and Anderson (2000), Dunlap, Gallup and Gallup (1992), Dunlap, Gallup and Gallup (1993), European Commission (2005), Särkimukka, Edlund and Svallfors (2000), Ester et al. (2003). A good overview is found in Ester et al. (2003: ch. 1).

An important theoretical background for the VBN theory can be found in Shalom Schwartz's norm-activation theory. Schwartz distinguishes between personal norms and social norms. Personal norms motivate individuals to act because activation is linked to their self-expectation. Schwartz writes that:

> I am proposing that individuals sometimes act in response to their own self expectations, their own personal norms. What distinguishes personal norms from social norms is that the sanctions attached to personal norms are tied to the self-concept. Anticipation of or actual conformity to a self-expectation results in pride, enhanced self-esteem, security, or other favorable self-evaluations; violation or its anticipation produce guilt, self-depreciation, loss of self-esteem, or other self-evaluations. (Schwartz 1977: 221)

Schwartz assumes that personal norms are activated by the awareness of adverse consequences for valued objects (AC) and the attribution of responsibility to oneself for bringing about or preventing those consequences (AR). Valued objects might be other human beings, but they might also be entities other than human beings, such as the natural environment. Such values have a central place in ecological belief systems.

3. The New Ecological Paradigm as a Belief System

In the present context, I want to concentrate on the NEP-scale and the concept of a belief system. Some items on the New Environmental Paradigm (NEP) scale were constructed by Riley Dunlap and K.D. van Liere to measure such beliefs. This scale originally consisted of 12 items, but was later extended to 15 items (Dunlap et al. 2000). Table 1 (below) shows the extended version of the NEP with data from a sample of residents in Washington State.

Table 1 *Frequency distributions (%) for New Ecological Paradigm Scale items*

	Do you agree or disagree that:	Strongly agree	Mildly agree	Undecided	Mildly disagree	Strongly disagree
1	We are approaching the number of people that the earth can support.	27.7	25.2	21.0	16.0	10.0
2	Humans have the right to modify the natural environment to suit their needs.	4.1	28.5	9.2	33.9	24.3
3	When humans interfere with nature it produces disastrous consequences	44.6	37.6	4.0	11.2	2.5

4	Human ingenuity will ensure that we do NOT make the earth un-livable.	7.8	23.5	21.5	24.4	22.7
5	Humans are severely abusing the environment.	51.3	35.3	2.6	9.3	1.5
6	The earth has plenty of natural resources if we just learn how to develop them.	24.4	34.8	11.3	17.5	11.9
7	Plants and animals have as much right as humans to exist.	44.7	32.2	4.7	12.8	5.7
8	The balance of nature is strong enough to cope with the impact of modern industrial nations.	1.1	7.4	11.3	30.9	49.4
9	Despite our special abilities, humans are still subject to the laws of nature.	59.6	31.3	5.4	2.9	0.8
10	The so-called 'ecological crisis' facing humankind has been greatly exaggerated.	3.9	17.9	13.8	25.9	38.5
11	The earth is like a spaceship with very limited room and resources.	38.0	36.3	7.3	13.4	4.8
12	Humans were meant to rule over the rest of nature.	13.5	20.4	8.2	23.9	34.0
13	The balance of nature is very delicate and easily upset.	45.9	32.8	24.2	27.9	24.6
14	Humans will eventually learn enough about how nature works to be able to control it.	3.2	20.1	24.2	27.9	24.5
15	If things continue on their present course, we will soon experience a major ecological catastrophe.	34.3	31.0	16.9	14.1	3.6

In a study from 1998, Örjan Widegren used a nationwide sample from Sweden to study the correlation between NEP (using a shorter 6-item version), personal norms and self-reported proenvironmental behavior (PEB). One of the findings was that personal norms (measured through expressions of guilt) were more strongly correlated with PEB than with the NEP scale (Widegren 1998). Another finding was that more than 40 % of the Swedes 'strongly agreed' with the NEP—and more than two-thirds 'strongly agreed' or 'agreed' with each of the six items of the NEP scale. On the other hand, only a minority of the

Swedes perceived local environmental problems to be 'serious' or 'very serious' (according to Gooch's study in 1995).

It must be emphasized that studies of the American population also find very strong support for the items on the NEP scale. In a nationwide American survey made by Dunlap in 1992, 86 % agreed that 'the balance of nature is very delicate and easily upset by human activities' (Dunlap, Gallup and Gallup 1992). More recent data from the World Value-Survey and the Eurobarometer suggest that environmental awareness on the part of Swedish citizens seems to follow a more general pattern found in many European countries as well as in the USA. Seventy-seven per cent of respondents would agree to an increase in taxes if the extra money were used to prevent environmental pollution. This figure is quite high in the USA, too, at 61%. But it is surprisingly low, at only 29 %, in Germany. Other data suggest that willingness to make sacrifices for the environment is high, not only in Sweden but also in a number of other Western countries including the USA, as well as in a number of third world countries, such as Vietnam.[3]

Table 2 *Comparison between the USA and Sweden (2006)*

	USA Agree strongly and mildly (%)	Sweden Agree entirely and partly (%)
The balance of nature is very delicate and easily upset.	79	85
The earth is like a spaceship with very limited room and resources.	74	72
When humans interfere with nature it produces disastrous consequences.	83	70

4. Ideologies in Sweden

Many of these surveys have included representative samples of the Swedish population and provided interesting comparisons to citizen attitudes elsewhere in the world. Other studies have been more limited in scope and more focused on the Swedish population. Examples of the latter are the ideological surveys carried out by researchers inspired by the work of Anders Jeffner, a former professor of theology at Uppsala. The study of ideologies as a specific academic field of enquiry dates back to the 1968–76, when Jeffner led a research project—'Ideologies in Modern Society'—with support from the Bank

[3] On the other hand Vietnam scored among the lowest in the world on the question if human beings should coexist with nature (53 %). Ninety-five per cent of the Swedes choose this alternative.

of Sweden Tercentenary Foundation. This project produced several reports on the study of ideologies, but the most lasting contribution of the project was a conceptual proposal made by Jeffner himself, namely a stipulative definition of ideologies or 'outlooks on life' (sv. livsåskådning). Presenting the new field of research for the quincentennial anniversary of Uppsala University in 1977, Jeffner summarized his proposal in the following terms:

> The Swedish word *livsåskådning* is very vague in everyday speech, but it is possible to give a stipulative definition which is in accordance with common usage and which also makes it possible to single out an interesting set of intellectual and emotional reactions. This is a certain complex whole, consisting of a person's central values and norms, the basic feelings which can be said to characterize his experience of life and those cognitive elements which influence, or are dependent on, the ethical and attitudinal components. (Gyllenkrok and Jeffner 1976: 129)

In essence, an ideology consists of three parts: (i) central values and norms, summarized more formally in ethics and morality; (ii) a comprehensive idea of reality, a cosmology; and (iii) basic attitude, optimism or pessimism, hope or despair.

Many studies followed Jeffner's conceptual proposal, especially studies of the wider Swedish public. The main results confirm earlier findings by sociologists of religion. The majority of the Swedish population (c. 78% in 2009) belong to the Lutheran church. Most people are baptized, most of them marry, and almost half of the fifteen-year-olds are confirmed in the Lutheran church of Sweden. But the figures are dropping, and according to many—if not most—indicators Sweden is one of the most secularized countries in the world.

The Uppsala study of ideologies and value systems in 1986 revealed a large zone of uncertainty between firmly-held religious beliefs and categorical unbelief—and showed that this is a neglected area of considerable interest. Many people in the intermediate zone have a great interest in existential matters. A book by the Norwegian theologian Pål Ketil Botvar has the poignant title *Religion without Church* (1993). Botvar estimates that about 70% of the Norwegian population belong to this group. In my opinion, the proportion in Sweden is similar. It appears that the number of such people is growing—at least in Western Europe. Jan Kerkofs, the former leader of the EVSSG-project, suggests that the group of 'open agnostics' is of key interest for the future. They do not deny the existence of a transcendent dimension, but they remain hesitant to characterize it in any way. While accepting the possibility of an opening into another dimension, they decline to give it a name. Typical of this group of 'open agnostics' is the following statement from a middle-aged woman interviewed in the Uppsala study of 1986. She gives the following answer to a question about whether the interview has captured what she thinks is important in life:

> Partly I have expressed most things, but it is difficult to describe the inner feeling. Emotions and thoughts, sometimes contradictory, sometimes strong. Do I believe in God?—I don't know, but still I know that there is something, for example, in the unknown. Do I have moral values?—Yes, but why? What are they founded on? Is it only something I have been taught? It is difficult to find an answer.

It is clear that in this intermediate area between belief and unbelief we find no clearly constructed systems of faith, no poignantly-declared confessional structures. Most people appear to have fragmented and loosely-connected thoughts on life and human beings—a tentative ideology, as it were. There are, of course, those who have a more clearly elaborated ideology, where elements of Christian belief are combined with non-Christian ideas. It is not unusual, for example, for people to combine ideas of heaven with ideas of reincarnation.

All this suggests that Swedish people's beliefs are nuanced and that the picture of a secularized Sweden might not be the whole truth. It can also be seen in some other survey findings. In the WVS survey carried out in 1990, representative population samples from different European countries were given the choice between four alternatives:

1. There is a personal God.
2. There is some spirit or life force.
3. Don't know.
4. There is no spirit, nor God.

It comes as no surprise that Sweden has the lowest population percentage in Europe who believe in a personal God. Only 15% of the Swedes believe this, compared with 67% of the Irish. More surprising, however, was the finding that 44% of the Swedes believe in a spirit or life force. This is the highest percentage in Europe—while the Irish percentage is among the lowest, at 24%.

How is this to be interpreted? The Swedish writer Birgitta Trotzig offers a challenging analysis. Against the flow of all theories of secularization, she writes:

> The average Swede is a strongly religious person, who finds the established religious symbolism offered by society quite unsatisfactory and therefore no longer wants to talk about it, turning instead to the deep eye of Nature with her life and her quest. But the Swede has powerful emotions reserved for a small number of significant moments in life: when a child is baptized, when vows are made at the altar, when the dead are buried to comfortable words of peace and resurrection, or when a candle is lit in the graveyards against the great darkness. (Trotzig 1987: 82)

I think that Birgitta Trotzig goes too far in her analysis. But she is surely right when she notices that a large stream of spiritual consciousness flows outside the established religious institutions. Where, then, do we find this churchless spirituality?

5. Nature as Religion

One answer to this question could be 'in the environmental movement'. Several social scientists and religious scholars have drawn attention to the close link between environmentalism and spirituality/religion. Needless to say, conceptual issues arise concerning this linkage. What is environmentalism? What is religion? In what way is spirituality different from religion? Considerable efforts have been devoted to these conceptual issues and the more specific relationships between environmentalism and religion (Gardner 2002). This is not the time to explore such a large field of enquiry, but a major distinction is important for what follows. One research domain concerns the relationship between established religions and ideologies and their increasingly positive response to environmental issues, namely studies of the 'greening of religion' (Taylor 2004). Historically, one or another of the world's religions has been blamed for fostering environmentally-destructive attitudes and behaviours, but there is clear evidence for a significant change within many of these religious traditions. Ecological theologies and environmental ethical systems have been developed and critically debated by scholars.[4]

If the first category of studies is concerned with the 'greening of religion', there is a second category closely entwined with the first but nevertheless dealing with a different phenomenon, namely the 'religion of greening'. Environmentalism and the environmentalist movement are often conceptualized as religion or as religious phenomena. Clearly, environmental organizations, green political parties and environmental protection agencies are seldom focused on a belief in God or a supernatural reality. Nevertheless, they display other characteristics of religion, such as

- promulgation of myths and rituals,
- expressions of sacredness,
- emphasis on ethics and morality,
- anchorage in a strong community, and

[4] A recent example of the importance of classical religious thought for contemporary ecological issues is Bergmann 2005. Bergmann opens up an extraordinary dialogue between former ecological theologies and the Doctor of the Church St Gregory of Nazianzus. Through the neglected topics of sociality, motion, suffering, and the Spirit, Bergmann expounds Gregory's doctrine of the liberation of creation. He connects ecological issues and patristic theology with contemporary liberation theology, concerned throughout to reaffirm the cosmos as something involved in redemption rather than merely a stage for the human drama of salvation.

- connection with elaborated doctrines.

Interpretation of environmentalism as religion is a popular theme in Western public debate. One noted example is a quotation from Mikhail Gorbachev (1997). When he was asked in an interview (published in *Resurgence*) about his spiritual beliefs, he responded:

> Well, I believe in the cosmos. All of us are linked to the cosmos. Look at the sun. If there is no sun, then we cannot exist. So nature is my god. To me, nature is sacred. Trees are my temples and forests are my cathedrals.[5]

Such quotations can often be found in the popular literature dealing with environmental issues—but not always with a positive connotation. For the author and film writer Michael Crichton, the religious character of environmentalism is a source of critical concern. In a speech entitled 'Environmentalism as Religion', he presented the following analysis:

> Today, one of the most powerful religions in the Western World is environmentalism. Environmentalism seems to be the religion of choice for urban atheists. Why do I say it's a religion? Well, just look at the beliefs. If you look carefully, you see that environmentalism is in fact a perfect twenty-first century remapping of traditional Judeo-Christian beliefs and myths.
> There's an initial Eden, a paradise, a state of grace and unity with nature, there's a fall from grace into a state of pollution as a result of eating from the tree of knowledge, and as a result of our actions there is a judgment day coming for us all. We are all energy sinners, doomed to die, unless we seek salvation, which is now called sustainability. Sustainability is salvation in the church of the environment. (Crichton 2003)

It may seem strange that environmentalism takes on religious characteristics in societies that are becoming more and more secularized and where Christian faith becomes more and more irrelevant for individuals. That would seem especially obvious for the Scandinavian countries. Does it mean that Crichton's analysis is less appropriate in Sweden, for example? He might have overstated his case but it is not without relevance, even in Sweden.

6. Ecological Belief Systems as Civil Religion

Let me now summarize my main point: the significance of Christianity is decreasing while the importance of environmentalism is not only increasing but has taken on some of the characteristics of religion, in the same way that Christianity once developed by adopting features of earlier religious traditions.

---

[5] Other examples are included in Taylor (2004).

In the last part of this chapter, I shall argue that environmentalism can also be understood as a form of civil religion, providing a kind of transcendent justification for political goals and aspirations inspired by the growing consciousness of challenges to the environment. During the nineteen-seventies and nineteen-eighties, the focus was on pollution and nuclear waste. Today, the focus has shifted to global challenges and climate change. We have popular films such as the *The Day after Tomorrow* and, more recently, Al Gore's film about global warming, *An Inconvenient Truth*. But there are also efforts by other political actors to revitalize their ideology and increase their power by incorporating green values and green ideologies into their value-systems.

Before pressing this point, I must clarify my terms. Social surveys using the NEP scale have made significant contributions to the study of value change in contemporary society. But the 'greening of society' is a very broad phenomenon. Some scholars have argued that there is place for a distinction between environmentalism in a broader sense and ecologism in a more narrow and specific sense. Andrew Dobson suggests that:

> Environmentalism argues for a managerial approach to environmental problems, secure in the belief they can be solved without fundamental changes in present values or patterns of production or consumption, while ecologism holds that a sustainable and fulfilling existence presupposes radical changes in our relationship to the non-human natural world, and in our mode of social and political life. The Queen of England does not suddenly become a political ecologist by having her fleet of limousines converted to lead-free petrol. (Dobson 2000: 2)

Moreover, Dobson argues for a 'maximalist' approach to ecologism. People and ideas have to pass stringent tests before they can properly be called ecological. 'Minimalists' cast their net wider, so that the definition of ecologism is subject to fewer and/or less stringent conditions. Dobson wants to describe the *ideology* of ecologism, i.e. its system of ideas. His point of departure is the number of thinkers and philosophers who have shaped the belief systems of green movements and green political parties in the USA and Western Europe. One of the most influential and original is the Norwegian philosopher Arne Naess (1973a). Others have followed him, explaining the metaphysical, ethical and—ultimately—political implications of his ecophilosophical principles, among them Fritjof Capra, Val Plumwood, Holmes Rolston III and Murray Bookchin.

Central to the ideology of ecologism is the concept of 'deep ecology', which has been the subject of an extensive literature. Originally, the concept derives from a lecture delivered by Naess in 1972 in Bucharest and subsequently published in the journal *Inquiry* (1973b). In it, the 'deep ecology' movement is contrasted with the 'shallow ecology' movement; in other words, a deep concern for the right of the non-human natural world to exist, irrespective of how useful it is for us, is contrasted with a shallow concern for pollution and resource depletion and the destructive effects it might have upon human life. Non-human nature has an intrinsic value.

The distinction between 'shallow ecology' and 'deep ecology' has been developed in different directions, and one of the most important developments has been made by the sociologist Bill Devall and the philosopher George Sessions, who refer to Naess's observation that 'the essence of deep ecology is to ask deeper questions' (Devall and Sessions 1985). Deep ecology focuses on the level of consciousness rather than on the level of technological development. It is not enough to change our policies; instead, we must change our way of thinking. We must question our inherited values and look for a new paradigm. One basic tenet of this paradigm is that nature has intrinsic value, 'biospherical egalitarianism in principle' (Naess 1973b: 95). It means that 'all the members in the ecosphere share equal rights to live and blossom' (Naess 1986: 12). This extended version of traditional social egalitarianism implies not only that nature has value as a resource for human beings but also that it has value irrespective of its use for human beings.

In sum, ecological belief systems are characterized by:

- a biospherical egalitarianism (in principle);
- a cosmology of the unity of life—everything is interconnected; the world wide web—and
- a basic attitude of respect and deference.

The substance and implications of 'biospherical egalitarianism' have increasingly attracted scholarly attention since the early nineteen-seventies. A number of studies devoted to the shift from anthropocentric to biocentric/ecocentric ethics have emerged (see, for example, Des Jardins 1997). For my present purpose, I shall reserve judgement on this literature in order to focus attention upon more popular ideas about the value of nature. Since the late nineteen-seventies, Sweden has seen several surveys of the basic value system of men and women in general, i.e. the basic value system as an aspect of the ordinary Swedish citizen's wider belief system. Some of these studies can also be compared to the results of international value surveys.

With these comments in mind, I proceed to some of the main political actors on the Swedish scene and the use that they have made of environmentalism/ecologism to strengthen their influence. I begin with the Royal Court of Sweden and His Majesty the King, Carl XVI Gustaf. On the Court's website, the king's engagements are presented in the following way. Nature and environment are first on the list:

> King Carl XVI Gustaf is actively involved in issues concerning nature and the environment and has great knowledge in both these areas.

> The King has personally instituted the King Carl Gustaf Environmental Competition and the 'Royal Colloquium', an international environmental symposium held in Sweden with participants from all over the world.
> The King has been chairman of the Swedish branch of the World Wide Fund for Nature (WWF) since 1988.[6]

Now, it could be argued that this is a trivial and predictable move for a contemporary monarch, having chosen the motto 'For Sweden—with the times'. But I would argue that not only environmentalism, but also ecologism is on the king's agenda. This is evidenced by some remarks in an important speech at an international environmental conference in Rättvik in 2005. After addressing a number of environmental problems—including the problem of climate change—the King concluded his speech in the following way:

> The word in Greenland for weather and climate is 'sila'. 'Sila' is also the word for universal consciousness, the all-pervading, life-giving force that is manifested in each and every person.
> 'Sila' integrates and connects a person with the rhythms of the natural world. So let us all listen to, understand and follow the deep sense of Sila. I have learnt a lot through 'Sila', but Sila never listens to me.
> Like nature, she finds her own way and follows her own rules with an amazing energy . . . Of course, I am talking about my dog. I thought it was a smart idea to call her Sila, to remind everybody in my surroundings about our responsibility towards nature.
> If we want future generations to survive, we have to listen to mother Earth, to act and to act now!

The clever twist towards the end may have distracted the listeners from the royal message about the universal consciousness, the all-pervading, life-giving force manifested in each and every person. It looks like a transcending holistic belief system of considerable depth and with far-reaching implications. This ecological belief system is closely associated with the spiritual concerns that have found their home in Green parties around Europe. These sentiments also find expression through interest in alternative and complementary medicine, which have had definite political consequences in Sweden. As I have indicated, the Social Democratic Party works in close cooperation with the Green Party and the former communists, the Left Party. In certain regional governments responsible for managing healthcare and hospitals, alternative and complementary medicine have been introduced under the aegis of a holistic ecological belief system emphasizing the unity of human body, soul and spirit.

6 http://www.kungahuset.se/royalcourt/royalfamily/hmkingcarlxvigustaf/Royal engagemnts.4.396160511584257f2180002112.html (last accessed 12 July 2012).

Similar ideas are found in the party's overall policy.[7] Scepticism towards scientific medicine and pleas for anthroposophy and ecological farming can be found at regional level (Jerket 2005). These sentiments are also reflected in a survey that I conducted in 2007. People who are sympathetic to the Green Party are clearly more spiritual than members in other parties. In the general population sample, 30% agree with the statement that there is a god, and supernatural power or force. But 50% of the Greens endorse this claim. The target statement 'Nature is animated by a power, which pervades all living things' is endorsed by 56% of Green sympathizers; the average for the total sample is 44%. And 48% of the Greens endorse the statement that 'I meet the holy foremost in nature'—contrasted with only 28% of the total sample.

These data might indicate that Green attitudes are formed by a more spiritual understanding of nature. Interestingly, they are not alone: such sentiments have also been visible at the highest level of the Swedish Social Democratic Party. Of course, this indicates a need for more extensive research into the Party's publications and also into its parliamentarians.

Nevertheless, I argue that there is sufficient evidence for the claim that the central ideology of the Swedish Social Democratic Party is shaped not only by a shared environmentalism but also by an ecological belief system with a spiritual dimension. One important point of departure is the former Social Democratic leader himself, Göran Persson, whose regard for environmentalism has been discussed by a Swedish political scientist, Stig Björn Ljunggren (2008).

Göran Persson came to power and became leader of the Swedish social democratic party and prime minister in 1997. He celebrated his election with a speech based on the vision of the 'Green public home' (in Swedish: 'det gröna folkhemmet'). He took up a slogan from his predecessor during the Second World War, Per Albin Hansson. Hansson compared his social utopia to a home, in which all family members are equal and live in solidarity with each other—under the father's mild but firm hand, of course. Persson fused this vision with a real concern for nature and sustainable development. In another speech in April 1997, he said:

> Our entire Western culture is in urgent need of a new humility in face of nature and the living world. What we need is a new 'wonder' about our moment on earth. A new, fresh feeling of holiness and awe, which in turn can make us more caring in our use of the resources of creation.

He added:

---

[7] 'Alternativ- och komplementärmedicinska utövare ska kunna arbeta tillsammans med sjukvården för patients bästa när så är lämpligt och önskvärt.' Retrieved on the 13th of May 2010 from the website of the Green Party (http://www.mp.se/templates/mct_177.aspx?number=167761).

> I see before me a specific and historically groundbreaking task, now at the millennium.... That task is about marrying ecology, the economy, and the struggle for jobs. It is a necessary and exciting challenge for all the nations of the world.

The plea for a green public home, an ecological welfare state, was not a passing impulse. Göran Persson returned to this vision time after time, particularly during the election year of 2006. He began his campaign on the island of Gotland in the middle of the Baltic and devoted almost half of his speech to the green welfare society. He returned to the subject in other speeches in his campaign. Moreover, Al Gore was invited to support Persson's vision ten days before election day—I might add, to no avail. The public have not responded positively and, in the opinion polls, environmental issues scarcely registered. Some would argue that the Swedish public's concern is shallow and lacking in commitment, but there is a further possibility. Public sentiments concerning ecology and sustainable development are real and powerful, but they are also sensitive to the efforts of powerful actors to instrumentalize their concern for short-sighted political purposes. One interesting question is, of course, whether Göran Persson maintained his ecological concern after his departure from the political stage. In his autobiography (Persson 2007), the environmental concerns are—generally speaking—left in the background.

7. Conclusion

I shall conclude this chapter with a distinction made by the Spanish sociologist Manuel Castells. Castells distinguishes between two types of identities, namely resistance identities and legitimizing identities. These identities are like Siamese twins, living in symbiosis with each other. Legitimizing identities are given to the roles that political and commercial power sets up for those who serve in their institutions. Resistance identities are given to the roles through which commercial or political power are opposed. These identities come in the form of social movements such as the environmental or ecological movement. They raise their voices against the abuse of nature and the environment. One response made by political power is suppression, another is repressive tolerance, while a third is positive assimilation: if you can't beat them, join them! But this last strategy comes with a risk—and that risk is loss of credibility and loss of inspiration. The Christian church was once a social movement with a set of clear resistance identities. Constantine finally turned that resistance movement into a state church.

I would like to suggest that something similar has happened to environmentalism, and even to ecologism. It is—and remains—a social movement providing identities of resistance towards postindustrial society, sometimes underpinned by an ecological belief system. In certain situations, it has been transformed into a set of legitimizing identities to support certain political actors and their striving for political power: if you can't beat them, join them. One example is Göran Persson's vision of the green welfare state, 'the green public home'. It has functioned by analogy to a civil religion, a set of ideas defining the basic goals of state policy.

References

European Commission (2005): 'The Attitudes of European Citizens towards the Environment'. In: *Eurobarometer*.

Bellah, R.N. and Hammond Ph. E. (1980): *Varieties of Civil Religion*. San Francisco.

Berggren, H. and Trägårdh, L. (2009): *Är Svensken Människa? Gemenskap Och Oberoende I Det Moderna Sverige*. New ed. Stockholm.

Bergmann, S. (2005): *Creation Set Free: The Spirit as Liberator of Nature*. Ed. by A.G. Padgett. Grand Rapids, MI.

Botvar, P.K. (1993): *Religion uten kirke: ikke-institusjonell religiøsitet i Norge, Storbritannia og Tyskland*. Oslo.

Crichton, M. (2003): 'Environmentalism as Religion'. http://www.crichton-official.com/speeches/speeches_quote05.html.

Des Jardins, J.R. (1997): *Environmental Ethics: An Introduction to Environmental Philosophy*. Second ed. Wadsworth.

Devall, B. and Sessions, G. (1985): *Deep Ecology: Living as if Nature Mattered*. Salt Lake City.

Dickens, P. (1991): 'People, Nature and Alienation'. In: *Working Paper* 82, Centre for Urban and Regional Research. Brighton.

Dobson, A. (2000): *Green Political Thought*. Third ed. London and New York.

Dunlap, R.E., Gallup, G.H., Jr., and Gallup, A.M. (1992): *The Health of the Planet Survey: A Preliminary Report on Attitudes toward the Environment and Economic Growth Measured by Surveys of Citizens in 22 Nations to Date*. Princeton.

——— (1993): 'Of Global Concern: Results of the Health of the Planet Survey'. In: *Environment* 9 (35), 7–15, 33–9.

Dunlap, R.E., et al. (2000): 'Measuring Endorsement of the New Ecological Paradigm: A Revised NEP Scale'. In: *Journal of Social Issues* 3/56, 425–42.

Ester, P. et al. (eds) (2003): *Culture and Sustainability: A Cross-National Study of Cultural Diversity and Environmental Priorities among Mass Publics and Decision Makers*. Amsterdam.

Gardner, G. (2002): *Invoking the Spirit: Religion and Spirituality in the Quest for a Sustainable World*. Ed. by J. Peterson. (Worldwatch Paper, Vol. 164).

Gorbachev, M. (1997): 'Nature Is My God'. In: *Resurgence: An International Forum for Ecological and Spiritual Thinking* 184, 14–15.

Gustafson, J.M. (1994): *A Sense of the Divine: The Natural Environment from a Theocentric Perspective*. Cleveland, OH.

Gyllenkrok, A. and Jeffner, A. (1976): 'Theological and Ideological Studies'. In: H. Ringgren (ed.) *Faculty of Theology at Uppsala University*. Uppsala.

Inglehart, R. (1997): *Modernization and Postmodernization: Cultural, Economic, and Political Change in 43 Societies*. Princeton.

Inglehart, R. and Welzel, C. (2005): *Modernization, Cultural Change, and Democracy: The Human Development Sequence*. Cambridge.

Jerket, J. (2005): 'Miljöpartiet Och Vetenskapen.' In: *Folkvett* 2.
Kardell, L. (1990): 'Svenskens Syn På Skogen'. In: *Sveriges Skogsvårdsförbunds Tidskrift* 6/87.
Lindgren, A., Strömstedt, M. and Norman, J.-H. (1987): *Mitt Småland*. Stockholm.
Ljunggren, S.-B. (2008): *Ideologier*. Third rev. ed. Stockholm.
Naess, A. (1973a): *Ecology, Community and Lifestyle*. Cambridge.
——— (1973b): 'The Shallow and the Deep, Long-Range Ecology Movement: A Summary'. In: *Inquiry* 16, 95–100.
——— (1986): 'The Deep Ecological Movement: Some Philosophical Aspects'. In: *Philosophical Inquiry* 8, 10–31.
Persson, G. (2007): *Min Väg, Mina Val*. Stockholm.
Ray, P.H. and Anderson, S.R. (2000): *The Cultural Creatives: How 50 Million People Are Changing the World*. New York.
Särkimukka, J., Edlund, J. and Svallfors, S. (2000): 'Åsikter Om Milöjön'. In: *Swedish Social Science Data Service*. Gothenburg.
Schwartz, S.H. (1977): 'Normative Influences on Altruism'. In: Berkowitz, L. (ed.), *Advances in Experimental Social Psychology*, San Diego, pp. 221–79.
Stern, P.C. (2000): 'Toward a Coherent Theory of Environmentally Significant Behavior'. In: *Journal of Social Issues* 4/56, 407–24.
——— (2005): 'Understanding Individuals' Environmentally Significant Behavior'. In: *Environmental Law Reporter* 11/35, 10785–90.
Stern, P.C. and Dietz, T. (1994): 'The Value Basis of Environmental Concern'. In: *Journal of Social Issues* 3/50, 65–84.
Stern, P.C. et al. (1995): 'Values, Beliefs and Proenvironmental Action: Attitude Formation toward Emergent Attitude Objects'. In: Journal of Applied Social Psychology 25, 1611–36.
Taylor, B. (2004): 'A Green Future for Religion?' In: *Futures* 36, 991–1008.
Trotzig, B. (1987): 'Det Sekulariserade Sverige: Det Sakralas Hemligheter'. In: Karlsson, I. (ed.): *Lycksalighetens Halvö: Den Svenska Välfärdsmodellen Och Europa*. Stockholm.
Widegren, Ö. (1998): 'The New Environmental Paradigm and Personal Norms'. In: *Environment and Behavior* 1/30, 75–100.

MISSION, COLONIZATION AND SECULARIZATION: A REFLECTION ON EVOLUTION WITHIN THE GLOBAL RELIGIOUS LANDSCAPE

Jean-François Zorn

The history of Europe since the Second World War has been dominated by the reconstruction of the continent, the search for peace between different European nations, and tensions between East and West. These terms have a primary connotation of countries in the Northern hemisphere. Although the de-colonization of countries in the Southern hemisphere also forms an integral part of this history, it has for twenty years been forced into the background of European preoccupations. A number of explanations may be found for this phenomenon: weakened by war, an introspective Europe was preoccupied with the healing of its own wounds and the demands of economic reconstruction; the political imperialism which had dominated Europe up until the end of the 1930s was no longer tenable; old empires were practically abandoned by European powers through rapid decolonization, on the assumption by political leaders of a straightforward transition process; and, furthermore, among strands of opinion particularly sensitive to questions of justice, this abandonment appeared to be an admission of failure and led to a wholesale rejection of the colonial enterprise. And so we saw a complete reversal of European public opinion: whereas, before the war, opinion had been largely favourable towards the process of colonization, in the years following the war, people were either indifferent on the one hand or outright anti-colonialist on the other. The post-colonial conflicts in Indochina and Algeria, to take the two most emblematic examples from a French point of view, illustrate very well the politics of abandonment. Europe did not want to enter into new conflicts with the South. In its abandonment there is, it seems to me, a measure of guilt, together with a desire to forget, which has prevented Europe from facing the facts about its colonial past and thus from accepting its responsibilities and accompanying the whole process of decolonization with both magnanimity and greater effectiveness.

We cannot rewrite history. But history writes itself, and we are indeed under an obligation today to re-read the past—not in order to justify it, but in order to understand it and better explain certain problems that we encounter today. These problems are: in the South, the general decline of those countries which we ourselves have largely created, leading in the North to two important consequences: immigration, and the establishment of religions other than Christianity, an establishment that has contributed to the changing European religious landscape. The first phenomenon is political: it is the consequence of the fact that those people whom the colonial agents called 'the natives', whose freedom they claimed to bring about, were unable to remain and to work with dignity in their own country. They therefore emigrated to our country; indeed, we ourselves even induced them to come in order to help our own reconstruction efforts. The second phenomenon is religious: it is the consequence of the failure of the great missionary project launched before the First World War and still vigorous up until the Second World War, to Christianize the world in a single generation. Many of the indigenous immigrants thus arriving are Christians, but most are Muslims, Hindus, Buddhists and Sikhs, a significant number of whom are fervent believers.

In Europe, these two phenomena, immigration and the establishment of new religions, are objectively connected although, for a long time, Europe has neglected this connection. In France, the link has been denied in consequence of a secular context incapable of understanding religious phenomena, and of a particular political assimilationist agenda, formally known as 'integration'. In other national contexts—in Britain and Germany, for example—the link between the two has been tolerated on account of cultural diversity and community distinctiveness, thus allowing immigrant communities to develop within their own traditions.

In this chapter, then, I propose to investigate the link between immigration and new religions in Europe as a consequence of colonialism. I shall develop my argument from the example provided by France, but since the French experience is comfortably situated within the European context it will not be difficult to extrapolate the argument to the experience of other countries.

1. Early Writings in Favour of Colonialism by French Utopians, Liberals and Republicans

In seeking to discover the theoretical foundations for the concept of colonial conquest in nineteenth-century France, we are confronted by the absence of any substantial writings on the subject prior to the final years of the Second Empire and the Franco-Prussian war of 1870. The first writings favourable to the colonial conquest came from both utopian socialists and liberal economists. Thus Jules Duval, a French magistrate of utopian persuasion living in Algeria, wrote in 1864 a work entitled *Les colonies et la politique coloniale de la France* (The Colonies and French Colonial Politics), in which he explained the goal of colonialism as, firstly, the realization of 'global economic unity', a condition necessary for the establishment of 'social harmony'; and secondly, 'the bringing together in one system encompassing different interests, sentiments and actions, the diverse elements of humanity who are dispersed throughout the continents and separated by the seas' (quoted in Girardet 1972: 45). From another perspective, Lucien Prevost-Paradol, a liberal politician, wrote in 1868 a book entitled *La France nouvelle* (The New France), in which he considered that the future destiny of the country could be envisaged in two ways only:

> Either we stay as we are, wasting away in powerless and sporadic agitation, plunging into shameful insignificance in a world occupied by the descendants of our former rivals, speaking their language, dominated by their customs and preoccupied by their affairs; or instead eighty to a hundred million French people, strongly established on both sides of the Mediterranean, will maintain through the course of time the name, language, and legitimate interests of France (quoted in Girardet 1972: 46–7).

We find in the writings of these men two key arguments in favour of the colonial enterprise, arguments that would subsequently be taken up by all of the European nations engaged in the colonial race, namely the universal argument justifying colonialism in the name of human rights, and the national argument providing it with the necessary administrative, technical and military means in the name of each individual nation state. A systematic doctrine of colonialism was elaborated a number of years later by the Saint-Simonian economist, Paul Leroy-Beaulieu. His work (1874), entitled *De la Colonisation chez les peuples modernes* (The Colonization of Modern Peoples), laid out the foundations for the colonial politics that the Republican Jules Ferry, who was also the founder of the secular education system in France, would defend in his turn and implement after his accession to power in 1880. Ferry identified three aspects of colonialism (quoted in Gaillard 1989: 530):

- *Economic*: Ferry declared that 'Colonial policy is the handmaid of industrial policy. In prosperous states, where capital is abundant and accumulates rapidly, and where the manufacturing base is in constant growth, attracting the blue-collar workers who are, if not the most numerous then at least the most enlightened and energetic, export becomes an essential factor in public prosperity. The deployment of capital and the demand for jobs can be assessed according to the extent of the export market' (Ferry 1890: 40–1).
- *Political*: 'In present-day Europe, with the competition among so many rivals that we see increasing around us, whether through naval and military advances or through the prodigious development of a constantly-growing population; in this Europe ... the politics of contemplation or of abstinence are quite simply the main road to decline. In the world in which we are living, nations attain grandeur only through the activities in which they engage' (Ferry 1885).
- *Humanitarian*: Ferry affirmed that the arrival of the European nations, and especially France, in Africa and India had led to an increase in justice, material and moral order, equality and social virtue. He thus clearly portrayed colonization as an act of emancipation (Ferry 1885). As the historian Raoul Girardet (1972: 83–4) has written, 'Colonial activity provides the means and the context for the century-long struggle pursued in the name of the spirit of Enlightenment against

> injustice, slavery and submission to forces of Darkness. How could France, the birthplace of human rights, herald of the great hopes of 1789, possibly shy away from this new crusade for freedom?'

These three perspectives at the heart of French colonial politics form the basis for global conquest as it is envisaged by every European nation. However, it is important to note that in France these perspectives were formulated in the aftermath of defeat by Germany in the war of 1870, a defeat which had led to the loss of Alsace and Lorraine. Republican politicians gaining power in the 1880s had no desire to add to this humiliating defeat an introspection perceived as an abdication of responsibility. Moreover, in the person of the chancellor Otto von Bismarck, Germany fully grasped that only a strong Franco-German axis would enable it to challenge, through its own colonial policies, a British imperialism that was considerably more advanced than France, which lagged twenty years behind, or than Germany, which had at that time no colonial empire at all. It was for this reason that in November 1884 Ferry and Bismarck convened in Berlin a so-called 'African' conference. It was this event that would fundamentally change the face of the world, from both a political and a religious perspective.

2. The African Conference at Berlin (1884–5): The International Legal Basis for Contemporary Colonization

The declared purpose of the Berlin African Conference was to maintain freedom of passage for shipping on the two great African rivers, the Congo and the Niger, and to condemn slavery, as indeed the Danube had also been internationalized and slavery condemned during the Congress of Vienna in 1815. In reality, the fourteen principal western nations present at Berlin—including the USA, Russia and Turkey, but without the presence of any of the African nations directly concerned—went on to set out the basis for partitioning the entire world (and not only Africa) into western zones of influence, thus establishing the right both to territorial colonization and to missionary activity. Thus articles 34 and 35 of the General Act of the Berlin African Conference state:

> Any power which henceforth takes possession of a tract of land on the coasts of the African continent outside of its present possessions, or which, being hitherto without such possessions, shall acquire them, as well as the Power which assumes a Protectorate there, [...] recognize the obligation to insure the establishment of authority in the regions occupied by them on the coasts

> of the African continent sufficient to protect existing rights, and, as the case may be, freedom of trade and of transit under the conditions agreed upon.[1]

The doctrine which underlies these articles, known in German as the 'Doctrine of the Hinterland', establishes the right and the duty of any nation alighting on the continent of Africa to occupy the surrounding area and to administer it. Negotiations with local chiefs and neighbouring colonial powers would enable the boundaries of the new colony to be clarified. Before articles 34 and 35, we find article 6, which states:

> All the Powers exercising sovereign rights or influence in the aforesaid territories bind themselves to watch over the preservation of the native tribes, and to care for the improvement of the conditions of their moral and material well-being, and to help in suppressing slavery, and especially the slave trade. They shall, without distinction of creed or nation, protect and favour all religious, scientific or charitable institutions and undertakings created and organized for the above ends, or which aim at instructing the natives and bringing home to them the blessings of civilization. Christian missionaries, scientists and explorers, with their followers, property and collections, shall likewise be the objects of special protection. Freedom of conscience and religious toleration are expressly guaranteed to the natives, no less than to subjects and to foreigners. The free and public exercise of all forms of divine worship, and the right to build edifices for religious purposes, and to organize religious missions belonging to all creeds, shall not be limited or fettered in any way whatsoever.

This article reveals a double association: on the one hand, between religious, scientific or charitable institutions; and on the other hand, between all such institutions and nation states with a duty to afford protection to indigenous populations, most of all in the campaign against slavery. There is a clear recognition here of the positive role played by religion in the humanitarian aspects of the colonial enterprise. The situation is totally unheard of from a French point of view. Whereas in France, religion—especially Catholicism—is associated more with obscurantism than with the spirit of Enlightenment, and religion was deliberately being detached from state-organized education, in the colonies religion stood to benefit from international public recognition and the Christian missionaries were associated with scientists (geographers) and explorers (philanthropists). All the same, the affirmation of freedom of conscience and religious tolerance, forming the basis of the Declaration of Human Rights, indicates that colonization does not seek to favour Christianity in particular but

[1] The French text is available online at http://mjp.univ-perp.fr/traites/1885berlin.htm; an English translation by Jim Jones is available at http://courses.wcupa.edu/jones/his312 /lectures/ber-cong.htm. This and the following quotation are taken from Jones's translation.

rather all religions whose public worship and missionary activity are publicly recognized. This paragraph is of considerable importance, and it was the subject of heated debate during the Congress. An early version of article 6 thus contains a reference to churches and chapels, which was subsequently replaced by the more general notion of 'religious edifices' at the request of the Turkish delegate.

Our reading of this internationally binding legal and diplomatic document permits us to confirm that in 1885 the Christian mission was officially granted the right to exist, to develop and even to be protected by the political powers in operation. Two consequences then followed: firstly, the Christian missions, many of which had been established for over half a century (and well before the colonial period), were then faced with considerable challenges; and secondly, the introduction of religious plurality would necessitate the particular recognition and support of indigenous religions, often at the expense of Christianity itself. Indeed, Christian missions found themselves disadvantaged by anticlerical French administrators, and they were even prohibited in certain territories where Islam had been long established.

In the following section, I give further consideration to the two rights, to colonization and to missionary activity, that were recognized by the Berlin African Conference, in order to assess their implications right up to the present day.

3. Christian Mission and Colonization: A 'Neurotic' Partnership

How did the missionary organizations interpret the colonial conquest as it was presented in the conclusions of the Berlin African Conference? In fact, the response was practically unanimous from both catholic and protestant perspectives: colonization was seen as a providential reality. It was 'a reality' because its existence could not be denied, neither could it be vigorously condemned; it was simply there, and people were obliged to deal with it realistically. It was 'providential' because, although it was not necessarily within the will of God, colonization could serve His glory if people knew how to interpret the signs of the times, both those pointing to God's glory and those threatening to detract from it.

It was thus that in 1885, immediately following the General Act, the pastor Alfred Boegner interpreted the Berlin African Conference. Boegner, the director of the Society of Evangelical Missions of Paris, was based in Lesotho from 1833 and in Senegal from 1836, before serving in Gabon, Zambezi and Madagascar. He asked:

> Which is the one event, at the outset of this new year of 1885, that will have the greatest impact on the course of history? Is it not the African Conference, where the destinies of the Dark Continent are studied and resolved? We can

> be certain that on the clock of history the hour has struck. (French original quoted in Zorn 1993: 17)

However, two years earlier, the same director had warned the mission supporters as follows:

> With the [colonial] expansion that is underway, we find ourselves faced with the considerable problem of the future direction to give to our work [...]. An error of judgment or a commitment insufficiently thought through could, it seems to me, throw our Society out of the path that God has traced for it, a path of unshakeable faithfulness to the obligations of the past and resolute acceptance of new obligations clearly indicated by God. (French original quoted in Zorn n.d.: vii)

On the Catholic side, a similar position was developed in 1902 by Bishop Alexandre Le Roy, superior-general of the Holy Ghost Fathers, established in Gabon since 1842 and more recently also in Central Africa. Le Roy stated:

> More debated—and doubtless more debatable—is the opportunity afforded by the European conquest. Is it a good thing? Is it bad? Certainly, it is a reality, a necessary reality, a providential reality. Let us seek therefore as far as we may to alleviate the inevitable harm by turning to good account the evident advantages through encouraging peaceful conquests. It is the best we can do. [...] Europe present in Africa remains, whether she desires it or not, the messenger of God [...]. She will break down the ramparts set up by Islam, she will crush the bloodthirsty tyrants that wreak havoc before her, she will ruin the slave-drivers, she will subdue the horrors of the slave trade, of bondage, of cannibalism, of infanticide and of all barbarian practices. She will open up roads, reduce distances, facilitate travel and transport, prolong the lifespan of man [...] Despite all the accidents, all the imperfections [...] and, on occasion, the crimes committed, all these are the fruit of Christian civilization, the route clearly laid out and along which the servants of the Gospel will travel (quoted in Comby 1992: 238).

This close association between Christian mission and human rights in the period leading up to the First World War corresponds exactly to the theories of colonization which we have already described. However, we know that the Colonial enterprise did not develop as those pioneers had anticipated. Were they therefore naïve, or unaware of the true issues involved in colonialism? Indeed, how was it possible to claim to colonize in the name of human rights while at the same time seeing these same rights imposed by force, leading to the loss of local sovereignty, the confiscation of land, and later also to demeaning treatment such as forced labour? Curiously, the arguments of the colonialists betray a contradiction that we would qualify today as fundamental, but which at the time was accepted without question: colonizing in the name of human rights was both an expression of Enlightenment ideals of equality, through the conviction that natives were as capable as anyone else of becoming fully civilized citizens, and also an affirmation that these same natives—called at the time 'races'—were inferior to the cultivated peoples of Europe. This contradiction leads to an essential question: in the minds of the colonizers, were the natives constitutionally inferior to Europeans (a biological distinction) or were they simply less developed than Europeans (an evolutionary distinction)? The colonizers were in theory evolutionists, but in practice they revealed themselves to be racist (although at the time the word employed was 'racialist'). For example, they took measures to create sub-categories of populations, either through native reserves or by the creation of native citizenships, which were not the same as the supposedly universal citizenship of the colonizing nation. The colonizers were stuck on the question of differences between civilizations. Their solution was to create specific or exceptional laws (the native code), leading to excesses that neither the French concept of direct assimilationist government nor the Anglo-Saxon model of indirect government were able to avoid.

4. French Colonization in the Face of Other Religions, Islam in Particular

By the time of the Berlin Conference, the aspirations of *jihad* cultivated by the principal Muslim chiefs, both in North Africa (Abd El Kader) and in Sudanese Africa (El Hadj Homar, and Samory Touré), had been subdued by French colonization. However a certain Faidherbe, governor in Algeria (1842–7 and 1849–52) and then in Senegal (1854–65), chose to rely on more or less Islamicized local dynasties, who were more easily influenced and won over to the colonial enterprise than the warrior chieftains who sought their missionary directives directly from Mecca. Moreover, Algiers, the first colonial conquest of France in 1830, had been won only when it was agreed that the act of capitulation signed by the Dey Hussein of Algiers should include a clause guaranteeing the protection of the Islamic religion and of its institutions. The result of this was to effectively render all Christian missionary activity impossible. It was at this price that France was able to gain a foothold in Algeria. Moreover, Algeria was henceforth to become an exemplar. From the moment that Islam agreed to take part in the French colonial enterprise, it would not be opposed but rather associated with the process of colonization. In principle, Christianity was to be treated in the same way, although with notable differences of treatment between Catholicism and Protestantism. In reality, the French State, which claimed to be secular or at any rate neutral as to religion, felt an obligation to avoid arbitration in Islamo-Christian disagreements. It could not allow the idea that the Christian religion was better than the Islamic religion—in other words, that Christianity was the religion of the colonizer and therefore the colonial religion. In those regions where Islam was the dominant religion, so long as it did not rouse the population to fanaticism the French colonial state considered it fittingly adapted to the local peoples and so encouraged the development of a Muslim élite committed to French interests. All of the colonizers' testimonies concur on this point. Thus, J.-C. Froelich, administrator of the French Overseas Territories for eighteen years, could write in 1962:

> We have deliberately sought to give preference to the tribal chiefs and we have organized tours for highly-regarded teachers of Sufism, asking in exchange that they placate the spirits. We have treated them with the greatest of honour and have constructed schools, madrasas and even Mosques at their request. (Froelich 1962: 85)

In this way, we observe that in its transition to tropical climates, the French secular system witnessed astonishing transformations.

In relating these events with their underlying motives, my intention is not to praise the process of colonization, even if honesty requires us to cast a more objective eye on this period than was the case in the past. It is rather to emphasize the fact that, in practice, the global religious boundaries that we know today all came into existence during the colonial period. Certainly, I have reasoned from a sole example, that of Islam in colonial-era Africa, but it would be possible to extrapolate my argument into other geographical and religious contexts, with the same basic conclusion: Buddhism, Hinduism, Islam and Christianity have all remained largely within the boundaries that were fixed during the nineteenth century, with some boundaries dating from earlier than that. Christianity, a missionary religion from Europe and the United States, was introduced during the nineteenth and twentieth centuries where traditional religions were already present, or in regions where religions with dogmatic structures were either disintegrating (such as in Korea) or struggling in the face of oppressed population groups like women or lower-caste men (such as the Dalits in India).

In conclusion, we need to consider two possible objections to this thesis. Firstly, how can we account for the revival of interest currently taking place in all of the world religions, including (so we are told) in Europe? Is it not indeed the result of profound changes in the religious map of the world? Secondly, surely the missionary religions—Christianity and Islam—have progressed in spite of everything in the last hundred years?

5. Religious Revivals: A Brief Survey of Some Internal Revolutions

The revival of interest in religion is universal, as numerous observers have demonstrated. But it seems to me that what we are currently witnessing is more an internal recomposition (and decomposition) of different religions than a true phenomenon of expansion. We might take a number of examples. It is frequently stated that Latin America is becoming increasingly Protestant. In the absence of evidence to the contrary, it appears to me that the substitution of Catholicism by Pentecostalism which seems to be taking place is (from a global perspective) an internal mutation of Christianity. Or again, the progress of Christianity in Asia—spectacular in South Korea, more undercover in China. In fact, the opening-up of South Korea to Christianity is not a recent phenomenon; its origins go back to the nineteenth century and may be explained by that country's religious and economic context. As for the position of Christianity in China, I am convinced that Christianity will remain as it has been since the first opening of the country to the western world—in other words, as a minority religion. Doubtless there exist in China numerous solid Christian communities living out their faith with great courage in adversity, but they will never be able to depend on the development of a Christianity in the image of ancient European Christendom. Moreover, it is perhaps to their advantage that they will not be able to fall in with religious authorities who are always more than ready to exploit religion for their own ends. As for Islam, the appearance of progress here and there (in the Balkans, Palestine, Indonesia, Pakistan, and Algeria) turns out in fact to be in every case an internal radicalization of a political and religious nature (which provokes of course an equally radical reaction in its adversary; thus Judaism in Palestine, Hinduism in south Asia, and so on). We have every reason to believe that on the day when such radicalization ceases, Mosques will be less frequented, and those who remain Muslim will do so from spiritual conviction and personal choice. Finally, in black Africa, despite certain situations which are indeed critical (Côte d'Ivoire, Nigeria, and Sudan), it is a largely peaceable form of Islam that is maintaining its presence more than it is expanding. Between Muslims and Christians, each group keeps a close eye on the other while maintaining regular contact. This is the case, for example, in the Bamoun region of Cameroun, where the situation vis-à-vis different religions has been stable since the beginning of the twentieth century. The Sahelian line of separation between Islam and Christianity has remained approximately the same for over a century. Recent missionary activity in the Sahel, whether by American protestants or the Muslim Brotherhood, has led to greater religious pluralization of Sahelian societies, but not to a total re-drawing of the religious map.

6. Is the Christian Mission Simply a Mirage?

The second objection to be raised does indeed appear to be a significant exception to the thesis. If we were to follow the argument to its logical conclusion, how could we explain the Christian expansion in complete continents (Africa, the Pacific) that had no knowledge of the Gospel prior to the arrival of missionaries in the nineteenth century? In response, we need to note that for the most part the regions touched by missionary evangelism knew only the existence of traditional religions, those of ancestor worship, or worship of the land and of the sea—religions known as 'animist' by their first serious observers. Such forms of religion were local, devoid of fixed doctrine or foundational texts, and as such were particularly fragile. Moreover, did not most (but not all of) the early missionaries deny these local religions by stigmatizing them with the attributes of paganism, namely idolatry, superstition and fetishism? It is true that the science of ethnography, invented by the missionaries themselves, made it possible to demonstrate that they were indeed religions, but religions in no way related in their essential structures to formally-constituted religions such as Judaism, Christianity, Islam, Hinduism or Buddhism. Traditional religions can be found everywhere, including in pre- and post-Christian Europe. It is precisely those religions which Christianity and Islam have always attempted to eradicate and yet which spring up again and again because they constitute the religious core belief common to humanity. It would be interesting to analyse the expressions of this core belief today through different manifestations of secularized popular religion. Such religious spirit is the exception which confirms the rule of my argumentation. Present everywhere, even if in a particularly identifiable form in black Africa (*voodoo*, Fang reliquaries and others), its boundaries are particularly permeable and evanescent. We can therefore conclude that Christianity and Islam have become substitutes for this religious spirit alone and not for other, formal religions. We have no contemporary example of a solidly Islamicized society that has been fundamentally Christianized or vice versa.

7. Conclusion: Nevertheless … a Mission of a New Type

I have sought to demonstrate that the 'geo-religious' configuration of the contemporary world has been more or less stable for a century. This does not mean that there have been no spiritual revolutions within each religion, neither does it mean that missionary projects have not been undertaken to enable men and women to convert freely to the 'true God', whether the God of Jesus Christ or the God of Israel or the God of Muhammad. This God is true for those who believe in Him and whose life has been changed by Him. However, it will always be as individuals before God that they will convert and not through a manoeuvre whereby missionary strategies turn into mass professions of faith. Furthermore, we must not forget that the task of evangelism is as much internal as it is external. Christians are called to conversion each day by driving out the idols that profane their God, their churches, other humans and the world. Other believers have the same responsibility, and it is probably when this task is honestly carried out within each religion that dialogue between them finds its true meaning.

It is doubtless in Europe and in North America, those continents in which the concepts of religious freedom and tolerance—or what in France we call 'laïcité'—originated, that this kind of experience might most easily develop. Here, the religious landscape is already fragmented, pluralist and highly individualized. Only time can tell if religious recompositions will be possible as a result of dialogue, principally religious, but perhaps also social and cultural—a dialogue rendered necessary in the face of new human challenges that are addressed only when religious *people*, and not simply the *institutions* they represent, gather together in order to speak and act.

References

Comby, J. (1992): Deux mille ans d'évangélisation. Tournai.
Duval, J. (1864): Les colonies et la politique coloniale de la France. Paris.
Ferry, J. (1885): Discours à la Chambre des députés. Session of 28 July 1885.
——— (1890): Le Tonkin et la mere patrie. Paris.
Froelich, J.C. (1962) : Les musulmans d'Afrique Noire. Paris.
Gaillard, J.-M. (1989): Jules Ferry. Paris.
Girardet, R. (1972): L'Idée coloniale en France de 1871 à 1962. Paris.
Leroy-Beaulieu, P.P. (1874): La Colonisation chez les peuples modernes. Paris.
Prevost-Paradol, L.A. (1868): La France nouvelle. Paris.
Zorn, J.-F. (1993): Le grans siècle d'une Mission protestante : La Mission de Paris de 1822 à 1914. Paris.
——— (n.d.): 1887–1987: 'Une maison une mission'. Manifestations à l'occasion du Centenaire de la Maison des Missions protestantes. Paris.

PART II

RELIGIOUS VERSUS SECULAR VALUES?

MODERATING RELIGION?

Patrick Vandermeersch

Should a modern state tolerate all forms of religion claiming the right to acceptance? Or must the state impose constraints on religions and define conditions for their practice? And does the state have the right to intervene in the ways that religion is lived within an individual's psychology? Should the State regulate the ways in which information about religion is presented to the general public? Should it guarantee that 'sound' theology is made accessible to everybody wanting instruction or even to those who aspire to become theologians? The rise of extremism, integrism[1] or fundamentalism in the contemporary world makes these questions particularly urgent.

We create unease when we ask these questions so bluntly. They seem to oppose everything to which modern society is accustomed: respect for religion as a private matter and reluctance to make any inquiry into what individuals believe in the secrecy of their hearts. But is the State not compelled to pursue an inquiry when public security is at stake? And would such an inquiry really be so different from what the state does in other domains? The state ensures that reliable information is provided on public health ('Smoking damages your health and makes you infertile!'), state universities have faculties under whose auspices the value of art and literature is discussed, and public bodies lay down rules for trade and financial affairs. This is not necessarily totalitarian. Smoking is not made impossible for you, you are not compelled to prefer romantic paintings and to hate surrealistic ones, and you are not obliged to buy a particular Toyota motor car nor to pay for it according to a mandatory hire purchase agreement. Consequently, we might ask why the state should not offer clear and trustworthy information about religion, in the same way that it takes pains to provide reliable information or to legislate basic rules in other domains? Is it not a shame that people get their knowledge of the history of religious culture from books such as the *Da Vinci Code* by Dan Brown? To put the question succinctly: should the state not establish faculties of theology so that people can make informed decisions about religious matters?

---

[1] The French word *intégrisme* has a different meaning from the English 'fundamentalism', although dictionaries suggest this translation. The etymology clarifies the difference: an 'integrist' sticks to all of his or her religion, down to the last detail. The fundamentalist sticks to the ancient, original form of the religion and declines to make any adaptation to present circumstances. So the two stances—although frequently identified—are characteristically different.

I will address this last question at the end of my enquiry. I begin with a more basic question, namely whether we are able to define 'moderate religion'. I will then analyse the concepts of 'belief' and 'faith' in order to elicit their complexities and to establish which elements require particular attention. That will bring us back to the relationship between religion and ethics, which seems to be the most urgent issue facing contemporary society. Finally, I will briefly discuss the status of faculties of Theology, whether linked to a church or—as is the case in Groningen—not so linked.

1. Moderate Religion: A Difficult Concept

'Moderate religion' is a strange term. It is unusual for things to appear to be improved by being moderate. Moderation has the connotation of being merely average. Is that an ideal? I never heard someone praising moderate art or moderate scientific research. Is art better when it keeps a low profile? Yes, of course there is pottery, and you can find it nearly everywhere, produced by both porcelain manufacturers and aged hippies, but is it art? The same question can be asked of scientific research and education. Is it best to study at an average university and to pursue scientific research that keeps a low profile?

Why, then, does it seem obvious that religion should be 'moderate'? When you ask people and insist on the point, you mostly get an answer along the following lines: It is not good that religious people are so devoted to their religion that they obey all its directives down to the last detail. That would be 'extremism', i.e. going too far in the observance of religion. This widely-shared opinion has aptly been expressed in a quotation carved into the pedestal of a bishop's statue in Viseu, Portugal. The inscription state that the bishop had been a hero in the civil war, fighting for greater freedom. It begins thus: 'To our bishop, the great revolutionary'. And the quotation to which I alluded runs as follows: 'Religion is like salt at dinner. You need a small amount of it, but too much spoils the meal.' I think that many of us could agree with the bishop's opinion. A good human being and a good citizen should possess inner freedom. Inner freedom is necessary in order to be someone who really cares about his or her neighbour. Without inner freedom we are not able to develop enough empathy to understand what our neighbours really need and to care for them.

But, to make things a little bit more complex—that is to say, both realistic and tricky—let us test the term 'moderate' in other domains, such as by applying it to driving a motor car. Would we say that a good driver, a 'moderate' driver, is someone who interprets the 50 km/hour sign merely as a general indication, whereas a driver who scrupulously keeps within the speed limit is an extremist? According to our interpretation of moderate religion, the traffic sign ought to be understood as announcing a particular traffic situation, but in the last resort it is up to the driver to decide what to do with that piece of information. We might be inclined to say, then, that someone who always limits his or her speed in order scrupulously to obey the traffic sign, even at night when there is nobody on the street, is an extremist and by no means a good driver. And the same would hold for tax-payers who insist on declaring the last eurocent they have earned. Should they not be considered dangerous people, these extremists?

In our heart of hearts, many of us will admit to having more sympathy for people who maintain a more liberated lifestyle—that is to say, for people who accept the general value of rules but who do not scrupulously conform to their requirements. On this view, such a free person is more reliable than someone who simply acts according to the law. Do we not meet here the core of the philosophy of Émmanuel Lévinas, who said that the only trustworthy basis for moral behaviour is the ethical appeal stemming from the face and the eyes of the other? Being open to the otherness of the other—if this is the core of ethical behaviour, should we not denounce extreme attachment to laws and stipulations as an attempt to escape from that prime experience of morality? Did we not learn how far the idea that *Befehl ist Befehl* (An order is an order) can lead human beings astray from truly ethical experience?

If that were really at stake with our antipathy towards extremism or integrism, it would imply that it is not because those people believe in certain things that we do not trust them, but because they display too much rigidity in human contact and are incapable of empathy. It would not mean that the content of the integrists' belief system is at stake; rather, it would mean that what is at stake is the (supposed) effect of the integrists' creed upon their capacity of true human relations. This shifts the topic of our enquiry from the integrists' creed to the integrists' psychology, and it prompts another question, namely whether this lack of capacity for empathy and sympathy is caused by the extremists' creed or whether matters are the other way round. Alternatively, we might ask whether both issues are the function of some inner psychological structure that remains to be explored.

2. Belief and Faith: A Complex Psychological Interaction

'A little religion is good, but too much of it is harmful.' Let us try to make further progress in the analysis of this phenomenon. Here we come across an historic distinction made by Christian theologians, to which a parallel can perhaps be found in Islamic theology. It is the distinction between what is called, in Latin, the *fides quae* and the *fides qua*, which can be rendered in English by the terms 'belief' and 'faith' and in French by *croyance* and *foi*.[2]

The *fides quae* (belief) points to the notional content of what a believer accepts as being real or true. In this way, you can believe that there is a God, that there was a Creation of heaven and earth in a distant past, that ghosts exist, that there is a reincarnation, that our body is subjected to a balance of energies,

[2] It is much more difficult to render the distinction in either German or Dutch, since *Glauben* and *geloof* can designate both *fides quae* and *fides qua*.

that there are flying saucers, and so on. Thus the *fides quae* points to the content of a certain creed, whose adherents are convinced that 'this exists' and that 'this is true'.

The *fides qua* is something different. The term points to the emotional side connected with the *fides quae*. *Fides qua* can often be translated into English as 'trust' or 'confidence'. In this sense it means faith, but there are also forms of *fides qua* based on fear, anxiety, or loss of personal identity.

The question is what comes first. Is it belief conceived in terms of a cognitive assessment, or in terms of faith, or of the experience of placing trust in someone, or, as a minimum, being encompassed by the Absolute (or yet other forms of *fides qua*)? The general public and many scholars in the social sciences give preference to belief. They assume that the notional side, the *fides quae*, comes first and that the experiential side, the *fides qua,* follows. In thinking thus, they imply that religious belief works in the same way that knowledge does: once you have discovered something and know it, you will act according to that knowledge. This is the reason why missionary activity often begins with preaching, after which the *fides ex auditu*, belief stemming from 'having heard', nurtures the development of sentiments belonging to the *fides qua*.

Nevertheless, important research in both the social sciences and theology has shown that the sequence *fides quae* → *fides qua* ought to be rejected. Social research has shown that in many cases faith comes first and the notional form of belief is only an implementation of an antecedent experience which was not on the notional level. And there have been intense debates among Christian theologians, especially between Catholics and Protestants, about the priority of knowledge over emotional experience.

Let us begin with the social sciences and take one of the most famous examples: Leon Festinger's *When Prophecy Fails* (Festinger et al. 1956). An American woman, practising spiritualism, received a message from heaven that God had decided to destroy his unfaithful creation by allowing the world to be flooded once more. Only a small group of elected people would be saved by a flying saucer, sent by God to pick them up. Immediately, the woman published announcements in the newspapers in order to warn the inhabitants of her home city. She gathered a small group of believers. Among them there were—how could it be otherwise?—a few researchers in psychology. The latter were curious, of course, to know what would happen once the promised flying saucer failed to appear. The saucer's arrival was delayed a few times, but fortunately a message from heaven announced each delay. Finally, the landing was firmly scheduled for the next night and the believers were waiting out of doors, ready to embark. But time passed and no flying saucer showed up. The psychologists had anticipated tremendous disappointment, but precisely the contrary occurred. With many hallelujahs, the little crowd thanked God that he had changed his plans because of their prayers and their leader promptly telephoned the newspapers to announce the good news.

As this example shows, there is no linear connection between a belief system, understood as the notional acceptance of representations, and the emotional, experiential aspect of faith. The contrary seems to be the case. First, there is the conviction of a special link with God, in whom the human being trusts, and this sustains some belief statements (in this case: that God will flood the world but save the group of the faithful by sending a flying saucer). If this particular statement of the creed appears to be wrong, however, faith remains unscathed and finds a different creed to express the initial faith.

There is another famous experiment in the social sciences supporting the same conclusion. It was carried out in the 1950s by Milton Rokeach, a social psychologist who has become famous for his research on social values. He brought three schizophrenic patients, each of them believing he was Christ, together in the same ward of a mental hospital. He wanted to find out if they would adhere to their creed once they were placed in a situation that clearly contradicted it (Rokeach 1981). Indeed, there was a brief quarrel about the right to bear Christ's identity, but very soon the three men were able to accept and even enjoy each other's company. They simply adopted different rationalizations in order to affirm their own identities without harming too greatly the identities of the others. This means that, even when people are deluded, their belief cannot be understood as mistaken knowledge, from which their behaviour and feelings stem.

If schizophrenic patients seem too unusual for any conclusion to be drawn from their case, let us look at the psychology of conversion. People do not become converted because they have been attracted by a clearly-outlined doctrine that they decide to accept as the 'real truth'. On the contrary, conversion nearly always starts with an encounter with a religious leader. The doctrine follows. Preceding the conversion experience, there is often a period of one or two years of mixed feelings of unhappiness, depression, and uncertainty about personal identity. Then one becomes attracted to a religious group or a leader, often met by coincidence. The leader is charismatic and gives the impression that he can make secure a new identity, while the group offers social support in that identity. Without knowing anything of the creeds affirmed by the group, one nevertheless becomes converted. Only afterwards does one become eager to learn more about those creeds (Ullman 1989). This is true of Zacarias Moussaoui, the man sentenced for participating in the 9/11 plot. We know a lot about of his life from the account given by his brother, who lives in Montpellier (Moussaoui and Bouquillet 2002). Both had lived in France since they were small boys. They spoke no Arabic and knew nothing about Islam. It was only later, while he was a university student in London and suffering from what we can interpret as an identity crisis, that Zacarias became attracted to Islam and, little by little became an extremist.

To conclude: it is widely held that religious belief is something like knowledge, the only difference being that religious beliefs lack a firm basis in reality. This is why some 'unbelievers' advocate that religious belief should be replaced by knowledge and that the advancement of scientific knowledge in modern society will render religious belief obsolete. Psychological investigation, however, shows that this assumption is wrong. Belief is intimately linked to faith, that is to say, to an affective experience. We should not immediately conclude that belief systems are *only* the expression of underlying faith neither should we conclude, even if that were the case, that any symbol or belief statement could serve to express faith. But we should acknowledge that the relationship is complex and that it completely misses the point to try to convince believers that one or other of their convictions is untrue, although such attempts are often found in newspapers and popular magazines.[3] Faith is something other than the result of unsupported 'knowledge'. In recognizing that, we merely accept what theologians have known for centuries.

3. Theologians on *fides quae* et *fides qua*

The distinction and the relationship between *fides quae* and *fides qua* have been a central issue in Christian tradition, especially in the debate between Reformation and Counter-Reformation theologians. The discovery of the original Greek text of the New Testament was crucial in this respect. Until the fifteenth century, only the Latin translation of the Vulgate Bible had been used and there the term *fides* refers to belief or faith, without making any distinction between them. In the original Greek, however, *pistis* is used, and this means 'trust' unequivocally. A great debate followed the discovery. Should people begin with trust and only later learn about the different religious statements—the 'dogmas' that had been elaborated during centuries of Christianity? Or should people nevertheless begin by learning about the Christian dogmas in order to assimilate over time what lies behind this knowledge (*fides ex auditu*)?

A central point in this debate addressed the problem of whether or not fear was a part of faith. According to the Roman Catholic Counter-Reformation, people had first to be warned about the existence of hell. In this way they could be moved by a 'sane fear of punishment', since this fear was needed to induce their faith in a redemptive God.[4] The opposite view was held by the Lutherans, who declared that faith was God-given and should eliminate every kind of fear.

---

[3] A striking example is a discussion, reported in *Le Monde,*,of the belief that a good Muslim would meet thousand virgins on his way to paradise. It was claimed that this belief stems from a bad translation of the Koran, since the 'thousand virgins' ought to be translated as 'thousand raisins'. However, on comparing the rival translations, readers maintain their opinion that, once it has been correctly read, the Koran is literally true.

[4] '[Adulti] disponuntur autem ad ipsam justitiam, dum excitati divina gratia et adjuti, fidem "ex auditu" concipientes, libere moventur in Deum, credentes, vera esse, quae divinitus revelata et promissa sunt, atque illud in primis, a Deo justificari impium per gratiam ejus, "per redemptionem, quae est in Christo Jesu", et dum, peccatores se esse intelligentes, a divinae justitiae timore, quo utiliter concutiuntur, ad considerandam Dei misericordiam se convertendo, in spem eriguntur ...' Concilium Tridentinum, *Decretum de justificatione* (13 Jan. 1547), in: Denzinger and Schönmeier (1967: nr. 1526).

Much earlier than the Counter-Reformation, one of the first Christian theologians posed the question about the existence of hell on a deeper level. Origen of Alexandria (c. 182–251) asks in his sermon on Jeremiah whether God deceives mankind. The question is triggered by a verse in the Book of Jeremiah: 'You have deceived me, o Lord, and I was deceived' (Jer. 20: 7). If you accept the Bible as the word of God, the following paradox will ensue: either the Bible tells the truth and God deceives mankind, or the Bible does not tell the truth and, consequently, God deceives mankind. Thus it is clear: God deceives mankind. How to understand this? We can summarize Origen's view as follows (Origen 1977: 261–73):

– Does hell exist?
– No, hell does not exist.
– Then I do not need to believe in the existence of hell?
– On the contrary. Certainly you should believe in the existence of hell.
– I do not understand. If hell does not exist, why should I believe that hell does exist?
– The answer is very simple: you must believe it in order not to go to hell.

Origen continues by saying that the portrayal of hell is a pious lie uttered by God. God is compelled to deceive mankind, just as a good father sometimes has to deceive his children. And Origen concludes: the Bible contains many such pious lies.

To put the issue in contemporary philosophical terms: religious creeds are often, and perhaps have always been, examples of performative utterances. They are not statements of fact; instead, they seek to effect change in the believer's inner life. Thus two things are needed, and these have been recognized since the beginning of Christianity (even though there have been controversies about their use): they are (i) a specific type of knowledge and (ii) a fruitful relationship with a good teacher.

4. The State's Responsibility for Making Sound Theology Available to the General Public

The interpretation of creeds was for centuries the sole responsibility of the church. Since the Enlightenment, however, secular authorities have become increasingly aware of the importance of making sound forms of hermeneutics and religious knowledge available to the general public. Nowadays, when many people believe that religions will quietly fade away, this role of the state is often overlooked. Let us therefore recall the central facts and issues.

European secularization basically consists in the fact that the authority of the churches has been challenged. Ecclesiastical authorities were refused the right to regulate people's daily lives. With the experience of hundreds of years of religious wars, Europe no longer trusted the idiosyncrasies of religions to pervade public life. First of all, this was a matter of societal law and order. The constitutions of most modern European states guarantee the individuals' right to hold their own religious opinions, and they set clear limits to what churches may do and what they should refrain from within the public domain. Although it was not made explicit, there was also a vivid concern about the psychological influence of religion. While individuals should have the right to believe and to act as they choose, it was axiomatic that those choices were freely made. Certainly, it was difficult to translate this deeply-anchored conviction into statutory form, but many of the European disputes between those in favour of more power for the churches and those opposed to it have addressed this question.

The USA was and remains quite different. We should not forget that it was founded by dissenters. Their influence shaped a constitution that guarantees to each religious group the right to live its own life, without disturbance from those outside the group. While the experience of intolerance was fundamental to Europe's separation of church and state, the experience of religious tolerance was America's foundational experience. This tolerance was not experienced as being in conflict with the fact that, within those groups, their members were expected to obey the rules. The USA is like the Father's house with many mansions (John 14:2) wherein one can be assured of finding a place, under condition of respecting the house rules. In a nation founded upon the coexistence of many churches, *God bless America* seems quite natural, whereas Europeans would be surprised, if not upset, were their governments to use such a religious terminology. As a consequence, America was reluctant to monitor what went on within a multitude of churches and denominations, where the management of psychological motives was more marked in groups that were smaller and more close-knit than they tended to be in Europe. In America, therefore, intervention in the unique psychological coherence of a religious group was felt to be a matter of great delicacy.

Here we have reached the intersection of two critically important questions. First, what psychological attributes do individuals need in order to grasp the meaning of a religious message without challenging their inner freedom? Second, can anyone impose, or even promote, such attributes without encroaching upon personal autonomy? The latter question is of course a variation upon the classic dilemma: does anyone have the right to compel another person to be free?

In the present context, I cannot address every aspect of these complex questions. Instead, I confine my attention to the following issue. One of the ways in which Europe was able to monitor the development of religion was to safeguard religious education in schools and universities. This seems to me, especially in the present day, an important duty for the state.

For several hundred years, universities have been the places where science is taught, research is undertaken and—last but not least—young citizens are educated in order to become open-minded and critical. I emphasize the last point, since it is often considered as being so self-evident that no attention is paid to it, nor to the question as to how this aim can be realized. From their beginnings, medieval universities knew better. Students learned to dispute, that is to say, to question their teachers' authority. I concede that the disputation was also a exercise in the acquisition of rhetorical skills and that it was the master's sentence which ended the disputation. However, the basis was laid for an intellectual discipline through which students could overcome blind adoration for their master—the first, but ideally transient, phase in the acquisition of knowledge and wisdom. Being attracted by a well-known master and then becoming able to put that master into perspective—this was, and ought to remain, the essence of the teacher-pupil relationship in a university. In this way, not only knowledge but also intellectual independence can be acquired (Vandermeersch 1996).

Universities have been of the utmost importance in the development of theology. While the monastic schools continued mainly to transmit the texts and opinions of the ancient authorities, the cathedral schools and universities began to question those authorities. It is true that modern scholars become irritated by the trivial or futile questions that were disputed—How many angels can sit on a needle? Would it have been possible for Christ to save the world if he had been incarnated in a bean?—but the students' opportunity—or rather, their obligation—to engage in disputation was an opportunity to liberate their thinking from blind acceptance of their master's opinions.

During the past two hundred years, new disciplines—biblical studies, ecclesiastical history, and religious studies—have replaced scholastic disputation as means to open young theologians' minds. When students are taught as they should be, their education does much more than inculcate factual knowledge. It implicitly teaches that the Bible has been written, translated and transmitted by many hands, that the history of a church is not just the history of a perfect ideal, that other religions partly resemble, and partly differ from, one's own, and that one can develop empathy with respect to them.

As I have been a professor at the University of Groningen for a long time, I hope that readers will forgive my advocacy of religious studies and my emphasis upon its origin as a theological discipline. Gerardus van der Leeuw, the pioneer of the phenomenology of religion, never had the impression that he was leaving the field of theology when introducing the new discipline. Nevertheless, an antinomy between theology and religious studies is often propagated, as if theology addresses the subjective viewpoint of believers whereas religious studies address the objective viewpoint of researchers committed to a 'methodological agnosticism'. If that were true, it would follow that a theological faculty should belong to a church and that a state university could not possibly have a faculty of theology. Moreover, state universities would then be restricted to religious studies, a term which generally connotes the study of 'foreign' religions.

After my observations at the beginning of this chapter, readers will recognize in these antinomian assertions a denial of European history. Europe's religious heritage emphatically does not belong to the churches alone, and sound theological reflection is required at a secular level if we are to be able to understand Europe's cultural history and to offer our critical assistance in the evolving conception of European citizenship. From this perspective, the idea of having state universities with state faculties of theology is neither bizarre nor novel.

In practice, such state faculties often work according to a *duplex ordo* model. This means that students of theology pursue for the two years a programme organized by a state university and only then follow the specific training demanded by their respective churches (such as courses on dogmatics and pastoral training). This system was established by Joseph II of Austria in 1786. In the Catholic world it disappeared rather quickly, but the idea was taken up again in 1876 in the Netherlands, where it still exists. It is the best system I am aware of.

I do not want to imply that in principle the churches are unable to run good theological faculties. Nevertheless, it seems to me that the complementarity between state faculties and church-based training is very fruitful and that the churches would harm themselves if they tried to undermine the state faculties and attempted to monopolize the teaching of academic theology. That would make of theology and religion something still more marginal and, moreover, it would foster yet more ignorance about matters of religion. Let us not forget that the worst enemy of religion is not unbelief, but ignorance.

References

Denzinger, H. and Schönmeier, A. (1967): *Enchiridion symbolorum definitionum et declarationum de rebus fidei et morum*. Thirty-fourth edition. Freiburg.

Festinger, L., et al. (1956): *When Prophecy Fails. A Social and Psychological Study of a Modern Group that Predicted the Destruction of the World*. Minneapolis.

Origen (1977): *Origène, Homélies sur Jérémie*. Vol. 1. (*Sources Chrétiennes* 238.) Paris.

Rokeach, M. (1981): *The Three Christs of Ypsilanti: A Psychological Study*. Second edition. New York (first edition: 1964).

Ullman, C. (1989): *The Transformed Self: The Psychology of Religious Conversion*. New York.

Moussaoui, A.S. and Bouquillet, F. (2002): *Zacarias Moussaoui: mon frère*. Paris. (Engl. transl.: *Zacarias My Brother: The Making of a Terrorist*. New York 2003).

Vandermeersch, P. (1996): 'Hooglerarenmoraal. De wijnschenker en de pentium-professor'. In: G. Hutschemaekers & M. de Winter (eds), *De veranderlijke moraal. Over moraliteit en psychologie*. Nijmegen, pp. 217–34.

RELIGION VERSUS LIBERALISM? ALASDAIR MACINTYRE'S HYPERDEMOCRATIC CRITIQUE OF LIBERAL DEMOCRACY

Marc Boss

In his book *Ethics after Babel*, Jeffrey Stout argues that while 'liberal democracies' and their 'distinctive modes of public discourse' result from a 'failure to achieve agreement on a fully detailed conception of the good', their 'arrangements and conventions' aim at limiting 'the damage of that failure by settling for a thinner conception of the good that more people could agree to, given the alternatives and until something better came along' (Stout 2001: 225). This is the most basic issue at stake in Stout's critical discussion of Alasdair MacIntyre's moral philosophy. The political utopianism that Stout discerns in MacIntyre's 'terminal wistfulness' originates, he believes, in some unwillingness to recognize our 'inability to imagine a full blown alternative to our society that would be both achievable by acceptable means and clearly better than what we have now' (Stout 2001: 229). According to Stout, this attitude is reflected in MacIntyre's (1984: 263) hyperbolic descriptions of 'the coming ages of barbarism and darkness' which make him sound like 'the Thomas Münzer of contemporary moral philosophy, intent on withdrawing into a sect until the time is ripe for virtue to triumph over vice' (Stout 2001: 223).

In his essay *Alasdair MacIntyre: une biographie intellectuelle* (2005), Émile Perreau-Saussine (1972–2010) castigates MacIntyre's religious and political antiliberalism in similar terms. In Perreau-Saussine's view (2005: 34), MacIntyre's reluctance to articulate an explicit allegiance to liberal democracy as a political form or regime constitutes a major weakness in his political thought: 'Something in him keeps him from clearly recognizing the worth of liberal democracy as a political regime, although he has no alternative to offer.'

Notwithstanding their harsh criticism of this antiliberal pathos, Stout and Perreau-Saussine both make the case that MacIntyre's outspoken antiliberalism should not dissuade his readers—especially those who do not share his political pessimism—from using some of his major conceptual tools for an improved self-understanding of liberal democracy itself. In this chapter I shall follow a similar path by suggesting that a hyperdemocratic critique of liberalism lies at the heart of MacIntyre's antiliberal rhetoric: his understanding of politics as a deliberative practice of rational investigation radicalizes the very concept of democracy in such a way that the liberal democracies we know are simply not democratic enough to meet its highly demanding standards. I shall substantiate this argument by discussing in turn Perreau-Saussine's and Stout's interpretations, before concluding that MacIntyre's political aims might be far less incompatible with liberal democracy than he himself seems inclined to believe.

1. Émile Perreau-Saussine's Proposal

Perreau-Saussine considers MacIntyre's anti-liberal rhetoric as the leitmotiv running across the different periods of his intellectual journey (Perreau-Saussine 2005: 15, 1999: 7). Considering the theological and political sources of this rhetoric, he argues that it tends to overlook the distinction that Aristotle himself established between ethics and politics; he furthermore sees MacIntyre's sociologism and historicism as incompatible with the epistemic foundations of Aristotle's politics.

1.1. Theological and Political Sources of MacIntyre's Antiliberalism

MacIntyre's reliance on 'community and tradition' as 'substitutes' (Perreau-Saussine 2005: 129) for the political institutions of liberal democracy can be traced well back into the early years of his philosophical career in Great Britain, when his views on liberalism were mainly influenced by Karl Barth's theological antiliberalism on the one hand and by the New Left's political antiliberalism on the other.

MacIntyre's early critiques of theological liberalism illustrate the deep impact of Barth's work on the British theological scene of the 1950s. As Perreau-Saussine observes (2005: 143), MacIntyre's 'first critique of abstract universalism was a critique of theological liberalism', and his 'first theory about incommensurability between conceptual schemes was a theory about the incommensurability between faith and reason, profane and religious language'. But Perreau-Saussine (2005: 129–30) insists that this theological antiliberalism, however 'profound and justified' it might have been, was unable—and certainly unwilling—to provide a political alternative to liberal society and its institutional arrangements. The utopian overtones detectable both in *After Virtue* and in MacIntyre's later work might therefore be construed as vestiges of a form of antiliberalism inclined 'to sacrifice the political community to a community of the believers which is not and cannot be its substitute' (Perreau-Saussine 2005: 126).

The other major source that Perreau-Saussine discerns in MacIntyre's early antiliberalism is the tradition of anti-state socialism partially retrieved by the British New Left in its attempts to recover 'forms of sociability' marginalized by the industrial revolution (Perreau-Saussine 2005: 51). 'The nostalgia of the community,' so Perreau-Saussine argues (2005: 51), 'is one of the dominant features of the first New Left and, more generally, of British socialist circles' in the 1950s and 1960s:

> British socialism had had a persistent anarcho-syndicalist tendency, freely romantic, oriented towards the pre-industrial era. … E. P. Thompson, one of the guiding lights of the New Left, was inspired by these currents of thought [and] … MacIntyre, who was to become an activist of the first New Left, had concluded *Marxism: an Interpretation*, published some years earlier, in the same spirit. (Perreau-Saussine 1999: 1–2)

Highlighting thereby the coherence of MacIntyre's intellectual trajectory, Perreau-Saussine argues (1999: 2) that 'he kept throughout his life, both a consistent philosophical problematic and the political radicalism of his youth' (Perreau-Saussine 1999: 2). Although he would eventually forsake 'his early dreams of revolution,' he would persistently seek 'norms for a restored communal society in pre-modern forms of social life'. Even his rehabilitation of the Aristotelian-Thomist tradition appears, in this context, as an attempt to give a new expression to the political concerns he had as a young New Left activist.

> MacIntyre presents Thomas Aquinas as an enemy of nascent bureaucracy—concerned, under Saint Louis, about the confiscation of administration by specialists having a monopoly of expertise—, and as a friend of local custom, against the great barons, the king, the ecclesiastical authorities, Frederick II, and more generally, I daresay, imperialism. To the nationalist and monarchist Saint Thomas of [the] Action Française, he substitutes a crypto-Marxist Aquinas! (Perreau-Saussine 1999: 12)

Though he still insists on the need to 'distinguish a "proto-MacIntyre" from a "deutero-MacIntyre"' (Perreau-Saussine 1999: 7), Perreau-Saussine tends, in one critical respect at least, to emphasize the continuity between the two: both are inclined to develop a 'romantic' conception of politics, 'somehow haunted by the theme of community and steeped in nostalgia for pre-industrial society' (Perreau-Saussine 1999: 1).

The case could be made that the continuity in MacIntyre's thought is perhaps not quite so evident as it is here suggested. It could be observed that the Thomism to which MacIntyre eventually turned involves a blunt rejection of Barth's theology, which he now dismisses for having proved unable to supply 'any practically adequate account of the moral life' (MacIntyre 1995: xx). It could likewise be noticed that MacIntyre's predilection for the politics of local communities against the politics of the modern state proceeds, on his own account, from a plain rejection of what he now depicts as the New Left's lasting illusions about state politics (MacIntyre 1995: xv). Yet the persistence of what Perreau-Saussine describes as a 'romantic' concern for community can hardly be overlooked in MacIntyre's work. As Peter Sedgwick had already noticed in his review of *After Virtue*, 'the theme of a possible recentering of morals, around one or other focus of shared human community, has been an uninterrupted concern of Alasdair MacIntyre ever since his New Left writings' (Sedgwick 1982). In his preface to *After Virtue* as well as in his introduction to the 1995 edition of *Marxism and Christianity*, MacIntyre suggests that by turning to the Aristotelian-Thomist tradition he was indeed less concerned with repudiating his earlier allegiances—be they political or theological—than with responding to the questions they had raised (1984: ix–x, 1995: xxi).

1.2. Ethics Absorbing Politics

According to Perreau-Saussine (2005: 34, 53, 61), the vestigial persistence of MacIntyre's early theological and political concerns in his later work explains his enduring—and rather puzzling—reluctance to articulate any clear commitment to liberal democracy. This is all the more regrettable, in Pereau-Saussine's view, since the tradition of the virtues is actually more compatible with 'the spirit of liberal democracy' than MacIntyre himself seems ready to admit (Perreau-Saussine 2005: 59). 'The laws of a liberal regime', he says, 'are not ethically neutral: they refer to morals that must be cultivated' (Perreau-Saussine 2005: 59). It is in 'liberal education' or in 'liberal arts' that Perreau-Saussine finds the pattern of such liberal cultivation of virtue that has to do with a 'certain form of excellence' (Perreau-Saussine 2005: 59). Insofar as the founding fathers of liberal democracy maintained a commitment to the good and the true, supporting and transcending their vision of political concord, the regime they tried to conceive should be distinguished, in Perreau-Saussine's view (2005: 56), from what liberalism has become for 'most of its contemporary theorists'. When liberalism is 'steered back to its highest and noblest sources,' he says (2005: 59), freedom must be reaffirmed as 'freedom to search for the good', and politics itself must be ultimately referred and subordinated to the requests of 'truth'. This account of what he takes to be 'true liberalism' explains why he sees in MacIntyre a potential renovator—rather than a mere critic—of liberal democracy.

Perreau-Saussine argues, in particular, that the neo-Aristotelian distinction between internal and external goods, which is at the heart of MacIntyre's moral philosophy, might provide a fruitful alternative to those classical justifications of liberal democracy that 'favor the avoidance of evil over against the search for the good' (Perreau-Saussine 2005: 17). Those who attempt to ground liberal democracy in Hobbes's anthropological pessimism conceive human relationships as being naturally antagonistic and competitive: the only goods they know are external. 'The more someone has of them, the less there is for other people' (MacIntyre 1984: 190). Internal goods, insofar as they are the goods of a social practice, are no less 'the outcome of competition to excel' (MacIntyre 1984: 190), but 'their achievement is a good for the whole community who participate in that practice' (MacIntyre 1984: 190–1). They involve an understanding of human relationships as being, so to speak, naturally social and cooperative. This is precisely what makes them suitable, on Perreau-Saussine's view (2005: 90–1), to provide a 'reformulation of liberal democracy's philosophical presuppositions'. As liberal democracy develops, extending its influence and proving its political viability, it becomes somewhat 'artificial', he argues (2005: 14), 'to insist on the primacy of evil' and more 'tempting to offer an Aristotelian reinterpretation of the regime' that would stress the 'dynamics of the good' more than the 'balance of evils'.

The problem with MacIntyre's neo-Aristotelianism, on Perreau-Saussine's account (2005: 126), is that it 'claims the legacy of a tradition that has never put politics at its center' and shows thus little concern for Aristotle's distinctively political thought. Neglecting 'the neo-Aristotelianism of German descent, in the context of which Hannah Arendt, Eric Voegelin, and Leo Strauss among others, have explored Aristotle's political thought', MacIntyre draws his main insights from 'the neo-Aristotelianism of analytic philosophers such as Elisabeth Anscombe, who are essentially interested in the philosophy of action' (Perreau-Saussine 2005: 126).

As a consequence, MacIntyre seems inclined to 'analyse internal goods in ethical rather than in political terms' (Perreau-Saussine 2005: 126) and appears, more generally, 'to sacrifice political philosophy for the sake of moral philosophy' (Perreau-Saussine 2005: 42) or 'to conceive the history of philosophy as the history of moral philosophy, to the detriment of political philosophy' (Perreau-Saussine 2005: 162). By ignoring Aristotle's own contention that 'the history of morals has to be interpreted in the light of the cyclical transformation of regimes or constitutions', such a de-politicized interpretation of Aristotelian ethics requires an assessment of Aristotle's politics that, strangely enough, ignores his 'most clearly political treatise' (Perreau-Saussine 1999: 11).

It is indeed no small paradox, as Perreau-Saussine observes, that MacIntyre's construal of Aristotelian politics is actually grounded not in Aristotle's *Politics*, as one could expect, but in the *Nicomachean Ethics.* In absorbing Aristotle's politics into his ethics, MacIntyre feels compelled to disapprove of liberal democracy insofar as it unblushingly claims its indifference towards virtue. Yet, in so doing, he forgets that 'Aristotle's very demanding views in ethical matters have as a counterpart a great flexibility in politics; he expects little from the people, and balances his moral "idealism" with a *caveat*—prudence and moderation are the most important political virtues' (Perreau-Saussine 1999: 16). Perreau-Saussine (2005: 162) chides MacIntyre for overlooking such political virtues while relating moral virtues 'to infra- or supra-political communities only, religious communities in particular'.

1.3. Sociologism and Historicism

Perreau-Saussine suggests that *After Virtue* suffers from a confusion between ethics and politics and that the combined influence of 'sociologism' and 'historicism' upon MacIntyre's thought is to be blamed for this confusion. Sociologism, in Perreau-Saussine's account, subordinates the political significance of a given political regime to the cultural significance it displays from the standpoint of the social sciences. As an illustration of MacIntyre's sociologism, Perreau-Saussine mentions his account of various political epochs in terms of the 'characters' in which their 'social order' is supposed to be embodied: the Explorer, the Engineer, and the Headmaster of Victorian England; the Prussian officer, the Professor, and the Social-Democrat of Wilhelmine Germany; or the aesthete, the therapist and the bureaucrat of contemporary democracies. Such characters are meant to 'reveal the spirit of the time', but MacIntyre does not ask how they relate 'to Victorian constitutional monarchy, to the Second Reich, or to today's democracies; they characterize a culture rather than a regime' (Perreau-Saussine 1999: 11). Notwithstanding his criticism of Weber's account of bureaucracy, MacIntyre remains here indebted to Weber's theory of ideal types.

In 'relating human types to social forms' this theory appears, in Perreau-Saussine's view (1999: 11), as a sociological substitute to the 'philosophical project of a classification of the regimes' that Aristotle has articulated in Book III of the *Politics*. While Aristotle sees the moral life as 'a function of an aristocratic or democratic ethos', MacIntyre sees it as a function of some 'particular sociology' (Perreau-Saussine 1999: 11).

MacIntyre's sociologism seems to provide no equivalent to Aristotle's universal truth claims about the nature of political regimes. Perreau-Saussine submits MacIntyre's historicism to a similar critique. Historicism, so he suggests, confers upon 'any thought a dimension which is profoundly social, and which at the same time denies the ultimate truth of any political perspective' (Perreau-Saussine 1999: 12).

The Aristotelian conception of politics involves a 'distinction of the eternal and the temporal, the theoretical and the practical' (Perreau-Saussine 1999: 14n54), which Perreau-Saussine sees as radically incompatible with MacIntyre's historicist theory of knowledge.[1] In blurring the difference between theory and practice, or the contemplative and the active life—a difference Aristotle, no less than Plato, was careful to maintain (Perreau-Saussine 1999: 12-13)—, historicism blurs also the difference between philosophy and politics. As 'action becomes quasi-philosophical, and philosophy, quasi-practical' (Per-

[1] Perreau-Saussine suggests that MacIntyre's historicist theory of knowledge 'drastically limits the possibility of politics' insofar as it involves a 'determinist' account of human agency. He grants that from the time of his 'moral critique of Stalinism' to the time of his later 'return to the *Nicomachean Ethics*', MacIntyre has never ceased 'to defend the autonomy of the human agent against social structures, and to assert a form of liberty' by criticizing 'economic, sociological, and psychological determinism' (1999: 10). Perreau-Saussine claims nevertheless that MacIntyre's description of practical reason as historically embedded 'reintroduces the very determinism which he had rejected' (1999: 10). Notwithstanding MacIntyre's critique of the Nietzschean concept of 'genealogy', the theme of the historicity of practical reason, which is the common denominator of his 'histories of ethics', displays more resemblances with the *Genealogy of Morals* than with the *Nicomachean Ethics* (1999: 9).

reau-Saussine 1999: 14), the boundless expansion of politics beyond its own particular sphere involves paradoxically the end of politics as such. In this coincidence of 'over-politicization' and 'de-politization,' Perreau-Saussine discerns (1999: 16), once again, a Marxist shadow over MacIntyre's neo-Aristotelianism: 'Marx,' as he recalls, 'wanted revolution only in order to end politics'.

Perreau-Saussine seems to believe that MacIntyre's retrieval of Aristotelian ethics and politics cannot succeed insofar as it is not grounded in Aristotle's own theory of knowledge, 'metaphysical biology' included (1999: 9). Perreau-Saussine rightly recalls that the 'opposition between reason and tradition', which MacIntyre's investigative concept of tradition is meant to overcome stands at the very foundation of Aristotelian epistemology and metaphysics (1999: 14). From the classically Aristotelian standpoint that Perreau-Saussine supports, MacIntyre's historicist account of the rationality of traditions obscures indeed the distinctions between 'reason' and 'history' or between 'nature' and 'convention', which are essential components of Aristotle's so-called 'metaphysical biology'.[2]

MacIntyre has admitted that Aristotelian teleology, expounded as Aristotle himself expounds it, presupposes a metaphysical biology: 'Human beings, like the members of all other species, have a specific nature; and that nature is such that they have certain aims and goals, such that they move by nature toward a specific *telos*' (1984: 148). One of MacIntyre's main purposes in *After Virtue* was to show that our participation in practices and traditions provides a conceptual framework alternative to these no more tenable metaphysical presuppositions and that we can thus dispense with them without abandoning the teleology itself. In *Dependent Rational Animals* (1999), MacIntyre provides a more charitable account of Aristotle's metaphysical biology, but even this softening of his earlier position does not meet the demands of classical Aristotelianism as Perreau-Saussine defines it: 'One can hardly see', he writes, how MacIntyre 'can admit the idea of nature' without 'renouncing his two most important concepts: "tradition of thought" and "practice"' (Perreau-Saussine 1999: 14n54).

There is no doubt that such historicist reinterpretation of Aristotelian philosophy would be unacceptable for Aristotle himself as well as for his medieval heirs. But why should this make MacIntyre's own proposal irrelevant? While Perreau-Saussine blames MacIntyre for having disconnected Aristotle's teleology from its epistemological and metaphysical presuppositions, Rorty and Sedgwick consider the very same disconnection in rather appreciative terms.

---

[2] Perreau-Saussine (1999: 9–10) insists that even Aristotle's contention that the human being is a 'political animal' implies distinctions of this sort. While MacIntyre sees the 'political' character of the human animal as a mere consequence of its 'historical' character, Aristotle subordinates the 'relative historicity' of our condition to our rationality: the *logos* being our most basic human characteristic, it is our rationality, not our historicity, which makes us political by nature.

Rorty (1991: 159n27) seems relieved to observe that, 'by the time MacIntyre gets rid of the nonsense in Aristotle (e.g., what he calls the "metaphysical biology"), Aristotle doesn't look much like himself.' Sedgwick (1982) likewise praises MacIntyre's 'committed zeal' to the refurbishing of 'crusty old Aristotle', suggesting that *After Virtue* 'has brought out the best in the Aristotelian structure' by substituting for 'fixed human nature' a 'fluid social teleology'. In the same vein, Jeffrey Stout claims (2001: 237) that his own reinterpretation of Aristotle's account of the virtues requires 'something resembling MacIntyre's metaphysically austere and historically informed teleological framework—Aristotelian in inspiration but without the "metaphysical biology"'.

2. Jeffrey Stout's Proposal

In the critical assessment of *After Virtue* that Stout has articulated in his book *Ethics after Babel*, he creatively combines a teleological reinterpretation of liberal democracy with a liberal construal of Aristotle's politics; his proposal consists in a 'stereoscopic' form of social criticism inspired by MacIntyre's reflections upon the ambiguous relationships of practices to institutions.

2.1. A Teleological Reinterpretation of Liberal Democracy

Stout contends that MacIntyre's efforts to recover a teleological framework in our morals and politics should not be dismissed all too hastily by those who claim their allegiance to liberal democracy: a 'teleological framework', he says, 'can be used not only to describe radical alternatives to the *status quo* but also to describe the so-called liberal society itself' (Stout 2001: 237).

Stout knows, of course, that Aristotelian teleology is commonly held in low esteem by theorists of liberal democracy, but he contends that the discursive practices of liberal societies still require—and achieve—agreement on what he calls a 'provisional *telos*' (Stout 2001: 212). Liberal societies are teleologically oriented, so he argues, by means of some 'self-limiting consensus on the good', involving the shared awareness 'that it would make life worse for us all, to press too hard or too far for agreement on all details in a given vision of the good' (Stout 2001: 212). One can claim to be teleological in this 'provisional' sense, so Stout claims, 'without supposing that we need to generate religious or philosophical agreement on anything so grand as the meaning of life or the ultimate purpose of human existence' (Stout 2001: 239). Given that such provisional conceptions of the good require the possession of virtues such as practical wisdom (*phronêsis*), which, according to Aristotle, 'allow us to alter our conception of the good in light of experience', Stout questions MacIntyre's belief that the institutional forms of modern politics express a 'systematic rejection' of Aristotelian tradition' (Stout 2001: 238).

> Does not our society embody the recognition, born of *phronesis*, and forged in the religious strife of early modern Europe, that the good life for us must make allowances for our inability to achieve perfect agreement on the good life? I believe it does. Where MacIntyre sees the social embodiment of emotivism, I see implicit commitment to a provisional, self-limiting conception of the good. (Stout 2001: 238)

Stout grants that the moral philosophy articulated in *After Virtue* 'takes full cognizance of the necessity for a provisional and corrigible conception of the "good"' (Stout 2001: 237), but he endeavours to draw its political consequences in a way that challenges MacIntyre's fundamental assumptions about liberal and Aristotelian politics.

2.2. A 'Liberal' Construal of Aristotle's Politics

The issue at stake is not only that liberal democracy, as Stout views it, displays certain parallels with Aristotelian teleology that MacIntyre overlooks; it is also that Aristotle's politics, as Stout construes it, provides an account of political conflict that is far more 'balanced and realistic' than MacIntyre suspects.

> To be sure, for Aristotle all forms of community involve something held in common. (…) What they share, however, is neither perfect agreement nor the bond that we, in contemporary English, call friendship. Otherwise, they wouldn't spend so much time using reasoned speech to argue about justice. Nor would they be as prone as Aristotle thinks they are to fall into conflict and mutual suspicion. To be members of a political community (…), they need only share enough agreement about standards to make argument about justice possible. (Stout 2001: 239)

Stout borrows this reading of Aristotle's politics from Bernard Yack (1985). He stresses Yack's contention that 'most recent interpreters of Aristotle, whether friends or foes of liberal society, "have disconnected Aristotle's analysis of political community from his analysis of political conflict"' (Stout 2001: 325n31). Such disconnection explains, in Stout's opinion, why MacIntyre, like so many contemporary readers, tends to 'exaggerate the extent of commonality Aristotle takes to be necessary for political community, thus creating a distorted caricature to be contrasted with liberal individualism' (Stout 2001: 325n31). In Yack's own terms, 'liberal justifications of political institutions in terms of individual calculation of interest and obligation' form the background of such misreading (Yack 1985: 93; cited in Stout 2001: 325n31).

> In [their] light (…), Aristotle's statements about the logical priority of the community to the individual in Book I of the *Politics* stand out and attract the great attention. Likewise, the analyses of political argument and conflict

> in the later books generally receive less attention since they do not contrast as sharply with widely accepted principles of liberal thought. Such a perspective distorts our understanding of Aristotle's concept of political community by making political community seem to be a form of identity and political conflict a divergence from political community. This may be the way in which some of Aristotle's antiliberal admirers understand political community. But it is not ... the understanding of political community developed in the *Politics*. (Yack 1985: 93; cited in Stout 2001: 325n31)

Stout argues that Yack's reading of Aristotle provides 'all the more reason for thinking that our politics, far from implicitly rejecting Aristotle's conception of community, in fact conforms to that conception rather closely' (Stout 2001: 239).

> If we take Aristotle to be saying what Yack thinks he is saying about political community and conflict, and carefully remove the outmoded metaphysics, recognizably Aristotelian habits of speech may prove surprisingly adaptable to our environment. (Stout 2001: 240)

Even though this assessment of Aristotle's *Politics* plays a key part in his argument, Stout does not claim that exegetical erudition will tell us any final truth about how we are supposed to understand Aristotle. His methodological ambition must be viewed in terms of an 'eclectic and creative' *bricolage* by virtue of which Aristotelian and modern vocabularies are made to appear far less unsuited to each other than it is the case in MacIntyre's dramatic historical narrative (Stout 2001: 240).

2.3. Practices and Institutions: The Moral Ambivalence of Liberal Democracy

On Stout's view, the method of *bricolage* that is so central to his appraisal of Aristotle should be applied to MacIntyre as well: while liberal democrats must reject MacIntyre's 'sense of belatedness and his account of moral diversity', they can still 'benefit greatly from his concept of social practices, his understanding of their relation to institutions, and his distinction between internal and external goods' (Stout 2001: 6, see also 193). If they do so, they will discover, Stout argues (2001: 221), that liberal societies are not 'as radically individualistic and unconcerned with the common good' as MacIntyre assumes that they are. Basing his proposal on examples taken from American society—though suggesting, quite incidentally, that similar examples could be found in other liberal democratic societies as well—Stout (2001: 271) blames MacIntyre for overlooking the numerous and highly-valued social practices with which his fellow citizens are actually surrounded. 'Doctors and nurses', he says, 'pursue goods internal to the practice of medical care, goods that cannot be achieved by any other practice or by any other means than by being a good doctor or nurse, acquiring and exhibiting the qualities, forms of excellence, or virtues particular to those roles' (Stout 2001: 269). In addition to medical care, Stout mentions a whole range of social practices including not only 'the arts and sciences' have promoted in official educational structures, but also 'the forms of music, dance, and sport that thrive on urban streets' and which all 'clearly qualify as social practices in MacIntyre's sense' (Stout 2001: 271). Each of these practices requires the cultivation of both technical skills and moral qualities that are to be acquired through imitation of role models and submission to the authority of those who are more experienced in the practice.

> My daughter, Little Leaguer and Yankee fan that she is, aims to run, hit and field not simply by the rules but as her favorite Yankee does. She studies him with the dedication of someone who needs no convincing that the goods internal to baseball are worth pursuing or that imitating excellence is the only way to achieve them. She takes instruction from her coaches and understands the meaning of their criticisms and prescriptions. (Stout 2001: 271)

There is hardly any room left here for the kind of 'unbridled individualism' that MacIntyre ascribes to liberal societies. 'We may parrot individualistic sayings on occasion', Stout says, 'but we also acquire the qualities needed to achieve, at least to some degree, the goods internal to the practices in which we participate, goods that are nobody's private possession and must be sought, if sought at all, for their own sake' (Stout 2001: 271). MacIntyre misconstrues our predicament insofar as his social criticism fails to put 'his own most valuable vocabulary to use' (Stout 2001: 289), thereby ignoring 'precisely the features of our society that make people care about it, the features that hold out some hope of transformation from within' (Stout 2001: 281).

Stout insists, however, that MacIntyre's social criticism rightly warns against our inclination to idolize external goods and the corruption of our most valuable practices by the demands of the marketplace and the bureaucracies (Stout 2001: 287). MacIntyre's inquiries into this 'uneasy relation' (Stout 2001: 275) between our social practices and their sustaining institutions provide indeed the conceptual framework for Stout's own attempt to conceive a 'stereoscopic social criticism' that 'brings social practices and institutions, internal and external goods, into focus at the same time' (Stout 2001: 279), accounting thus for 'the tendency of the capitalist marketplace and large-scaled bureaucracies to provide material conditions that permit social practices to flourish, while at the same time they undermine the moral conditions needed to achieve goods internal to such practices' (Stout 2001: 289).

From these premises, which he shares with MacIntyre, Stout draws his own conclusions: liberal democracy is not bound to protect only 'private bonds and the individual pursuit of external goods', but it provides also political resources of its own to grant 'right to life' and 'room to flourish' for the 'goods internal to worthy social practices' and to protect them against 'the proliferation, distribution, and merchandizing of external goods' (Stout 2001: 290).

MacIntyre's influence becomes noticeable again as soon as Stout asks which practices are actually 'worthy' of such protection. Recalling MacIntyre's warning that practices are not virtuous as such and should not be approved of indiscriminately (MacIntyre 1984: 200), Stout argues that we must move 'beyond the first stage of MacIntyre's analysis, which pertains to social practices and institutions, to the second and third stages, which pertain to the possibility of living a good human life within the extant configuration of practices and institutions, and the possibility of sustaining communities over time' (Stout 2001: 290).

Stout claims to be confident that his liberal democratic reassessment of MacIntyre's vocabulary should suffer no breakdown once it is raised to levels two and three. As far as level two is concerned, 'we have reason to suppose', he says, 'that a good human life is not likely to flourish under conditions where the tyranny of external goods goes unchecked—reason, in other words, to protect such social practices as medical care, baseball, family life, and democratic government from being overwhelmed and corrupted' (Stout 2001: 287). On level three, the critical question that must be raised is whether the pluralistic society of a liberal democracy can 'achieve sufficient continuity over time' to be identified as an 'ongoing tradition' that can be criticized and transformed 'both reasonably and radically from within'. Stout's response is affirmative: 'I believe it already has' (Stout 2001: 288).

As Stanley Hauerwas and Phil Kenneson (1997: 102) have correctly noticed in their critical appraisal of *Ethics after Babel*, the book provides no argument for this conclusion. Retrospectively, however, it appears that Stout's laconic response was in fact less a conclusion than a programmatic outline of his later work, most notably his essay *Democracy and Tradition* (2004). In his postscript to the second edition of *Ethics after Babel*, which reflects his subsequent intellectual trajectory, Stout (2001: 348) suggests that 'discursive improvisations of the kind that descend from [Ralph Waldo] Emerson' offer democratic and liberal grounds for a distinctive tradition in MacIntyre's sense of the term. Such a tradition provides standards that permit us to determine which elements in other traditions are to be valued and which are to be discarded. It displays none of the features ascribed to the 'amorphous entity' that liberal society is commonly thought to be (Stout 2001: 346). It can hardly be reduced, Stout argues (2001: 348), to 'something neutral that operates procedurally at the level of a metatradition'. It entails 'normative commitments', including commitments to pluralism understood as a 'normatively charged openness to difference' (2001: 348).

In the concluding words of *Ethics after Babel*, Stout suggests that liberal democracy as he understands it is not incompatible with some sort of 'civic republican talk about the virtues and politics as a social practice directed toward the common good' (2001: 292). Yet his attempt to redescribe liberal democracy with conceptual tools borrowed from MacIntyre's virtue ethics appears, on the whole, to be more concerned with moral-political than with legal-political issues. He claims—quite persuasively—that the fate of the virtues in the actual practices of liberal society is not so hopeless as MacIntyre believes, but he shares to a great extent MacIntyre's worries about the corruptive power of institutional arrangements upon practices. To be sure, Stout takes care to distinguish 'practice enhancing arrangements' such as 'ballot boxes and constitutions' from practice-threatening arrangements such as the marketplace and the bureaucracies (2001: 352). But as he puts it himself, one of the aims he pursues 'is to place ethical-political *discussion* on the practice side of MacIntyre's practice-institution distinction, so that democratic individuality, participation, and rationality' may come into sight 'as internal goods of a valuable discursive practice' (2001: 351). Such insistence on the moral value of liberal practices, as opposed to the moral perils and ambiguities of liberal institutions, may partly explain why Stout seems concerned with the moral-political dimension of liberal *societies* rather than with the legal-political dimension of liberal *regimes*, or why his talk about liberal democracy as a political form seems so difficult to separate from his talk about 'America', its moral tradition, its moral substance, and its moral community.

3. Concluding Perspectives

In the postscript to the second edition of *Ethics after Babel*, Stout draws a suggestive parallel between MacIntyre and Hauerwas, both of whom he gratefully acknowledges as inspiring mentors: 'There are few intellectuals to whom I owe more', he writes. 'But the more I thought about the virtues needed to sustain a self-critical and democratic ethos, the more I saw the posture being assumed in recent years by Hauerwas and MacIntyre as a threat to commitments I hold dear' (2001: 342). While Stout sees in both authors 'a splendid example of individuality, forged in the crucible of democratic exchange', he fears that their message 'may well be contributing to the erosion of habits and virtues essential to democracy' (2001: 342). Hauerwas, he says, 'has used MacIntyre's arguments to persuade Christians that democratic collaboration in the struggle for justice is a "bad idea" for the church' (2001: 342–3). Furthermore, Hauerwas 'invokes Aristotle to argue for a view of ethics that is "elitist" and not "democratic"', suggesting thereby that 'democratic exchange should not be seen as a basis for hope and that rational discourse on ethical topics is beyond the capacities of anyone not docile in relation to authority' (2001: 343). On Stout's account, the same hopelessness about 'democratic exchange' (2001: 343) forms a significant part of MacIntyre's own message as well, at least if we consider those passages in *After Virtue* that seem to advise 'withdrawal from democratic engagement into a circle of virtuous, like-minded souls at the margins of society' (2001: 342).

Stout has certainly voiced a discomfort widely shared by the readers of *After Virtue*, in suggesting that anyone giving credit to MacIntyre's account of liberal politics and their moral implications 'would clearly have trouble remaining rationally committed to the discursive practices of democracy' (2001: 342).

Yet, as I shall argue, MacIntyre's discontent with liberal politics can hardly be described as 'antidemocratic'. Quite to the contrary, such discontent is rooted in what I suggest should be labelled a 'hyperdemocratic' conception of politics as a deliberative practice of rational investigation. MacIntyre does not criticize liberal democracy for its commitment to the rational and critical features of democracy. Rather, he chides it for actually lacking such features in actual practice. In other words, it is not moral authority but democracy that he sees primarily missing in liberal democracy. Its lack of moral authority is but a consequence of its falling short of a truly democratic commitment to rational deliberation.

It is noteworthy that Mark Murphy draws attention to these epistemic implications of MacIntyre's political thought. *After Virtue*, as we have noticed, ascribes to the political institutions of human communities 'all the characteristics of a practice' (MacIntyre 1984: 194). But as Murphy persuasively argues—drawing mainly on MacIntyre's later clarifications—politics is not just a practice among others. It has a special status by reason of its 'role as a master practice organizing the various other practices' (Murphy 2003: 164). As such it appears to be an 'intensely cognitive activity' made of 'common practical reasoning about the common life' (Murphy 2003: 163). The 'goods internal to political life' are therefore 'goods of inquiry', and the role of governing institutions is to provide the ground on which 'rational investigation into the good can be pursued' (Murphy 2003: 164). This is why political communities require a local setting and a shared culture. The first of these two requirements 'is not based on some love of the local as such', but it is a practical condition for excluding no-one from common deliberation (Murphy 2003: 165). The requisite of a shared culture has a similar purpose: it is but another condition for a common rational inquiry into the good. In fact, the culture to be shared must itself be a 'culture of deliberation' which has to allow for a critical investigation into one's very own cultural traditions.[3] In giving such a central attention to MacIntyre's descriptions of the 'good of politics' as a 'good of inquiry' (Murphy 2003: 165), Murphy's construal offers, incidentally, a sensible account of why, in MacIntyre's view, some totalitarian 'evil' threatens the modern state's project to favour and promote a certain conception of the good. Whether we label it 'republican' or 'communitarian', such a project is to be rejected insofar as it is 'imposed from above without adequate rational inquiry into the defensibility of that conception of the good and without adequate participation

[3] Murphy 2003: 165. See also p. 166: 'MacIntyre's point is that a political community, when in good condition, is just that sort of community in which one *is* enabled to engage in rational criticism of one's own political community in the light of potentially competing goods.'

in decisionmaking by those whose lives will be governed by that conception' (Murphy 2003: 159).

Such fighting against elitist and authoritarian features of the modern state in the name of a socially sensitive conception of democracy is indeed utterly consistent with MacIntyre's valuing of the Christian catalogue of virtues over and above the aristocratic virtues of the Aristotelian catalogue—and, moreover, consistent with his consequential claim that the readers he wishes to write for are the people whose professional activities are despised as insignificant by those who hold dominant social positions. As Perreau-Saussine rightly suggests, MacIntyre's persistent 'sympathy for democracy' owes more to his early commitments to Marxist Christianity than to Aristotle's political thought (2005: 128–9).

It would be a mistake, however, to reduce MacIntyre's concern with democracy to a merely social issue. The kind of democracy he calls for is not only socially sensitive; it is also participatory and deliberative, critical and investtigative. In this outlook, social and epistemic concerns are intermingled to such point that MacIntyre identifies 'oppression with deprivation of the capacities and opportunities for rational inquiry' (Murphy 2003: 160).

It is hard to see how such views about the nature and purpose of political life could endanger our rational commitments to the 'discursive practices of democracy'. It could be objected, however, that while MacIntyre's critique of liberal democracy is not directed towards *democracy* as such, it still entails a clear dismissal of its *liberal* qualifier. As he puts it in the introduction to the 1995 edition of *Marxism and Christianity*,

> liberalism is the politics of a set of elites, whose members through their control of party machines and of the media, predetermine for the most part the range of political choices open to the vast mass of ordinary voters. Of those voters, apart from the making of electoral choices, passivity is required. Politics and their cultural ambiance have become areas of professionalized life, and among the most important of the relevant professsionals are the professional manipulators of mass opinion. (MacIntyre 1995: xxi–xxii)

All the motives of what I have called MacIntyre's 'hyperdemocratic critique' of liberal democracy are here gathered in a single argument: liberal democratic societies are not democratic enough. The manipulative partnership of their electoral structures and of their mass media force most people into political passivity, excluding them 'from any possibility of active and rational participation in determining the form of community in which they live' (MacIntyre 1995: xxii). Liberal democracy thus fails to protect them from 'the corrosive effects of capitalism and the depredations of state power' (MacIntyre 1995: xxvi). This is why MacIntyre urges that 'a politics of self-defence' (1995: xxvi) is needed for all those forms of life whose goods are pursued 'rationally and critically' (1995: xxviii) in 'local societies that aspire to achieve some relatively self-sufficient and independent form of participatory practice-based community' (1995: xxvi).

But we might ask at this point what this insistent appeal to local politics actually implies for those distinctive institutional features and governmental structures of liberal democracy that MacIntyre identifies with the 'modern state'. The response is once again somewhat puzzling.

Notwithstanding the massive presence of antiliberal rhetoric in *After Virtue* and in his later work, MacIntyre has repeatedly refused to articulate any large-scale alternative to the state institutions of liberal democracy. At times, he even acknowledges their relative value and legitimacy (MacIntyre 1984: 255, 1995: xxi, 1999: 133). He deems, to be sure, that any global endorsement of its pretensions is to be refused from the standpoint of local communities owing allegiance to the tradition of the virtues; he insists, however, that refusing any global consent to the modern state does not preclude some *ad hoc* acquiescence with and taking part in its particular tasks and responsibilities (MacIntyre 1984: 255).

As Murphy (2003: 170) has observed, these concessions raise some serious questions 'about whether practitioners of the politics of local community, if there were no state, would find it necessary, or highly desirable, to invent it'. Murphy argues that if 'several local communities saw the point of putting into place a statelike institution' (2003: 171), some striking resemblances would emerge between such a 'quasi-state' and 'the modern state that MacIntyre criticizes' (2003: 172), the most significant one being that, very much like the neutralist state of liberal democracy, the ideal quasi-state of local politics would proceed 'on the basis of a thinner theory of the good than that endorsed by any of the communities that it seeks to serve' (2003: 172). MacIntyre himself is not far from admitting the need for such a 'thinner theory of the good' when he approves of the liberal appeal to a neutralist state in order to oppose any alternative project requiring that a specific conception of the good be defended or promoted by means of state politics.

To be sure, MacIntyre's political philosophy still needs to be amended if it is to be reconciled with liberal democracy. Yet such a reconciliation requires no rejection of his Aristotelian teleology. As both Stout and Perreau-Saussine correctly suggest, it should rather proceed from a renewed understanding of the relationship that Aristotle establishes between ethics and politics. I take them to mean, with different but converging arguments, that the distinction which Aristotle draws between politics and ethics—or between civic and moral virtue—overlaps to some extent with Rawls's distinction between 'thin' and 'thick' conceptions of the good. As Stout (2001: 325n35) puts it, Rawls 'is not denying that the citizens of a liberal society share common aims or ends. Neither is he denying that his own liberal theory of justice as fairness needs to make certain thin assumptions about the good, assumptions that fall well short of a full-blown view of the meaning, value, or purpose of life.'

An Aristotelian interpretation of liberal democracy will concede to MacIntyre that justice and the good are intermingled to such an extent that it would be deceptive to admit Rawls's contention that the 'right' is prior to the 'good'. Yet it will uphold Rawls's distinction between 'thin' and 'thick' conceptions of the good as a safeguard against MacIntyre's inclination to conflate moral and civic virtue. In politics as in ethics, it is the good—and not merely some procedural form of justice—that is pursued, but the good pursued by means of political virtues is not quite as thick or substantive—even to Aristotle himself—as the good pursued by means of moral virtues.

References

Hauerwas, S., and Kenneson, Ph. (1997): 'The Flight from Foundationalism, Or, Things Aren't As Bad As They Seem'. Reprinted in: S. Hauerwas, *Wilderness Wanderings: Probing Twentieth-Century Theology and Philosophy*. Boulder, CO, pp. 97–110.

MacIntyre, A. (1984): *After Virtue: A Study in Moral Theory*. Second edition. Notre Dame.

——— (1995): *Marxism and Christianity*. Second edition. London.

——— (1999): *Dependent Rational Animals: Why Human Beings Need the Virtues*. Chicago.

Murphy, M. (2003): 'MacIntyre's Political Philosophy'. in M. Murphy (ed.): *Alasdair MacIntyre*. Cambridge, pp. 152–75.

Perreau-Saussine, É. (1999): 'Alasdair MacIntyre Between Marx and Aristotle'. Translated by Stéphane Douard and Jonathan Hand. University of Chicago Political Theory Workshop, February 1999. Formerly available online at www.src.uchicago.edu/politicaltheory/saussine99.pdf.

——— (2005): *Alasdair MacIntyre. Une biographie intellectuelle*. Paris.

Rorty, R. (1991): *Essays on Heidegger and Others, Philosophical Papers*. Vol. 2. Cambridge.

Sedgwick, P. (1982): 'The Ethical Dance: A Review of Alasdair MacIntyre's After Virtue'. Available online at: www.marxists.org/archive/sedgwick/1982/xx/macintyre.htm.

Stout, J. (2001): *Ethics After Babel: The Languages of Morals and their Discontents*. Second edition with new postscript. Princeton.

——— (2004): *Democracy and Tradition*. Princeton.

Yack, B. (1985): 'Community and Conflict in Aristotle's Political Philosophy'. In: *The Review of Politics* 1/47, 92–112.

TOWARDS THE POSTSECULAR: RAWLS AND THE LIMITS OF SECULAR PUBLIC REASON

Christoph Jedan

In much contemporary thought, the renewed visibility of religion in the public domain is acknowledged and even applauded. Theorists such as Jürgen Habermas, who cannot be suspected of a hidden religious agenda, have even begun to speak of a new 'postsecular' age in which the old antagonism between religion and secular reason in the public domain may be overcome (see e.g. Habermas 2005, Molendijk, Beaumont and Jedan 2010). Although scholars in the field of religion find much to applaud in such a vision, the resurgence or renewed visibility of religion in the public sphere finds no equivalent in terms of a postsecular political philosophy that would strive to make sense of the terms on which religion (or rather, religious reason) could play a legitimate role in public political debate. Habermas, for instance, seems willing to recognize religion as a worldview that supports pro-social values, but he remains reluctant to allow a genuine role for religious reason in the realm of 'official' political determination.

In this chapter, I want to ask how a postsecular political philosophy might allow a legitimate place for religion in the political arena. Since much of the discussion about the (post)secular is conducted in terms laid down by John Rawls's *Political Liberalism*, I will conduct my inquiry as an interrogation of Rawls's project for a justificatory 'political' liberalism, which attempts to restrict the participation of religious reason in public political argument for the sake of the stability and harmony of a society deeply divided along the lines of incommensurable worldviews.[1]

In the first part, I present my perspective on Rawls's political liberalism. In the second part, I discuss frequently-voiced critiques of Rawls's project that are to my mind largely misguided because they ignore the extent to which Rawls takes his inspiration from a particular historical experience, namely that of the USA. I argue that the historical situatedness of Rawls's theory allows us to understand better why Rawls concludes that it is right to regulate the access of religious reason to the public political domain. In the last part, I offer five

[1] The first edition of Rawls's *Political Liberalism* appeared in 1993. Rawls revised his theory of public reason in a new introduction to the paperback edition, which appeared in 1996. He restated his ideas in an article 'The Idea of Public Reason Revisited', first published in the *University of Chicago Law Review* in 1997. The revisions and the restatement are included in the new expanded edition of *Political Liberalism* (Rawls 2005). My references are to the page numbers of the 2005 edition.

suggestions as to what directions political philosophy ought to develop in order to allow religious reason a legitimate role in public political argument.

1. Rawls's Political Liberalism

If we want to understand what Rawls's concept of public reason is about, we can take our cue from his characterization of the ways in which *Political Liberalism* deviates from the theory he had previously proposed in *A Theory of Justice* (1971). He still upholds the ideal of a well-ordered society that he had famously advanced in *A Theory of Justice*, but he now points to what in his view was a major shortcoming of that work: it did not make sufficient allowance for the fact that a plurality of reasonable comprehensive doctrines is the norm in our modern democratic culture (2005: xli).

With the expression 'comprehensive doctrines' Rawls points to the fact that there is 'a diversity of opposing and irreconcilable religious, philosophical, and moral doctrines' (2005: 3–4), many of which are perfectly reasonable. Such doctrines are called 'comprehensive' if they

> include conceptions of what is of value in human life, and ideals of personal character, as well as ideals of friendship and of familial and associational relationships, and much else that is to inform our conduct, and in the limit to our life as a whole. (2005: 13)

Rawls now asks how a society characterized by a plurality of irreconcilable comprehensive doctrines can be just and remain stable over time (2005: 4). It is to this end that Rawls feels bound to constrain the use of religious reason in public political exchanges.

At first sight, it might seem odd that justice and the stability of a democratic society demand a constraint on the use of religious reason, but we can understand this demand better once we see it as a corollary of Rawls's stance on democracy and the concept of legitimacy in democratic societies. While many other democratic theorists consider voting to be a fair way of arbitrating conflict between rival political standpoints, on Rawls's view such an aggregative view of democracy is insufficient: recourse to the sheer fact of a majority of likeminded voters falls short of the moral demands that liberal democracy imposes. Even if a clear majority of likeminded voters is foreseeable, the majority owe it to those who disagree with them to give reasons for their decision. Rawls's view of democracy has a strong 'deliberative' or 'discursive' bent, and sees legitimacy as the provision of reasons that every rational citizen can, in principle, understand and share.[2] To Rawls, the exercise of political power is legitimate if and only if the justification of a coercive law can be made with reasons that every rational citizen can in principle understand and share. In

[2] Bohman and Rehg 1997; Gutman and Thompson 2004.

consequence, Rawls emphasizes reason-giving as a moral duty for citizens. More is at stake, however, than the moral duties of citizenship. Where the giving of reasons is denied or insufficiently discharged, or so Rawls argues, the stability of society is at risk. In Rawls's view the harmony in a society, the 'ties of civic friendship', cannot be attained as a matter of course but are a fragile achievement that is placed at risk when the justified demand for accessible reasons is denied (2005: 253). Citizens whose right to reasons is violated then feel trifled with and they might ultimately cease to give full-hearted support to the society in which they live.

At this point, the concept of public reason enters the picture. What could count as a basis for political reasoning acceptable to citizens holding a diversity of irreconcilable comprehensive doctrines? With his 'idea of public reason', Rawls addresses the problem of a common ground of reason-giving in pluralistic, liberal democracies. Given the thoroughgoing pluralism of incompatible comprehensive doctrines, Rawls argues, it is vitally important that common ground is found, at least in the 'constitutional essentials', namely the structures and procedures outlined by the constitution in addition to the citizens' basic rights, liberties and opportunities. These essentials should be embraced in the form of an 'overlapping consensus' from within all reasonable comprehensive doctrines. In order to be the object of an overlapping consensus, public reason cannot put forward values in the way embodies in a comprehensive doctrine, of which the scope is the whole truth as one sees it. It can do no more than conceptualize certain 'political' values *for the public-political realm*. Citizens are free to realize or disregard those values in their non-public lives (for instance, in a religious affiliation to which they might adhere). Only subject to this condition can public reason acceptably contain one or other of the family of broadly liberal conceptions of justice that support the constitutional basis of liberal democracies, including a certain priority of freedoms and rights over perfectionist ideals (2005: 223).

In addition to a system of common liberal values, public reason will also embody common 'guidelines of inquiry'. As an upshot of these guideline, Rawls posits that 'we are to appeal only to presently accepted general beliefs and forms of reasoning found in common sense, and the methods and conclusions of science when these are not controversial' (2005: 224).

From this depiction of public reason, it follows that religious contributions to public political arguments must be eyed with suspicion. Yet—and this is highly significant in our present context—Rawls does not ask for religious reason to be kept out of public political discourse absolutely. In the paperback edition of 1996, he further adjusts his concept to be more accommodating to religious reason in the public political realm.

In the first edition of *Political Liberalism*, Rawls explicitly rejects the absolute exclusion of religion from public political discourse (the 'exclusive view'), and prefers an 'inclusive view', 'allowing citizens, in certain situations, to present what they regard as the basis of political values rooted in their comprehensive doctrine, provided they do this in ways that strengthen the ideal of public reason itself' (2005: 247). The inclusive view is flexible. Whereas citizens in a well-ordered and perfectly just society will not see any reason to invoke comprehensive doctrines, citizens in a nearly just society might assuage doubts about the sincerity of their adherence to political values by invoking their comprehensive doctrine and show that their support of the political value in question is sincere and more than 'a mere modus vivendi' (2005: 249). In societies characterized by fundamental injustices, finally, citizens will want to invoke their comprehensive doctrines in order to 'give sufficient strength to the political conception to be subsequently realized' (2005: 254). Rawls claims that by its flexibility the inclusive view 'best encourages citizens to honour the ideal of public reason and secures its social conditions in the longer run in a well-ordered society' (2005: 248).

Rawls remained, however, not long satisfied with this explanation. In the new introduction to the paperback edition of *Political Liberalism* and in the more detailed paper 'The Idea of Public Reason Revisited', Rawls argues for a further relaxation of the restrictions imposed by the ideal of public reason on political reason-giving by citizens and embraces what he terms 'the wide view of public reason'.[3] He declares:

> I now believe (...) that reasonable [comprehensive] doctrines may be introduced in public reason at any time, provided that in due course public reasons, given by a reasonable political conception, are presented sufficient to support whatever the comprehensive doctrines are introduced to support. (2005: xlix–l)

Rawls calls this condition for the introduction of comprehensive doctrines into public debate 'the proviso'. He argues that this relaxation of the requirements for introducing comprehensive doctrines into public reason-giving

> [H]as the further advantage of showing to other citizens the roots in our comprehensive doctrines of our allegiance to the political conception, which strengthens stability in the presence of a reasonable overlapping consensus. (2005: l)

2. Critiquing Rawls

Rawls's concept of public reason and his regulation of religious reason in public political discourse has attracted numerous critiques. 'Is Rawls' conception of public reason incomplete?' is one of the questions asked most frequently (e.g., de Marneffe 1994, Bohman 1995, Lehning 1995, O'Neill 1997, Perry 1997). 'Is the proviso formulated well or could it be improved?' is another question,

[3] On 'The Idea of Public Reason Revisited' see Hayfa 2004.

mostly asked with a view to relaxing the proviso (Reidy 2000, Weithman 2002: ch. 5, Jedan 2006[4]). The most radical critics of the proviso have even asked if it might be abandoned altogether (Quinn 1997, Wolterstorff 1997, Eberle 2002, Schuster 2010), while a very few voices have advocated a more stringent exclusion of religion from the public realm than Rawls had envisaged (most notably, Audi 1997a, 1997b, 2000).

Interesting as such attempts may be, they are largely technical exercises that miss a crucial point: Rawls develops his accounts of public reason, the inclusive view and the wide view as an engagement with a concrete historical experience, the constitutional history of the USA. This point is regularly missed in the criticisms of Rawls, probably because of the awkward way in which he presents his reflections upon history as conceptual exercises.[5] What I shall be doing here is to analyse the intersection between historical experience and philosophical conceptualization. Understanding why Rawls is driven to constrain religious reason in public political argument will aid an enquiry into the principles of a political philosophy accommodating religious reason in the public political sphere. To this end, it is necessary to take stock of how Rawls relates his concept of public reason, both the inclusive view and the wide view, to historical exemplars of non-secular reasoning.

As I have mentioned before, it has already been noticed (Stout 2004) that Rawls offers in his development of both views some rather awkward references to historical precedents in political oratory. While unfolding the inclusive view, Rawls raises the cases of the abolitionists (who argued from the 1830s onwards that the South's institution of slavery was contrary to God's law) and the civil rights movement spearheaded by Martin Luther King, Jr., in the twentieth

---

[4] My own attempt (which I present here in more detail because it was published in German) takes its cue from Weithman's (2002) differential treatment of public advocacy and voting (with stricter limitations applying to the latter). It allows for substitutive justification by other participants in the public discourse and avoids gambling on future states of public reason (*pace* von Rautenfeld 2004). I differentiate as follows between a 'proviso for public reason-giving' and a 'voting principle':

(Proviso for public reason-giving:) A citizen (unless in an official role—as a government official, member of parliament or member of the judiciary—in which case stricter limitations apply) may at any time introduce comprehensive doctrines into the public debate to support a political proposal, provided that the person introducing such a doctrine is sincerely convinced that at that very moment proper public reasons—and not reasons given solely by comprehensive doctrines—can be presented that are sufficient to support whatever the comprehensive doctrines introduced are said to support.

(Voting principle:) When voting, citizens have a moral duty (entailed by the virtue of good citizenship) not to support (candidates promising to support) proposals for which proper public reasons have not yet been given.

[5] The most important exception is Jeffrey Stout's (2004) critique of Rawls, but even Stout does not give Rawls's engagement with US constitutional history its full due: he points at Rawls's awkward comments on political oratory without offering a full analysis of Rawls's understanding of US history.

century. He recognizes that these are two major examples of political argument steeped in religious language (2005: 249–50). He then writes:

> Did the abolitionists go against the ideal of public reason? Let us view the question conceptually and not historically, and take for granted that their political agitation was a necessary political force leading to the Civil War and so to the destruction of the great evil and curse of slavery. Surely they hoped for that result and they could have seen their actions as the best way to bring about a well-ordered and just society in which the ideal of public reason could eventually be honored. (...) On this account the abolitionists and the leaders of the civil rights movement did not go against the ideal of public reason; or rather, they did not provided they thought, or on reflection would have thought (as they certainly could have thought), that the comprehensive reasons they appealed to were required to give sufficient strength to the political conception to be subsequently realized. (2005: 251)

Rawls then claims that the above-mentioned cases fulfil the proviso and offers in a footnote the following argument:

> I do not know whether the Abolitionists and King ever fulfilled the proviso. But whether they did or not, they could have. And, had they known the idea of public reason and shared its ideal, they would have. (lii, n. 27)

It is obvious that these counterfactual ascriptions of motives fulfil neither the inclusive view nor the proviso. What is more, they are motives that are, in an important sense, anachronistic and may, therefore, surely be called 'in-accessible' to the historical figures to whom Rawls attributes them.

It might be tempting to blame Rawls simply for a lack of historical understanding, the more so since he expressly states in my first quotation that he intends to make a conceptual rather than an historical point. This, however, will not do. Rawls's repeated attempts to come to terms with the religious language in exemplars of political oratory from the constitutional history of the U.S. show that his initial advocacy of the inclusive view as opposed to the exclusive view, and his subsequent move to the wide view of public reason, are triggered by his wish to allow for this kind of public oratory. Moreover, throughout *Political Liberalism* he repeatedly signals his preparedness to make room for historical experience. We find this preparedness even at the methodological level. As in *A Theory of Justice* (1971: 20–1, 48–51), he employs the method of 'reflective equilibrium', the attempt to balance considered judgments with theoretical construction. In line with his reflective equilibrium approach, Rawls stresses in *Political Liberalism* that the starting-point for his political concept is the result of historical experience in a concrete political tradition.[6] The impact

[6] He thus states: 'We start, then, by looking to the public culture itself as *the shared fund of implicitly recognized basic ideas and principles*' (2005: 8, my italics). Shortly

of his method can be found in many aspects of his theory of public reason. For instance, he expresses his conviction that some basic decision problems (pertaining to constitutional essentials) have no 'universally best' solution and that a solution must depend on the historical political experience of a nation.[7]

Rawls not only acknowledges his dependency on history at a methodological level, but his own delineation of public reason is deeply rooted in the constitutional history of the USA. His hints as to what the content of public reason is supposed to be are heavily indebted to the US constitutional framework, and in particular to the Bill of Rights, evident, for example, from his minimalistic circumscription of the structure of the political process and a very limited list of rights. Other constitutions include a far greater range of values, many of which Rawls is either silent about or excludes from the content of public reason. Pertinent examples are the ban on capital punishment,[8] the protection of the environment[9] or the public provision of recreational facilities, which can be found in the Dutch constitution but not in the US constitution. Rawls follows the US constitution and does not argue for the more extensive lists of rights found in other constitutions.[10]

Rawls's departure from the US historical experience is revealed both in his wish to make his political liberalism acceptable to groups that are opposed to autonomy as a personal ideal and also in his description of a well-ordered society as a 'social union of social unions', previously formulated in *A Theory of Justice* (1971: 527). Moreover, his pessimistic view of the fragility of the ties of civic concord (see above) seems to be derived from the history of the USA. Nor should we forget, as Patrick Vandermeersch emphasizes in his contribution to this volume, that the USA was the creation of dissenters who wished to maximize the freedom accorded to different religious groups. Rawls's account overemphasizes the differences between those groups and therefore maximizes

---

afterwards, he remarks that 'justice as fairness starts *from within a certain political tradition*' (2005: 14, my italics).

[7] A point in question is how to protect the citizens' basic rights. Should, for instance, basic rights be entrenched, as in the German constitution, or is a parliamentary supremacy with no Bill of Rights preferable? Rawls sides with Robert Dahl, who declared that 'specific solutions need to be adapted to the historical conditions and experiences, political culture, and concrete political institutions of a particular country' (Rawls 2005: 235, n.21). Another example is his emphasis on 'successful practice' as a decisive factor determining the legitimacy of constitutional reform (Rawls 2005: 239).

[8] Article 114 of the Dutch constitution. Its place among the articles concerning the judiciary had merely procedural reasons and does not affect its character as fundamental right (van der Pot and Donner 1989). Rawls is silent on the death penalty, as is the US constitution, in spite of its ban on cruel and unusual punishment (Amendment VIII).

[9] According to Rawls, this is only derivatively a constitutional essential. He grants only that questions of environmental protection 'may *become* ones of constitutional essentials once our duties and obligations to future generations and to other societies are involved' (2005: 246, n.35, my italics). See Article 21 of the Dutch constitution.

[10] Article 20.3 of the Dutch constitution.

the need for a common basis of 'political' values, which would have to be independent of religious or other comprehensive doctrines. I argue that a need for the uncompromized independence of, and difference between, social unions has not been felt so keenly in Europe, with its long tradition of state interference in matters of religion.[11]

In Rawls's theory, this historical experience is tied to an excessively radical interpretation of democratic legitimacy. Rawlsian legitimacy, as I have argued elsewhere (Jedan 2010), is an all-or-nothing affair. It implies a moral duty on the part of individuals to offer reasons that are generally accessible in a situation where (as explained above) the common ground of understanding and accessibility is delineated far too narrowly. Again, this very idealistic and demanding notion of the democratic process, which is both deliberative and demotes the aggregative function of voting, is coupled to a pessimistic view of civic harmony and the threats to which it is exposed. All this makes of Rawls's ideal of public reason a highly situated concept.

In saying that, I do not mean to imply that Rawls advances an excessively precise delineation of the moral duties of citizenship, turning what was meant to be a vague ideal into a reified moralizing concept.[12] The truth of the matter is that Rawls is fully cognizant of the vagueness surrounding the delineation of the inclusive and the wide view.[13] This appears to be a corollary of his emphasis upon historical experience and is exemplified by his laboured attempts to allow classical oratory of US constitutional history to meet the criteria for the inclusive and the wide view. Vagueness is therefore not an effective critique of Rawls's concept of public reason, of the inclusive and the wide view. The real problem with Rawls's theory is that it combines an unrealistic all-or-nothing concept of political legitimacy based on deliberative democracy with a highly situated and overly defensive stance on what might be common ground for such

[11] See also Vandermeersch in this volume.

[12] This has been claimed by Stout 2004: 75.

[13] Rawls recognizes, e.g. in 'The Idea of Public Reason Revisited', that 'the details about how to satisfy this proviso must be worked out in practice and cannot feasibly be governed by a clear family of rules given in advance' (Rawls 2005: 462). In fact, his whole conception of public reason should best be interpreted as a postulate in the Kantian sense. Rawls posits that *some* common ground for public reason-giving is necessary for the sake of (perceived) legitimacy of coercive law in liberal democracies. Taking this postulate as his starting point, he attempts to reconstruct, rather tentatively and minimalistically, the scope and content that public reason should have in order to fulfil its function as a necessary condition for the legitimacy of coercive law in pluralistic, liberal democracies. In line with the postulatory character of the idea of public reason, Rawls begins with what he sees as the most urgent and at the same time most promising case: the necessity for common ground where constitutional essentials are concerned (2005: 227). Only if we give the postulatory character of Rawls's concept of public reason its full due, we can understand his demands that (1) public reason must be complete (i.e. can solve all or most problems to be decided) and (2) that the citizens employing public reason must be convinced that public reason is complete.

discursive practices. If we wish to analyse how the renewed visibility of the religious presence in the public domain could legitimately extend to the realm of the political, we will have to step outside the Rawlsian framework. In the final part of the chapter, I shall outline in five suggestions what I see as pivotal in a theory of political postsecularity.

3. Towards a Postsecular Political Philosophy—Five Suggestions

1. If we can learn from history at all, there is one lesson of note: the appreciation of historical events shows that much more can be understood, can be appreciated, and is 'accessible' across the divide of incommensurable worldviews than is allowed for in Rawls's political liberalism and kindred philosophies requiring non-religious reason as the basis for public political argument. Rawls unwittingly corroborates this by his attempts to allow political oratory steeped in religion to meet his criteria for the inclusive and the wide view. Such contributions to public political discourse can be perceived as exemplary and a model of 'discursive excellence', their religious content notwithstanding (Stout 2004). Rather than disuniting, on account of its religious content, such oratory can be felt to be a uniting, moving force. A political philosophy that attempts to theorize the renewed presence of religion in the public sphere will take care not to make such contributions to the public realm appear to be defective.

2. The single biggest issue with Rawls's conception of public reason is his all-or-nothing account of democratic legitimacy, which moreover ties legitimacy to overly restrictive ideas about the accessibility of arguments across incommensurable worldviews. If we want to come to terms with the renewed presence of religion in the public sphere, the Rawlsian concepts of legitimacy and accessibility must be replaced by notions of legitimacy and accessibility that are pluralism-proof.

3. In this vein, the Bill of Rights model of a single non-comprehensive basis of public political argument that stands behind Rawls's account, as well as much contemporary political thought, must be abandoned.

4. Just as with Rawls's Bill-of-Rights account of public reason, so his ideas about the fragility of civic harmony were developed in response to U.S. political history. In spite of Rawls's engagement with history, however, we ought to be sceptical about excessively radical claims with regard to fragility, particularly where they serve to burden religious (as well as other comprehensive) contributions to the public debate. Such claims might easily conjure up the spectre of disunity they are designed to banish.

5. Instead of attempting to exclude religious voices from the public political debate, we should foster what I would like to call the *symbolic presence of religion in public political argument*. In a situation of worldview pluralism, politicians are well advised to show how the values and coercive laws they promote can be derived from within one (or a number of) particular religious

tradition(s). Such attempts will be particularly valuable where they are symbolic, in the sense that they are undertaken by politicians who do not themselves belong to the religious tradition(s) in question.

Rawls recognizes the usefulness of employing comprehensive doctrines to reinforce the ideal of public reason.[14] In his view, however, such arguments may be used to muster support for the sake of a number of predefined general political values. What I propose here, instead, is a pluralistic, and also symbolic, public use of such arguments. Religious arguments can be employed in full cognizance of the controversial nature of concrete proposals of coercive law. While such arguments are to be employed in the sincere hope of raising support for the proposals under consideration, a second equally important goal is the attempt to show how religious arguments can perform a legitimate as well as a constructive role in public political argument.

It is clear that this fifth proposal goes against the grain of a recent tendency to negative representation, even caricature, in the public political representation of—particularly Islamic—religion by political entrepreneurs in the Netherlands as well as abroad. By drawing religious arguments into the realm of serious public inspection, religious convictions are taken out of the private realm of wounded pride and thus gain public recognition. I do not wish to invoke the spectre of civic disunity, but it is hard to see how citizens of faith can realize their full potential unless they feel that their religious convictions are taken seriously by their partners in the democratic process and are seen as an asset rather than a liability. We all stand to gain from a constructive symbolic representation of religion in public political argument.

References

Audi, R. (1997a): 'The State, the Church, and the Citizen'. In: P.J. Weithman (ed.) *Religion and Contemporary Liberalism*. Notre Dame, pp. 38–75.

——— (1997b): 'Liberal Democracy and the Place of Religion in Politics'. In: R. Audi and N. Wolterstorff, *Religion in the Public Square: The Place of Religious Convictions in Political Debate*. Lanham, pp. 1–66.

——— (2000): *Religious Commitment and Secular Reason.* Cambridge.

Bohman, J. (1995): 'Public Reason and Cultural Pluralism: Political Liberalism and the Problem of Moral Conflict'. In: *Political Theory* 23, 253–79.

Bohman, J., and Rehg, W. (1997) (eds.): *Deliberative Democracy: Essays on Reason and Politics.* Cambridge, MA.

Dombrowski, D. A. (2001): *Rawls and Religion*. Albany.

Eberle, C.J. (2002): *Religious Conviction in Liberal Politics.* Cambridge.

Greenawalt, K. (1994): 'On Public Reason'. In: *Chicago-Kent Law Review* 69, 669–89.

——— (1995): *Private Consciences and Public Reasons*. Oxford.

Gutman, A., and Thompson, D. (2004): *Why Deliberative Democracy?* Princeton.

[14] Rawls calls this use 'conjecture' (2005: 465–6).

Habermas, J. (2005): 'Religion in the Public Sphere'. Holberg Prize Lecture.
Hayfa, T. (2004): 'The Idea of Public Justification in Rawls's *Law of Peoples'*. In: *Res Publica* 10, 233–46.
Jedan, C. (2006): 'Das Recht zu reden: Eine sozialethische Theorie über die Präsenz von kulturell-religiösen Minderheiten im öffentlichen Diskurs'. In: *Nederlands Theologisch Tijdschrift* 60, 235–53.
——— (2010): 'Beyond the Secular? Public Reason and the Search for a Concept of Postsecular Legitimacy'. In: A. L. Molendijk, J. Beaumont and C. Jedan (eds) *Exploring the Postsecular: The Religious, the Political and the Urban*. Leiden and Boston, pp. 311–27.
Larmore, Ch. (2003): 'Public Reason'. In: S. Freeman (ed.) *The Cambridge Companion to Rawls*, Cambridge, 368–93.
Lehning, P.B. (1995): 'The Idea of Public Reason: Can It Fullfill Its Task? A Reply to Catherine Audard'. In: *Ratio Juris*, 8/1, 30–9.
Marneffe, P. De (1994): 'Rawls's Idea of Public Reason'. In: *Pacific Philosophical Quarterly* 75, 232–50.
Molendijk, A.L., Beaumont, J., Jedan, C. (eds) (2010): *Exploring the Postsecular: The Religious, the Political and the Urban*. Leiden and Boston.
O'Neill, O. (1997): 'Political Liberalism and Public Reason: A Critical Notice of John Rawls, Political Liberalism'. In: *The Philosophical Review* 106, 411–28.
Perry, M.J. (1997): *Religion in Politics: Constitutional and Moral Perspectives*. Oxford.
Pot, C.W. van der, and Donner, A.M. (1989): *Handboek van het Nederlandse staatsrecht*. 12th edition. Zwolle.
Quinn, Ph. A. (1997): 'Political Liberalisms and Their Exclusions of the Religious'. Reprint in: P.J. Weithman (ed.) *Religion and Contemporary Liberalism*. Notre Dame, 138–61. (Original in: *Prodeedings and Addresses of the APA* 69 (1995), 35–56.
Rautenfeld, H. von (2004): 'Charitable Interpretations: Emerson, Rawls, and Cavell on the Use of Public Reason'. In: *Political Theory* 32, 61–84.
Rawls, J. (1971): *A Theory of Justice*. Oxford.
——— (1997): 'The Idea of Public Reason Revisited'. In: *University of Chicago Law Review* 64, 765–807 (included in Rawls 2005).
——— (2005): *Political Liberalism*. Expanded edition. New York.
Reidy, D.A. (2000): 'Rawls's Wide View of Public Reason: Not Wide Enough'. In: *Res Publica* 6, 49–72.
Scanlon, T.M. (2003): 'Rawls on Justification'. In: S. Freeman (ed.) *The Cambridge Companion to Rawls*. Cambridge, pp. 139–67.
Schuster, A. (2010): 'Public Reason and Inclusionism as Pseudo-Inclusionism'. In: A. L. Molendijk, J. Beaumont and C. Jedan (eds) *Exploring the Postsecular: The Religious, the Political and the Urban*. Leiden and Boston, pp. 343–55.
Solum, L.B. (1994): 'Inclusive Public Reason'. In: *Pacific Philosophical Quarterly* 75, 217–31.
Sterba, J.P. (1999): 'Reconciling Public Reason and Religious Values'. In: *Social Theory and Practice* 25, 1–28.
Stout, J. (2004): *Democracy and Tradition*. Princeton.
Waldron, J. (1993): 'Religious Contributions in Public Deliberation', *San Diego Law Review* 30, 817–48.
Weithman, P.J. (2002): *Religion and the Obligations of Citizenship*. Cambridge.

Williams, A. (2000): 'The Alleged Incompleteness of Public Reason'. In: *Res Publica* 6, 191–211.

Wolterstorff, N. (1997): 'Why We Should Reject What Liberalism Tells Us about Speaking in Public for Religious Reasons'. In: P.J. Weithman (ed.) (1997): *Religion and Contemporary Liberalism*. Notre Dame, 162–81.

RETHINKING RELIGION AND POLITICS IN POSTSECULAR EUROPE

Erin Wilson

The critique of secularism and the secularization thesis has become a familiar refrain for social scientists. Where once the secularization thesis was so dominant that it was almost largely considered fact, the 21st century political environment makes clear that religion is by no means a spent force. Even in Europe, frequently considered the exception to the 'desecularization' of global politics (Berger 1997: 34–5), there is reason to think that the place of religion in European politics and public life is anything but settled.

Yet despite the now widely accepted view that the secularization thesis is at best, problematic and, at worst, simply wrong, there has been little discussion of where we go from here. The secularization thesis and the assumptions of secularism have been analysed and enumerated by scholars from within almost every discipline in the social sciences, all of which is helpful and important. Nonetheless, having exhausted all the possible angles from which to highlight the problems with the secularization thesis, there is a need to consider alternative ways to make sense of the relationship between religion and politics in the 21st century postsecular context.[1]

In this chapter, I suggest one such possible alternative framework. I take the multiple critiques of secularism and the secularization thesis as my point of departure and develop a theoretical framework through which we might rethink our understandings of both religion and its relationship with politics. I consider these issues in the European context, since the confusion about religion's newfound public profile seems greatest here. The strong reactions in the European public sphere to the wearing of headscarves, Turkey's membership to the EU and the debate around the preamble to the European constitution all indicate that religion is anything but a settled issue for Europe. Rather it is a vibrant, dynamic area of activity and debate for European identity and public life.

I take issue with two key sets of assumptions about religion and its relationship with politics and public life that secularists and adherents of the secularization thesis frequently make: 1) assumptions about the 'correct' way

[1] The term postsecular, like most other terms associated with discussions of religion, politics and secularism, is highly contested. In this chapter, I use postsecular to mean a period when secularist assumptions are increasingly questioned. In addition, while Taylor (2007: 13) asserts that a secular age is one in which belief is no longer the default position, I suggest that in a postsecular age, unbelief is no longer the default position, that in fact, there is no longer a default position when it comes to religion.

that the relationship between religion and politics should be organized; and 2) assumptions about the nature and definition of religion itself. I argue that the secular worldview has engendered a dualistic understanding of religion and politics as permanently separated by the public/private divide and has promoted a limited definition of religion as institutional, individual and irrational in order to reinforce assumptions about the need to separate religion and politics and privatize religion. Not only have these assumptions restricted our understanding of the role religion plays in politics and public life, it has also affected our assumptions regarding the role that religion *should* play in the public domain. As numerous scholars have pointed out, if we are indeed moving into a postsecular phase, scholars must reconsider such long held assumptions (Bretherton 2010: 15; Habermas 2006; 2008).

I begin by outlining the main assumptions held within the European context about the role that religion does and should (or rather, should not) play in politics and public life and the nature of religion itself, all assumptions which, I argue, stem largely from the secularization thesis and the secularist worldview. I highlight critical shortcomings of these assumptions before spending time outlining the relational dialogist framework, an alternative means for understanding both religion and its role in public life. This framework draws on the work of Julia Kristeva (1986) and Raia Prokhovnik (2003) and enables scholars to keep in mind the fluid dynamics of all social phenomena, but particularly religion. Religion is not static, but changes in meaning, practice, doctrine and experience over time and through interactions with other elements of society. As such, a static, rigid definition of religion is inadequate for explaining and capturing the full implications of religion's apparent resurgence in the 21st century. I conclude by considering what preliminary insights a relational dialogist framework can reveal concerning the postsecular European context.

1. Secularism, Postsecularism and Europe

Europe presents something of a conundrum for scholars exploring the relationship between the religious and the secular. There are widely held assumptions that Europe as a whole is the most secular continent in the world (Davie 2002: ix–x; Katzenstein 2006: 1). While some countries within Europe may be more or less religious than others, the general portrait frequently painted of religion and secularism in Europe is that secularism has triumphed. Politics and public life are now conducted according to secular liberal democratic principles. Religion has been successfully privatized and even in the realm of private, personal beliefs, religion is losing ground (Bruce 1992; Pollack 2008).

Yet several recent studies raise a number of questions regarding the validity of Europe's assumed secularization. The significant debate over including reference to common Christian heritage in the European Constitution and more particularly the on-going unease around Turkey's membership of the EU has highlighted that Europe's secular nature cannot be taken for granted (Challand

2009; Hurd 2008; Leuestean and Madeley 2009). Foret (2009: 38) acknowledges that while religion in Europe is constrained by the predominantly pluralist and relativist nature of contemporary politics in most European states, it still exercises political influence 'as a cultural raw material.' Casanova (2006: 66) has claimed the very formation of the EU is rooted in Christian thought and practice. '[T]he initial project of a European Union was fundamentally a Christian Democratic project, sanctioned by the Vatican, at a time of a general religious revival in post-World War Two Europe, in the geopolitical context of the Cold War when "the free world" and "Christian civilization" had become synonymous' (Casanova 2006: 66). There is little acknowledgement of this apparently intimate relationship between Christianity and modern European identity, owing to the on-going secularist bias within Europe that sees the presence of religion in public life as problematic, pre-modern and even embarrassing or shameful (Casanova 2009: 1058–9; Leuestan and Madeley 2009: 4). Europe's secular nature is emphasized over its Christian connections and the dominant narrative told about Europe's historical development is the successful separation of religion from politics and law to establish communities of peace and tolerance (Willaime 2009: 24).

There are two key sets of assumptions within this traditional narrative concerning the religion/politics nexus in Europe that provide clues to the deep and pervasive influence of the secularist worldview on this issue. Firstly, the privatization of religion is highlighted as a success. Jose Casanova (2008) provides a succinct re-telling of the European myth surrounding the privatization of religion, in which religion is essentialized as being intolerant, divisive and generally 'bad'. Religion's removal from politics and public life is critical to the long-term stability and survival of European society. This myth has institutionalized the first key assumption I take issue with—that religion *should* be privatized and excluded from public life, that it is both possible and necessary to separate religion from politics.

The second key set of assumptions informs the first and is evident in the way religion is defined in this traditional story about religion and politics in Europe. In general, such narratives are concerned with a particular type of religion, Christianity, and with a particular embodiment of this religion—the organized, institutionalized churches. If one limits one's definition of religion to the institutionalized Christian churches, then it is very easy to argue that secularism has won. The marginal place that Christian church institutions hold in public debates in Europe and the recent growing trend amongst individuals to be 'debaptized' from the institutionalized churches (Bryant 2012) is merely the latest in a long line of events that demonstrate the diminishing power and influence of traditional Christian institutions in European politics and public life.

The institutional aspect of religion is but one of its many characteristics. The continued equation of 'religion' with ecclesiastical institutions within discourses around religion and politics in Europe is, I argue, an indication of the pervasive influence of secularist assumptions regarding religion and its proper role in politics and public life.

These traditional stories about religion and public life in Europe also assume that religion is primarily a matter of personal, individual belief and that religion is largely irrational. As a question relevant mainly to individuals, public discussion of religious beliefs is not acceptable within the realm of secular liberal democracies. Religious reasons and justifications are also not suitable contributions to debates about public and social policy, since such arguments are only acceptable to the religious members of a particularly society (Dombrowski 2001: 3, 9; Eberle 2002: 13; Rawls 1999: 151–2). Consequently, regardless of how many people in a society profess either religious or spiritual beliefs, (a number that is surprisingly high in Europe for a secularized continent (EVS 2012)), the fact that these individuals do not attend church and do not discuss their beliefs publicly is seen by social scientists as further evidence of both the need for and the success of the secularization project in Europe (EVS 2012; Halman, Sieben and van Zundert 2011).

Further, as an irrational system of belief, something that cannot be proven through visible, tangible evidence, religion has no business contributing to public debates and public reasoning (Eberle 2002: 313–14). Consequently, religion *should* be separated from politics and public life.

A number of respected political theorists and philosophers have recently challenged this assumption that has long been an implicit part of secular liberalism. Jeffrey Stout (2004: 9–10) argues that the requirement for religious adherents to leave their beliefs in the private realm when contributing to public debate is inherently undemocratic. Jürgen Habermas (2006: 13) concurs, arguing that this requirement by secular liberal political philosophers lays an unequal burden on religious citizens. Further, Habermas states that society loses something if religion is excluded from the public sphere, since religions act as important carriers of meaning in society and 'have special power to articulate moral intuitions' (Habermas 2006: 10; Chambers 2007: 214).

This secular liberal requirement that all religious reasoning be excluded from the public sphere is premised on a series of implicit assumptions concerning how reason and rationality are defined. Such 'common sense' notions about what is rational and reasonable generally exclude religion, emotion, and aesthetics, amongst other things, and are informed through the cultural preconditioning of secularism (Eberle 2002: 313–14). With the growing critique of secularism, there is a need to rethink our understanding of what is rational and reasonable and to acknowledge that aspects of human life previously excluded from 'rational' public debate, possess their own logic, their own reason and can make fruitful contributions to public life (Bleiker 2009: 29; Wilson 2012). These criticisms make clear that the assumptions implicit in the secular worldview need to be reconsidered.

2. Secularist Logic—Four Key Moves

Secularism, I argue, makes four cognitive moves, influenced by and developed throughout key historical and philosophical moments, which work to produce a view that religion is mainly institutional, individual and irrational, and consequently that religion and politics should be separated.

2.1. The Possibility and Necessity of Separating Religion and Politics

The first of secularism's four moves involves establishing that it is both possible and necessary to separate religion and politics from one another. In order to establish the possibility for separating religion and politics, these two aspects of society had to be conceptualized as belonging to two different spheres of existence. Charles Taylor (2009) refers to this as the 'secular/religious dyad'. Once a clear distinction was made between the two, it became possible to conceive of the two as separate.

The possibility for separating religion and politics is hinted at in the work of a number of philosophers and theologians, one of the most significant being Martin Luther. Luther suggests that the Christian lives in two realms—the spiritual and the secular or temporal (Luther 1972: 468–9). He states that the church holds authority over the spiritual realm and the temporal authority, ordained by God, has jurisdiction over the civil realm (Luther 1972: 468–9). In Luther's theology, the two realms are distinct but equal, both under the authority of God, but neither one subordinated to the other. Nonetheless, by distinguishing between the two, Luther sets up the conditions necessary for secularism's first move, establishing the possibility of separating religion and politics.[2]

Alongside Lutheran theology, the wars of religion of the sixteenth and seventeenth centuries have been and continue to be critical aspects of the justification for the need to separate religion and politics, as well as crucial events in the story told about Europe's secularization (Casanova 2008; Thomas 2000). According to Scott Thomas (2000: 819), 'what the wars of religion unequivocally indicate [for liberal secular scholars] is that when religion is brought into international public life it causes intolerance, war, devastation, political upheaval, and even the collapse of the international order.' It is here we see the emergence of the argument for the *necessity* to exclude religion from politics, not merely the possibility of doing so. This argument is central to secular liberal accounts of how the relationship between religion and politics should be arranged and managed in Western democracies. Liberal secularism presupposes that religion *had* to be 'removed' from society in order to put an end to sectarian conflict that disrupted the social order (Thomas 2000: 819).

As William Cavanaugh (2009: 4) has argued, 'the attempt to create a transhistorical and transcultural concept of religion that is essentially prone to

[2] For a detailed discussion of Luther's doctrine of the two kingdoms, see Wilson 2012: 44–5.

violence is one of the foundational legitimating myths of the liberal nation-state.' This 'myth' concerning the violent, irrational nature of religion 'tries to establish as timeless, universal and natural a very contingent set of categories—religious and secular—that are in fact constructions of the modern West' (Cavanaugh 2009: 6). Thus, the myth of religious violence is a crucial part of secularist ideology and its efforts to contain, control and remove religion from public life. The idea of religion as inherently violent ties in with one of the three main characterizations of religion in the social sciences, as being largely irrational and consequently unsuitable for participation in public debate.

2.2. Excluding Religion from Politics

The emergence of the modern state was the primary way in which the exclusion of religion from politics was made possible in practice (Thomas 2000) and the Peace of Westphalia is a critical component of that story. According to the secular liberal account, the Peace of Westphalia encapsulates the death of religion as a characteristic feature of European society. Prior to Westphalia, Christianity was the organizing principle and defining feature of Europe, known then as *Respublica Christiana* (Philpott 2001: 77). After Westphalia, the collective loyalty of the people was directed more towards the state, in particular the nation as a source of identity, and less towards the church (Philpott 2009: 188). Christendom became forever divided after Westphalia and ceased to be a salient political community.

Dominant secular narratives concerning this period assert that there existed an almost mutually exclusive relationship between religion and politics. One of the apparent triumphs of the Westphalian states system is the removal of religion from politics and public life, replacing it with liberal, secular, universal values arrived at through reason and rational debate. Religion and politics were forever separated. The modern state emerged as the dominant organizational unit in society, rather than the churches, and thereby 'saved' the world from a continuing spiral of violent sectarian conflict (Bellen 2008: 318). Religion was subordinated to the state and became a private, personal matter of little consequence in public life.

2.3. Enforcing Religion's Exclusion through the Public/Private Divide

The third move of secularism is then directed towards maintaining religion's separation from and subordination to politics. Building on ideas encapsulated in Luther's Doctrine of the Two Kingdoms and other writings that established the distinction between religion/politics and church/state, the notion of the public/private divide was articulated by scholars such as John Locke and Emile Durkheim (2008 [1915]: 36–42).

Locke wrote on the idea of the public and the private realms in his musings on the problem of religious intolerance (Ingersoll and Matthews 1986: 39). Locke's idea was that, in order to ensure tolerance, it was important to make a clear distinction between the business related to religion and the business related to civil government (Locke 1965[1689]: 171). Locke held that the state or the civil government should be primarily concerned with issues that had a direct impact on all citizens. He argued that this included 'life, liberty, health and indolency of body; and the possession of outward things, such as money, lands, houses, furniture, and the like' (Locke 1965[1689]: 172) because it is these things that should be available to all citizens to enable them to live. 'The care of souls', Locke (1965[1689]: 172–3) argued, is not the responsibility of any man. Individuals are responsible for their own salvation and their own souls (Locke 1965[1689]: 172–3).

In Locke's writing, the division of public and private is done primarily with reference to religion. Religion is the only matter specifically restricted to the private realm. The influence of dualism on understandings of the relationship between religion and politics in the West is evident here. Locke's prescription for tolerance divides society into public and private realms and restricts religion to the private, separating it from politics and public life.

Religion, and to a lesser extent, morality, continue to be the obvious targets of exclusion in relation to the public/private divide. In the case of religion, its exclusion from the public realm is articulated in the principle of the separation of church and state. In part related to Locke's notion of the separation of the private and the public realm (Ingersoll and Matthews 1986: 39), the church is associated with the private realm and the state with the public. Religion, more than any other issue, caused intolerance and chaos when permitted in the public realm, with the Thirty Years' War (amongst other examples) apparently demonstrating this (Eberle 2002: 27, 152; Thomas 2000: 819).

Yet, ironically, ideas and principles from religion itself have played a significant role in shaping the concept of the separation of church and state and the public/private divide. Religious thought influenced the rise of political principles such as the separation of church and state, the public/private divide and the rule of law (Wilson 2012: 111–13). It is somewhat paradoxical that the very phenomena secularists sought to exclude from political life in the West influenced the development of arguments to justify the separation of religion and politics.

2.4. Promoting Secularism and the Exclusion of Religion as the Ideal for a Progressive, 'Developed', 'Civilized' Society

The fourth move of secularist thinking further contributes to the subordination of religion to politics by constructing religion as primordial and premodern, something that decreases in influence with processes of secularization and modernization. With economic development and political modernization, religion would no longer exercise any influence in the public sphere, being restricted to individual personal matters. Authors such as David Apter (1965) and Donald E. Smith (1974) exemplify this attitude. Apter suggests that, in the process of political value formation, the purposes and needs of individuals that had previously been served by church religion, are transferred to political religion. Where church religion provides a sense of purpose and triumph over death in relation to the supernatural, political religion does the same in relation to the nation-state. 'Individuals in a political community are made to feel that they are products of lives lived before theirs within the context of the nation. This feeling is translated into family and kinship commitments as secured within the state' (Apter 1965: 268–9). Commitments to the state thus become the 'religion' of a community rather than commitments to a supernatural being or deity. The usurpation of religious commitment by commitment to the state is, according to Apter, a critical component of the process of modernization. In Apter's work, then, we see the fourth move of secularist thinking in action. For processes of modernization to succeed, the authority and influence of the church must be usurped by the state and all references to God and transcendental belief removed from public life.

Donald E. Smith's 1974 study, *Religion and Political Modernization,* also articulates the dominant assumption that secularization and the decline of religion are essential for political modernization. 'Political modernization includes, as one of its basic processes, the secularization of polities, the progressive exclusion of religion from the political system' (Smith 1974: 4).

Smith confines his study to societies embedded in four of the major religious 'systems', as he calls them: Hinduism, Islam, Buddhism and Catholicism (Smith 1974: 7). His focus is on 'South and Southeast Asia, the Middle East, North Africa, and Latin America' (Smith 1974: 3). He does not consider Western communities, such as Europe and North America. Consistent with secularization theory, Smith's work assumes that political modernization for Western communities occurred around the time of the Peace of Westphalia. He considers Western states already modernized and consequently secularized, with religion no longer having a significant role in Western society (Philpott 2002: 67–9).

The implication of this line of thinking is that once political modernization has occurred, religion will not have a significant role in the politics of a community, as the West, particularly Europe, supposedly exemplifies. Political modernization and development requires secularization. According to secularist thinking, a society cannot be considered modern and developed unless religion has been privatized and subordinated to the public realm of secular liberal democratic politics.

These four moves of secularist ideology, I contend, are underpinned by dualistic thinking and result in relationships of privilege and subordination. Public is privileged over private; reason is privileged over emotion; men are privileged over women; progress and development are privileged over tradition, history and culture; and politics is privileged over religion. Further, public, reason, men, progress, development and politics become connected with one another and juxtaposed against private, women, emotion, tradition, history, culture and religion, which also become connected with one another.

Secularism's four cognitive moves are consistent with the twin influences Casanova (2009: 1052) has identified—philosophico-historical and political. The philosophico-historical theme in secularist thinking constructs religion as an historical artefact, consigning 'religion to a superseded age' (Casanova 2009: 1052). The political theme assumes that 'religion is either an irrational force or a nonrational form of discourse that should be banished from the democratic public sphere' (Casanova 2009: 1052). These assumptions reflect the underlying dualism that permeates secularist thinking. Secularism divides the world into either rational or irrational, either historical or modern, either part of the public realm or the private realm. These processes do not occur instantaneously but, as Casanova notes, occur as part of a gradual process. 'Eventually, however, as a result of this particular historical process of secularization, "the secular" has become the dominant category that serves to structure and delimit, legally, philosophically, scientifically, and politically, the nature and the boundaries of "religion."' (Casanova 2009: 1063). Yet such clear neat divisions are, in general, only useful in theory. Relationships between different facets of society are much more complex in reality. Religion is not simply rational or irrational, but contains elements of both. Religion also is not simply historical or modern. It has had historical influence on the development of international society and politics and continues to have influence in modern contemporary political settings, albeit in different forms. Finally, it is increasingly obvious that religion is not merely a part of the private realm but exercises influence in the public realm of modern Western and international politics. Yet dualistic assumptions concerning religion and its place in modern European politics persist and are played out in the four cognitive moves of secularist thinking.

3. Religion: Three Dichotomies

The second set of assumptions that I take issue with in this chapter concern the definition of religion itself. Dominant assumptions about the nature of religion, I suggest, have been heavily affected by dualism and operate around three dichotomies. These dichotomies relate to the ways religion influences politics and society. The three dichotomies are: institutional/ideational, individual/communal and irrational/rational.

The first of these dichotomies relates to religion as an institution or religion as a set of ideas. Religion, I propose, is both institutional and ideational, not one or the other. The overall tendency within the social sciences, however, is to focus on the institutional aspects of religion. The institutional element of religion is observable and tangible, and thus, easier to examine, in contrast to religion's ideational influences, which are more subtle, implicit and intangible.

This focus on the institutional element of religion, coupled with the separation of church and state and the public/private divide in European society, highlights in part why religion's influence on European politics and society is often underexplored.

The second dichotomy refers to whether religion exercises influence at an individual level or at a broader communal level. Again, I argue that religion's influence operates at both levels. However, social scientists often assume that the influence of religion functions primarily at the individual level in Europe. The public/private divide reinforces this perception of religion as mainly important to individuals. Liberal advocates of secularism also promote the idea that religion *should* only function at the individual level and should not influence politics and society (Cudd 2002: 125 n.19; Dombrowski 2001: 4; Thomas 2000: 819). Assumptions that religion has been successfully and wholly excluded from the public realm in general and politics in particular in Europe have led social scientists to either dismiss or downplay the influence of religion in politics.

The third dichotomy involves whether religion is seen as rational or irrational. Overwhelmingly, social science research assumes religion is irrational. The effect of this assumption is that religion is often considered relevant only to analyses of developing societies or communities of non-European 'others' arriving in European states. The dichotomous view of religion as predominantly institutional, individual and irrational contributes to continued confusion about the role and influence of religion in European politics and society. This is why developing a framework for analysing religion that encompasses all six elements and values them equally is essential for overcoming the effects of dualism on perceptions of religion and politics in Europe.

4. An Alternative Approach

In contrast to the inflexibility of dualism, the Bakhtinian notion of dialogism, as posited by Julia Kristeva, highlights the ongoing interaction of ideas, emphasizing fluidity and change, rather than rigidity (Kristeva, 1986: 39–40). In Kristeva's analysis, dialogism is both 'subjectivity and communication'. The text is telling a story, describing a series of events, but also communicating with texts and events that have come before and will come after. Kristeva (1986: 39) refers to this as intertextuality. This intertextuality contrasts with dualism, particularly as part of secularist thinking, which claims objectivity and universality (Hurd 2008), establishes fixed barriers limiting communication between dichotomized pairs, such as reason/emotion, man/woman, politics/religion, and maintains the meaning of these different categories as fixed and unchanging.

The aim of dialogism, Kristeva argues, is not to arrive at a finite point of understanding and definition, but to strive 'toward harmony, all the while implying an idea of rupture (of opposition and analogy) as a modality of transformation' (Kristeva, 1986: 58). This approach recognizes that ideas are constantly developing and changing, that they can exist both in harmony and in opposition to one another, often at the same time. Changes occur through interactions with other ideas within and across texts and historical events. There will be moments of agreement and 'harmony' about what ideas mean and what their implications are for analysis and for broader society. Yet dialogism highlights that such moments are not conclusive. There is always the possibility of shifts and changes in ideas and how they interact, how texts communicate with each other and with broader society.

Dialogism suggests that views of religion and politics as separate and irelevant to one another and of religion as institutional, individual and irrational are not fixed, permanent, objective, universal conclusions, but merely thoughts that will shift after interactions with other ideas. Thus, Bakhtinian dialogism refracts and unsettles our established understandings of religion and politics. In Kristeva's articulation, dialogism represents a condition of constant rupture, with few moments of agreement or fixity. While such rupture is beneficial for shifting our current confined definitions of religion and politics, it creates a somewhat debilitating situation, in which there is no means for agreeing on new definitions or understandings, since they are always in constant rupture. Thus, while dialogism assists in the project of displacing secularism as the dominant thought mode in the social sciences, it leaves us without any substantial means for moving passed secularism. It does not necessarily provide us with 'other ways of talking about and enacting the relations between "religion" and "secularism"' (Pellegrini 2009: 1345), other than to note that these relations are in a constant state of rupture.

It is at this point that combining the insights from Kristeva's interpretation of Bakhtinian dialogism with Raia Prokhovnik's (2003) critique of dualism is useful for developing other modes of thinking about religion and politics. Prokhovnik's model of relational thinking provides one means of moving forward from this potentially debilitating point of constant rupture. Understanding concepts as existing in relationships provides a way for managing these concepts and using them in practice, all the while remembering, in line with dialogism, that the meanings associated with these terms are infinite and open to change. Using the relational thought model, connections amongst ideas are understood in much the same way as relationships amongst people, an ever-present, constant component of society yet always containing possibilities for change and a level of uncertainty.

The dualism present within secularist approaches to religion and politics endeavours to remove this uncertainty, to establish fixed understandings of particular ideas. As part of this process, dualism separates concepts that actually exist in close relationship with each other. In separating the public realm from the private, man from woman, reason from emotion, politics from religion, dualism disguises the relationship between each of these dichotomous pairings that is integral to their definition. 'Woman' is central to definitions of 'man', just as 'man' is central to definitions of 'woman'; 'emotion' is central to definitions of 'reason,' just as 'reason' is a critical part of definitions of 'emotion' and so on. The two concepts are intimately and interdependently connected. In contrast to dualism, Prokhovnik (2003: 14) highlights that relational thought seeks to emphasize the connections that exist within these dichotomous pairings, arguing that there are numerous 'intellectual and social benefits' in recognizing the relationships that are present both within and across existing dualisms. Thus, religion and politics are not separated from one another but are in constant relationship and dialogue, both contributing to shaping what we understand as 'politics' and 'religion' and the identities and goals of political and religious actors within the public realm.

In contrast to dualism's restrictive 'either/or' pattern, relational thought proposes a 'both-and' approach, assisting transcendence of barriers established across existing dualisms. Using this model, it is not a question of whether politics and the public realm should be 'secular' or 'religious.' Elements of both exist within the public political realm and should be recognized as such. The secular and the religious shape and define one another, so that what is considered secular is affected by what is considered religious. Further, regarding religion itself, it is not a question of whether religion is primarily institutional or ideational, primarily individual or communal, or primarily irrational or rational. Religion is made up of all of these elements, although obviously the manifestation of these elements differs across religions. At different times and in different contexts, some aspects of the relational dialogist understanding of religion will be more important to consider and analyse and will have more significant influence on aspects of politics than others, but all should be incorporated into the way in which religion and its relationship with politics are understood in the European context.

Combining Kristeva's (1986) interpretation of dialogism and Prokhovnik's (2003) model of relational thought develops a framework that acknowledges connections amongst elements in religion that are not fixed, but are fluid, shifting and changing as they interact with each other, with other ideas, other texts and with people's practical experiences, past, present and future. This opens up possibilities for rethinking and reassessing traditional secularist assumptions about the relationship between religion and politics and the nature of religion that have restricted studies of this issue within the European setting.

5. Undoing the Four Moves of Secularism

Relational dialogism enables scholars to overcome or subvert the four moves of secularism. Firstly, the possibility of separating religion and politics is recognized as nigh on impossible, since politics and religion are not purely defined by their institutions, but also by their history and their philosophical and doctrinal/ideological beliefs and ideas. Politics and religion are not purely carried out by 'rational', autonomous individuals, but by communities of people who may act in their common interests and according to the logic of their own worldview, not necessarily the liberal secular worldview. This does not make them wrong; it simply makes them adherents to one worldview that offers an alternative perspective to the secularist worldview. Following on from this, the argument that it is necessary to exclude religion from politics becomes void, largely since it is not possible to do so, but also because it is not simply religion that causes chaos and disorder in public life, but any passionately held set of beliefs, including secularism, that is also not tempered with critical reason (Bernstein 2009: 1047). Equally, however, critical reason, uninformed by faith, should not be considered the ultimate source of truth (Ager and Ager 2010: 8).

Secularism's second move, the actual exclusion of religion from public life, is negated by the changes relational dialogism brings to how we understand religion. The separation of religion and politics was primarily justified through defining religion as mainly institutional and establishing the legal requirement for church and state to be separate. I am not suggesting that political authorities should be able to exercise authority and influence over doctrinal issues within churches, nor am I saying that religious groups should be able to dictate the laws of any particular country. What I am saying is that, like it or not, the ideas from the one do permeate and influence the other. Aspects of political philosophy and practice influence how religious believers, institutions and communities exercise their faith (such as democratic principles that now govern church synod meetings and the election of vestry members for congregations). Equally, however, elements of religion permeate and influence the way we think and talk about politics and public life (Wilson 2012: esp. ch. 5). Understanding religion as both institutional and ideational enables recognition of these multiple influences.

Relational dialogism also helps to circumvent secularism's third move, enforcing religion's exclusion from politics through the establishment of the public/private divide. Part of reviewing secularist assumptions about the relationship between religion and politics involves rethinking the division of Western society and international politics into public and private spheres, the primary method by which religion and politics have been kept separate. Relational dialogism reveals that these two spheres are not separate but interact in multiple ways. If the nature of the connection between religion and politics is to be more comprehensively understood, then the public/private divide also has to be thought of as fluid and shifting, rather than permanently fixed. Indeed, it may be beneficial to entirely do away with the categories of public and private realms and instead view European society in more relational terms. Again, dialogism's emphasis on history is useful here. Ways in which religion and politics have interacted in the past continue to influence how they interact now and into the future, rendering the relatively recent imposition of the public/private divide even more problematic.

Finally, by breaking down barriers between concepts traditionally positioned in binary opposition to one another, relational dialogism undermines the assumption that religion is incompatible with modernization and development.

Religion is not purely historical but is an important influence on contemporary politics. Religion's separation from modernization and development is also undermined by the changes relational dialogism brings to how we understand religion itself. Through a relational dialogist framework, religion is no longer considered purely 'irrational'. Neither are contemporary politics and public life considered purely 'rational'. Consequently, this opens up space for acknowledging religion's presence in the modern public sphere and its influence on various dimensions of politics in Europe.

6. Reconceptualizing Religion

The second set of secularist assumptions that relational dialogism addresses relate to definitions of religion itself. Current secularist understandings of religion are highly dualistic and confined primarily to religion's institutional, individual and irrational elements. Relational dialogism questions these dominant definitions and develops an alternative understanding of religion itself, one that overcomes the limitations of dualistic secularism. Rather than viewing religion as primarily institutional, individual and irrational, excluding its ideational, communal and rational elements, within the relational dialogist framework, all of these elements are understood as existing relationally, each influencing the others to varying degrees. The elements do not exist in defined positions against each other but shift and interact. A further category of experience, which intersects with the institutional, communal, individual, rational and irrational, must also be included, following insights from Grace Davie (2006: 29) and Ivan Strenski (2010). Further, the very concepts of 'rational' and 'irrational' are undermined, since what is considered 'rational' and 'irrational' has been defined from a secularist standpoint (Eberle 2002: 313–14; Wilson 2012: 18, 140–5). Indeed, within the relational dialogist framework, notions of rational and irrational become analytically unhelpful. Yet this raises the significant question of what concepts should replace them. For the present, I propose utilizing notions of intellectual reason, emotional reason and spiritual reason as alternative ways of thinking about elements previously considered to be either rational or irrational. By referring to them as different types of reason, this acknowledges both that the nature of reason is subjective, conditional and internal to a particular area of life, rather than being objective, natural, unconditional and external. By using three new characteristics to replace the previous dichotomy of irrational/rational, I hope to move thinking about religion further away from the influence of secular dualism. For the moment I am suggesting such a conceptual move purely in the context of understanding religion. Such categories remain useful when discussing the idea of public reason, but require significant rethinking and redefinition in order to accommodate other forms of knowledge, logic and reasoning traditionally excluded from debates in the public sphere.

7. Relational Dialogist Insights on Religion and Politics in Postsecular Europe

The implications of utilizing this alternative approach in the European context are many and varied. To begin with, analysts can no longer focus predominantly on the roles of religious institutions or the personal beliefs of individuals in their efforts to determine the influence of religion on politics and public life. These factors remain an important part of determining religion's influence in a society, but not the main or primary focus. In addition, the relational dialogist framework encourages scholars to more closely examine the influence of religious ideas on communities, societies, nation-states and civilizations, not just the actions of individuals. These ideas may be prominent, such as the many affirmations of the existence of God that constitute aspects of American political culture, but they may also be deeply embedded implicit assumptions relating to fundamental questions of ethics, good and evil, the purpose and progress of history and other basic assumptions that exist within a society's subconscious or imaginary (Galtung 1996). These implicit embedded assumptions make the use of religious language, narratives, phrases and ideas as framing devices for representations of political events and justifications for particular policy actions more acceptable and legitimate.

Another implication of utilizing the relational dialogist framework in the European context is that the dominant narrative regarding religion and politics in Europe becomes increasingly untenable. The birth of the secular state as the 'felicitous response to [the] catastrophic experience' of religious conflict (Casanova 2008) is a myth that must be abandoned. Alternative accounts of Europe's recent history and the birth of the nation-state that include open and free acknowledgement of the historical role that religion has played in shaping the politics and identity of the nation-states that constitute Europe, as well as the emerging identity of the European Community and the European Union, must be told. Rather than denying, ignoring or dismissing the period of European history where religious wars irrevocably altered the political landscape, as is often the case (Casanova 2008; Eberle 2002; Thomas 2000), scholars also need to acknowledge that this period contributed to positively shaping the philosophical and political values and institutions that now constitute the modern liberal democratic state and that religious ideas too played a significant and positive role.

Such an acknowledgement of religion's significant historical, philosophical and cultural contribution to European politics and identity may lead to a second, rather more uncomfortable conclusion—that the question of religion and politics in Europe has not been as successfully 'settled' as has generally been assumed. The very concept of the secular within the European context implicitly assumes that religion, secularism's 'antagonistic, bipolar opposite' (Bleiker 2001), is not just any religion but is a particular type of religion (Christianity) that can comfortably co-exist with the idea that religion and politics can and should be separated. Not all religions, not even all forms of

Christianity, can conform to such an assumption, and, as Grace Davie (2000: 22–3) has highlighted, the changing religious demographics within Europe mean that we can no longer speak of 'European religion' (if indeed we ever could), but must now instead refer to the 'religions of Europe.' The shift to a postsecular societal context raises questions as to how to manage the relationship between a secular public domain and the religions that do not easily co-exist with the idea that religion should not be present in the public sphere. Perhaps the most important question to start with is why, given the numerous erroneous assumptions in secularist thinking, religions should be excluded from the public sphere at all. The challenge for political theorists and philosophers is to develop theories and philosophies of religion that allow for such variation and diversity and move beyond the assumptions about the nature of religion, politics and rationality contained within the secular worldview.

References

Bellin, E. (2008): 'Faith in Politics: New Trends in the Study of Religion and Politics', World Politics 60/2, 315–47.

Berger, P.L. (1997): 'Against the Current'. *Prospect* (March 1997), 32–6.

Bernstein, R.J. (2009): 'The Secular-Religious Divide: Kant's Legacy', *Social Research* 76/4, 1035–48.

Bleiker, R. (2009): *Aesthetics and World Politics*. Houndsmill.

——— (2001): 'East-West Stories of War and Peace: Neorealist Claims in Light of Ancient Chinese Philosophy'. In: S. Chan, P. Mandaville and R. Bleiker (eds), *The Zen of International Relations*. New York, pp. 177–201.

Bretherton, L. (2010): *Christianity and Contemporary Politics*. Chichester.

Bruce, S. (1992): 'Pluralism and Religious Vitality'. In: S. Bruce (ed.), *Religion and Modernization*. Oxford, pp. 170–94.

Bryant, E. (2012): 'Flood of 'De-Baptisms' Worries European Church Leaders', *Religion News Service* 18 January 2012. Available at http://www.religionnews.com/politics/government-and-politics/growing-de-baptisms-reflect-europes-secular-drift (accessed 20 February 2012).

Casanova, J. (2009): 'The Secular and Secularisms', *Social Research* 76/4, 1049–66.

——— (2008): 'Public Religions Revisited'. In: H. de Vries (ed.), *Religion: Beyond the Concept*. Fordham, pp. 101–19.

Cavanaugh, W.T. (2009): *The Myth of Religious Violence*. Oxford.

Challand, B. (2009): 'From Hammer and Sickle to Star and Crescent: the Question of Religion for European Identity and a Political Europe', *Religion, State and Society* 37/1, 65–80.

Chambers, S. (2007): 'How Religion Speaks to the Agnostic: Habermas on the Persistent Value of Religion', *Constellations* 14/2, 210–23.

Cudd, A.E. (2002): 'Preference, Rationality and Democratic Theory'. In: R.L. Simon (ed.), *The Blackwell Guide to Social and Political Philosophy*. Malden MA, pp. 106–30.

Davie, G. (2006): 'Is Europe an Exceptional Case?', *The Hedgehog Review* 8/1–2, 23–34.

——— (2002): *Europe: The Exceptional Case*. London.

——— (2000): *Religion in Modern Europe: A Memory Mutates*. Oxford.
Dombrowski, D. (2001): *Rawls and Religion: The Case for Political Liberalism*. Albany, NY.
Durkheim, É. (2008 [1915]): *The Elementary Forms of the Religious Life*. Mineola, NY.
Eberle, C.J. (2002): *Religious Conviction in Liberal Politics*. Cambridge.
European Values Survey (EVS) (2012): 'Religion'. Available at http://www.europeanvaluesstudy.eu/evs/research/themes/religion/, accessed 24 February 2012.
Foret, F. (2009): 'Religion: a Solution or a Problem for the Legitimisation of the European Union?', *Religion, State and Society* 37/1, 37–50.
Galtung, J. (1996): *Peace by Peaceful Means: Peace and Conflict, Development and Civilization*. London.
Habermas, J. (2008): 'Notes on Post-Secular Society', *New Perspectives Quarterly* 25/4, 17–29.
——— (2006): 'Religion in the Public Sphere', *European Journal of Philosophy* 14/1, 1–25.
Halman, L., Sieben, I. and van Zundert, M. (2011): *Atlas of European Values: Trends and Traditions at the turn of the Century*. Leiden.
Hurd, E.S. (2008): *The Politics of Secularism in International Relations*. Princeton.
Katzenstein, P.J. (2006): 'Multiple Modernities as Limits to Secular Europeanization?'. In: T.A. Byrnes and P.J. Katzenstein (eds), *Religion in an Expanding Europe*. Cambridge, pp. 1–33.
Kristeva, J. (1986): 'Word, Dialogue and Novel'. In: T. Moi (ed.), *The Kristeva Reader*. New York, pp. 34–61.
Leustean, L.N. and Madeley, J.T.S. (2009): 'Religion, Politics and Law in the European Union: An Introduction', *Religion, State and Society* 37/1, 3–18.
Locke, J. (1965 [1689]): 'A Letter Concerning Toleration'. In: C.L. Sherman (ed.), *Treatise of Civil Government and A Letter Concerning Toleration by John Locke*. New York, pp. 167–224.
Luther, M. (1972): 'Romans Chapter Thirteen'. In: H.C. Oswald (ed), *Luther's Works Volume 25 Lectures on Romans*. Saint Louis, pp. 468–84.
Pellegrini, A. (2009): 'Religion, Secularism and a Democratic Politics of "As If"', *Social Research* 76/4, 1345–50.
Philpott, D. (2009): 'Has the Study of Global Politics found Religion?', *Annual Review of Political Science* 12, 183–202.
——— (2002): 'The Challenge of September 11 to Secularism in International Relations', *World Politics* 55/1, 66–95.
——— (2001): *Revolutions in Sovereignty: How Ideas Shaped Modern International Relations*. Princeton.
Prokhovnik, R. (2003): *Rational Woman: A Feminist Critique of Dichotomy*. Manchester.
Smith, D.E. (1974): 'Religion and Political Modernization: Comparative Perspectives'. In: D.E. Smith (ed.), *Religion and Political Modernization*. New Haven, pp. 3–28.
Strenski, I. (2010): *Why Politics Can't Be Freed from Religion*. Chichester.
Taylor, C. (2009): 'The Polysemy of the Secular', *Social Research* 76/4, 1143–66.
——— (2007): *A Secular Age*. Cambridge MA and London.
Thomas, S.M. (2000): 'Taking Religion and Cultural Pluralism Seriously: The Global Resurgence of Religion and the Transformation of International Society', *Millennium* 29/3, 815–41.

Willaime, J.-P. (2009): 'European Integration, *Laïcité* and Religion', *Religion, State and Society* 37/1, 23–35.

Wilson, B. (1992): 'Reflections on a Many-Sided Controversy', in R. Wallis and S. Bruce (eds.), *Religion and Modernization: Sociologists and Historians Debate the Secularization Thesis.* Oxford, pp. 195–210.

Wilson, E.K. (2012): *After Secularism: Rethinking Religion in Global Politics.* Basingstoke.

PART III

RELIGIOUS POLITICAL PARTIES—DUTCH PERSPECTIVES

RELIGIOUS PARTIES IN A SECULAR SOCIETY: THE DUTCH PARADOX

Paul Lucardie

At first sight, Dutch society looks very secular. When we stroll through the streets of a city like Groningen, we see more prostitutes than priests, monks, mullahs or any other people wearing religious robes or religious symbols. There may be quite a few churches, but on Sundays they are rarely crowded and some are filled only on special occasions such as weddings. When we observe the behaviour of Dutch people more closely and listen to their conversation, we find few references to religious values or traditions—with perhaps one major exception: many Dutch curses still contain the word 'God'. And of course we have observed—or at least heard about—gay marriage, abortion and euthanasia, pornography and prostitution—all of which were legalized in spite of disapproval or opposition from churches, synagogues and mosques.

If we probe a little more deeply, it seems that we can confirm those first impressions. In this chapter, however, I will argue that some qualifications are necessary. The World Values Study, a survey undertaken in more than forty countries between 1990 and 1993, shows that the Netherlands figure among the most secular countries. Only half the population, 51 per cent, belonged to a religious denomination, fewer than in any other country apart from former Socialist states like China or Russia, Bulgaria or Estonia (Inglehart, Basañez and Moreno 1998: V143). Slightly more Dutchmen considered themselves religious (61 per cent) and believed in God (64 per cent), yet religious services were attended once a month or more by only 31 per cent (Inglehart, Basañez and Moreno 1998: V151, V166, V147). In 2005, the number of believers was roughly the same, but membership of Christian churches had dropped to 44 per cent of the population, whereas the number of Muslims and Hindus had risen to about 6 per cent (Becker and de Hart 2006: 34, 52). These figures are below the 'world average' but not among the very lowest. Perhaps the Dutch stay away from formal or institutional religion while still retaining religious attitudes and practices?

However, while almost all Dutch denominations are declining in membership, religious parties still flourish in the Netherlands—more so than in most European countries. Not one but three parties in the Dutch parliament claim to be Christian: the Christian Democratic party (in Dutch: *Christen-Democratisch Appèl*, CDA), the Christian Union (*ChristenUnie*, CU) and the Calvinist or Reformed Party (in Dutch: *Staatkundig Gereformeerde Partij*, SGP). Islamic parties have not yet entered parliament but the 'Islamic Democrats' won a seat on the municipal council of The Hague in March 2006 and managed to retain it in 2010. Until quite recently, the three Christian parties have occupied a third of the seats in the lower house. The German Christian Democrats are better represented than that in the *Bundestag* (239 out of 622 seats at the elections of 2009), but their party manifesto appeals not only to Christians but also—explicitly—to Conservatives and Liberals (CDU 1994: 5). Christian or Christian Democratic parties in Central and Eastern Europe and Scandinavia tend to do less well; only the Christian Socialist People's Party of Luxembourg has achieved substantially better results. In Britain and Southern Europe, as well as in Australia, Canada and the USA, Christian parties are not represented at all—either because they do not exist or because they are too small. This fact can be explained to some extent by those countries' electoral systems. Pure proportional representation without electoral thresholds, as practised in the Netherlands, implies that a party needs less than 1 per cent of the popular vote to gain a seat in parliament. If Canada or Germany had introduced a similar system, small parties like the Christian Heritage Party or the *Partei Bibeltreuer Christen* would have won a few seats in the House of Commons or the *Bundestag*. Even then, however, religious parties would probably be stronger in the Netherlands than in those two countries.

Hence we are confronted with a paradox: religious parties seem to flourish in a secularized society. In order to resolve this paradox, we have to know more about the history and the ideologies of the religious parties as well as about their status and function in the Dutch political system. In my opinion, a religious party can be distinguished from secular parties not only by its name but also by its policies and, perhaps, by its voters. In other words, a religious party can be defined as a party that protects and promotes religious organizations such as churches and faith schools, by legislating for moral behaviour and by politicizing the rift between religious and secular divisions in the population.

1. A Brief Historical Survey

A hundred and fifty years ago, there were no religious parties in the Netherlands. In fact, political parties in the modern sense of the word did not exist at all before the 1870s. Yet people referred to 'parties' in parliament, by which they meant informal networks of like-minded men—women were not allowed to vote or to be elected until 1919. Most men did not have the right to vote, either; the franchise was limited to the wealthy and well-educated upper-middle class. One party would support the government while the other led the opposition. Since 1848, the government needed the support of a parliamentary majority. Most of the time, the government depended on the Liberal party, while the Conservatives were in the opposition. Whereas the Liberals fought for the modernization and secularization of the state, on the basis of individual liberty and equal rights, the Conservatives defended tradition and privileges—especially the powers of the monarchy and the Dutch Reformed Church, which had been the privileged church in the Netherlands since independence. Until

1852, the King would appoint the church council or synod (Blei 2000: 85). At that time, the Dutch party system did not seem to differ very much from the Belgian, Danish, Swiss or United Kingdom party systems.

Gradually, all over Western Europe the franchise was extended as a consequence of economic development, rising levels of education and urbanization. The growing electorate required more formal organization, both nationally and locally. The Dutch Liberals set up a Liberal Union in 1885. The Conservatives tried to establish a national organization as early as 1868, but it had already disintegrated by 1875 (de Jong 2000: 243–5). In 1891 the last Conservative member of parliament lost his seat. Conservative voters had switched to other parties, mainly to the Anti-Revolutionary Party (*Anti-Revolutionaire Partij*, ARP), founded as a formal organization in 1879, and to the Catholic party, which remained an informal network of local associations until 1904. Some of the more secular Conservatives might have preferred their old rivals, the Liberals, to the religious parties. The demise of the Conservative party is usually explained in terms of the 'school struggle', the question of who would control the mass education that every modernizing nation required.[1] The Liberals introduced legislation promoting 'public schools', funded and controlled by the state, which would teach (rather vaguely defined) Christian moral principles, whereas the Anti-Revolutionaries and Catholics called for 'private schools', i.e. faith schools associated with particular churches or denominations, but also funded by the state. The Conservatives had defended a public (state) school system inspired by Christian principles, but this position differed very little from the Liberal policy and it alienated most of their Catholic and Protestant supporters (de Haan 1998: 205).

2. ARP

Like the Conservatives, the ARP cherished traditions—particularly with respect to Protestantism and the sovereignty of the House of Orange, which had ruled the Netherlands since independence. When the French Revolution reached the Netherlands in 1795, the Prince of Orange fled. Almost a hundred years later, the Anti-Revolutionaries were still fighting against the spirit of the French Revolution with its radical-democratic ideas about the sovereignty of the people and 'emancipation of the nations from the sovereign authority and legal authority of the omnipotent God' [*emancipatie der volken van onder het souverein gezag en de rechts-autoriteit van den almachtigen God*] which resulted in 'breaking the tie that linked us to God and His Word' [*de band die ons aan God en zijn Woord bond*] as Abraham Kuyper, the founder and ideologue of the party, put it (1880: 13). They argued that God had entrusted sovereignty to the House of Orange. They believed that the eternal principles of God's Word

[1] Similar conflicts took place in Belgium, France, and Germany—the *Kulturkampf* (see Gould, 1999).

should guide political life, but only through the individual conscience of the political leaders; and no church should seek to give orders to politicians (ARP 1911: 59). Unlike most Conservatives, the ARP did not want to grant privileges to the Dutch Reformed Church, or indeed to any other established church. In fact, most of its leaders felt that the Dutch Reformed Church had become too liberal and modernising in the course of the nineteenth century. Some had left the old Dutch Reformed Church (or in Dutch: *Nederlands Hervormde Kerk*) as early as 1834, and many others would do so in 1886. In 1892 most of them joined the new Reformed Church (*Gereformeerde Kerken*) established by Abraham Kuyper—a church minister who happened also to be president of the ARP and founder of the Free (Protestant) University (Blei 2000: 101–6).[2]

3. CHU

A minority within the ARP continued, however, to be loyal to the old Dutch Reformed Church, but in a sense they were closer to the defunct Conservative party. In 1894 most of them left the ARP, not so much for theological reasons as because of disagreements about electoral reform and party discipline, and on account of personality clashes as well (Janssens 2001: 90–1; van Spanning 2001). With two other Protestant groups, they went on to found the Christian Historical Union (*Christelijk-Historische Unie*, CHU) in 1908. Its manifesto seemed to be more theocratic and clerical than that of the ARP. It proposed that the Netherlands should be governed 'as a Christian state in the Protestant sense' [*als een Christelijke staat in Protestantschen zin*], inspired by the Holy Bible and by the wisdom of the Christian Church [*het oordeel der Christelijke Kerk*] (CHU 1911: 65). Yet, in practice, the CHU turned out to be a far from militant but rather a moderate and governmentalist party, willing to co-operate even with the Social Democrats (van Spanning 1988: 282–6, 429, 452).

4. SGP

To a lesser extent this was true of a third Protestant party, which was founded in 1918: the Political Reformed Party (*Staatkundig Gereformeerde Partij*, SGP). Most of its members belonged (and still belong) either to small pietistic Calvinist churches that had refused to join the *Gereformeerde Kerk* or to the pietistic tendency within the Dutch Reformed Church (Janse 1985: 66–8). Until the introduction of the universal and compulsory vote in 1918, they had usually abstained from political activity. They rejected the Neo-Calvinism of Kuyper and kept to the orthodox doctrine, emphasizing the incomprehensibility and omnipotence of God and the sinful nature of mankind who, they believed, should

---

[2] In Dutch there is a subtle difference between 'Hervormd' and 'Gereformeerd' which is lost in the English translation 'Reformed'.

humbly accept the predestined events in their lives rather than try to control them (Fieret, 1990: 28). For this reason, the SGP has always opposed insurance and immunization against diseases (SGP 1924: 143). It would also like to ban cinema and theatre, dancing, swearing and birth control (Fieret 1990: 82ff.). The government, they argued, ought to act according to God's Law as revealed in the Scriptures (SGP 1924: 142). The SGP interpreted this law in a strict sense: the government was to ban any meeting where principles would be promulgated that would dishonour God and the authority of the government [*in alle samenkomsten te verbieden het verbreiden van beginselen, die de eere Gods en het gezag der overheid aanranden*, SGP 1924: 143]. This might refer not only to events like the performance of the American entertainer Madonna hanging on a cross (in Amsterdam, 3 September 2006) but also to the Catholic mass, as Catholicism was regarded by the orthodox Calvinists as a false religion (Fieret 1990: 81). Given its aversion from Catholicism and its self-image as a prophetic party setting out to promote principles rather than to maximize its vote or gain power, the SGP did not join any coalition.

5. KVP

The Catholic party was very different. It was formed in the nineteenth century as a loose network of local electoral associations around the Catholic notables who supported Liberal or Conservative cabinets. Catholics had been treated as second-class citizens in the Dutch Republic (1588–1795) and to a lesser extent also in the Kingdom before 1848. Gradually, however, they gained self-confidence. In 1883 a Catholic priest, Hermanus Schaepman, drafted a programme for the Catholic party he was trying to build despite the resistance of conservative Catholics and Catholic Conservatives. In Schaepman's eyes, the Conservatives were 'nothing but retarded Liberals' (1883: 25). He felt more affinity with the Anti-Revolutionaries and agreed with their ideas about sovereignty, faith schools and Sunday observance, even if he objected to their hegemonic ambitions. In 1888 Catholics and Calvinist Anti-Revolutionaries overcame their traditional hostility—the legacy of the Dutch War of Independence—and formed the first Christian coalition government. The government lasted until 1891, but the coalition continued. In 1918 it came to be led by a Catholic nobleman, the first Catholic prime minister in the Netherlands. The introduction of universal suffrage had helped the Catholic party to win 30 out of 100 seats, which was more than the Social Democrats, Liberals, ARP or CHU had won. It would continue to be the dominant party in Dutch politics until the 1970s. Gradually, it developed a more centralized organization and a more coherent programme. In 1946 it was renamed the Catholic People's Party (*Katholieke Volkspartij*, KVP). It based its programme not directly on the Bible, like the ARP and other Protestant parties, but on 'principles drawn from the revelation, as interpreted by the doctrinal authority of the Church' [*Die beginselen put zij uit de Openbaring, gelijk deze door het Kerkelijk Leergezag wordt vertolkt*] as well as from 'the natural demands of personal and social life' [*de natuurlijke eischen van het persoonlijke- en het gemeenschapsleven*] (KVP 1946: 93). Like other Catholic parties, it argued for co-operation between Capital and Labour, employers and employees, in a corporatist framework (KVP 1946: 97; see also van Wissen 1982: 24–6, 41–2). Its predecessor, the Catholic State Party, had done the same in the 1920s and 1930s, but its protestant allies, the ARP and CHU, showed very little enthusiasm for corporatist arrangements. After the Second World War, however, the KVP switched partners and governed together with the Labour Party (*Partij van de Arbeid*, PvdA), which was more favourably disposed to corporatist experiments, insofar as they accorded well with the construction of a social welfare state. When the experiments met with growing resistance, especially from employers, the KVP gradually gave up on corporatism and shifted towards more liberal socio-economic policies (van Wissen 1982: 202–43). At the same time, it began to prefer coalitions with the ARP, CHU and the Liberal party (People's Party for Freedom and Democracy, *Volkspartij voor Vrijheid en Democratie*, VVD).

Coalitions restricted to the three Christian parties became uncommon after 1933, even though the parties continued to win parliamentary majorities until 1967. A stable government seemed to require a broad coalition, in the opinion of the Dutch political elites who usually preferred accommodation and 'consociationalism' (as political scientists would call it) to polarization and confrontation (Lijphart 1969; Koole and Daalder 2002). Thus all parties had to compromise their principles to some extent. At first, the Christian parties had tried to accept the modernization of Dutch society with respect to technology and economic development, while blocking or containing it in the moral and cultural sphere. Even though the ARP, CHU and KVP did not go so far as the SGP, they introduced film censorship, they banned prostitution, they tried to maintain strict Sunday observance, and they sought to ban married women from employment in the public sector—in order to protect the family and Christian morality. They argued that if cultural modernization could not be avoided it should be contained, by being channelled through organizations controlled (usually indirectly rather than directly) by religious leaders. Thus Catholics were encouraged to send their children to Catholic schools, to read Catholic newspapers and to listen to the Catholic radio network, to join a Catholic soccer club and a Catholic trade union. This process is usually referred to as 'pillarization' (*verzuiling* in Dutch). Furthermore, the Catholic elites, and to a lesser extent the Protestants, hoped to avoid or control socio-economic conflicts through corporatist arrangements, binding arbitration and consultation of 'recognized' (or pillarized) trade unions.

It proved to be an uphill task. Modernization continued at an increasing speed after the Second World War. Both Catholics and Protestants refused to be pillarized and began to watch secular television and to join secular clubs (Koole and Daalder 2002: 26–7; Pennings 1997). Church attendance declined and increasing numbers of people left the church altogether. In parliament, the Christian parties lost their majority at the 1967 elections and have never won it back. The PvdA became the largest party in parliament, winning more seats in 1977 than the ARP, CHU and KVP together. By then, the three parties had already combined their lists in the elections and planned to merge into one Christian Democratic party—the *Christen-Democratisch Appèl* or Christian Democratic Appeal (CDA).

6. CDA

The merger between ARP, CHU and KVP was a slow and complicated process, which began in 1967 and ended in 1980 (ten Napel 1992). The task of bridging four centuries of religious conflict took time. Resistance came especially from leftwingers within the parties, who feared that the CDA would turn into a right-wing party like the German CDU; however, resistance also came from orthodox Protestants and, although to a lesser extent, from orthodox Catholics. The orthodox Protestants objected to the decision not to base the new party's manifesto directly on the Bible, as ARP and CHU had done; for them, it was to be 'the answer to the appeal made by the Bible' [*antwoord op de oproep van de Bijbel*] and would be tested against the Bible (CDA 1980: 5). The CDA attached importance to the statements issued by the Christian churches but did not feel obliged to implement them (as the KVP and to some extent the CHU had done). The government should serve God, they believed, in delivering justice (CDA 1980: 5). The Christian Democratic party was to be guided by four principles: public justice, stewardship, differentiated responsibility, and solidarity. Justice was a biblical notion that should be constantly redefined according to the circumstances of time and place (Wetenschappelijk Instituut voor het CDA 1990: 116). Stewardship (*rentmeesterschap*) referred to mankind's responsibility for God's creation, and in particular to the protecting the environment. Differentiated responsibility (in Dutch: *gespreide verantwoordelijkheid*) implied support for institutions that mediate between the state and its individual citizens—civil society or, in another typical Dutch expression, *het maatschappelijk middenveld* (the mid-field or centre-field of society). These were institutions such as trade unions and employers' associations, in addition to welfare societies, broadcasting networks and faith school or private school governing bodies. In combination with solidarity, we might consider this a very faint reflection of an admittedly faded corporatism. Jan Peter Balkenende, one of the young ideologues of the CDA who was elected party leader in 2001, and who served as Dutch prime minister from 2002 until 2010, interpreted it in a rather abstract communitarian sense as a moral prescription rather than an argument for corporatist institutions (2002: 25–30).

In 1980 the Christian Democrats still criticized capitalism to some extent, just as their predecessors had done. They held that production should become more 'meaningful' and that power should be shared between Capital and Labour (CDA, 1980: 8), but by the time that the party manifesto was revised in 1993 these demands had disappeared. The spirit of the age (*Zeitgeist*) seemed to demand more liberal rather than socialist policies. Yet the CDA did not embrace economic liberalism wholeheartedly. The state, it believed, should shield and protect the weak [*treedt de overheid op als schild voor de zwakke*] and should promote the non-profit sector (CDA 1993: 17; see also Balkenende 2002: 113–27). Nevertheless, several senior party members criticized the party's evolution. Bert de Vries, who had been minister of social affairs in the 1980s and the party chairman from 2001 to 2002, observed a shift towards neo-liberalism and neo-conservatism, which in his opinion was far too radical (de Vries 2005: 31–2).

7. Christian Democracy and Conservatism

'Conservatism' however, seems to be a taboo word among Christian Democrats. In 2003 a law professor and member of the Senate, Alphons Dölle, suggested that his party should adhere explicitly to social conservatism—partly in order to appeal to the secular conservatives, whose numbers seemed to be increasing (Dölle 2003). His proposal met with strong resistance, however (van Houten 2003). Another senator, Henk Woldring, immediately brushed the idea aside (2003). The ideological debate did not proceed very far, partly because 'conservatism' proved to be an ill-defined and highly-contested concept. Critics like Woldring did not see conservatism as a coherent ideology but more as a state of mind. In his opinion, Christian Democracy was a 'moderate progressive movement' (1996: 303–4). Yet in 2010 Woldring—together with Bert de Vries—left the party because he believed that it had betrayed its principles by joining a government with the VVD, which needed the support of the national-populist Freedom Party (*Partij voor de Vrijheid*, PVV) (Woldring 2010).[3]

It is true that the Christian Democrats and their predecessors had played a major part in the construction of the Dutch welfare state. Nor did they shy away from reconstructing it, even if critics might prefer the term 'deconstructing'. The coalition of Christian Democrats and Liberals led by Balkenende turned the Dutch health-care system upside down and reformed the broadcasting system as well as the social security system more drastically than any Social Democrat would have done. However, if Conservatism is spelled with an upper-case 'C' rather than a lower-case 'c', it may be quite compatible with reformism. International experts in the study of ideology, like Michael Freeden, regard Conservatism as one of the three major ideological families, next to Liberalism and Socialism. Conservatism should be seen not as 'an attempt to forestall change ... but to render it safe' (Freeden 1998: 332). Freeden specified three core concepts of Conservatism: preference for organic growth, belief in the transcendental origins of the social order and an antithetical or mirror-image tendency (1998: 333–8). All three concepts can be found in policy and other documents of Dutch Christian Democrats, albeit with some qualifications.

[3] For Woldring's take on Christian Democratic thought, see his contribution to this volume.

'Renewal in order to preserve' was the well-chosen title of a Christian Democrat report on social security (CDA 1982). It was also an expression favoured by Ruud Lubbers, political leader and prime minister from 1982 to 1994 (Lubbers 1986: 23). The Christian Democrats object to revolutionary and planned change, as do most Liberals and even many Socialists today. Yet, unlike Liberals and Socialists, they refuse to submit (at least in theory) to the sovereign will of the people; and they reject the absolute autonomy of the individual as well as that of the state, believing that both the individual and the state should serve God—obviously a 'transcendental origin of social order'. The antithetical character of the Dutch Christian Democrats has declined since the days of Abraham Kuyper—who called for an 'antithesis' between secular and Christian parties—but was given new meaning when they were excluded from the government benches in 1994—for the first time since 1918. The CDA did not actually oppose the socio-economic policies of the coalition of Labour, Liberals and Democrats (PvdA, VVD and D66) that ruled the Netherlands until 2002, but they objected to the legalization of euthanasia and the institutionalization of gay marriage, the toleration of soft drugs and the (relatively) liberal immigration policy. Secular conservatives did not approve of these policies either and might have voted in 2002 for the CDA—if they did not vote for the (fairly conservative) populist Pim Fortuyn (van Holsteyn and Irwin 2003: 48–9). The Balkenende government probably satisfied quite a few of them, given the relatively strong performance of the CDA at the 2006 elections. Yet when Balkenende formed a government with the PvdA and Christian Union, his popularity began to decline. In 2010 the CDA lost most of its secular voters and reached only 21 seats, or less than 14 per cent of the vote (see also van Kersbergen, 2011). In 2012 the CDA reached even less, only 15 seats.

The Dutch Christian Democrats have adopted liberal ideas in many respects—as, in fact, many Conservatives in other countries have done. Besides, the CDA cannot govern alone and it depends on either Liberal or Social Democratic allies. Euthanasia and gay marriage are not to be banned again. Soft drugs are not legalized but still tolerated. Immigration has been reduced effecttively, however, and 'multiculturalism' is no longer a popular idea. In my view, the ideology of the CDA—and possibly other Christian Democratic parties—should be seen as—and I hope readers will pardon the rather frivolous metaphor—a distant and estranged cousin of the Conservative family who has had affairs with members of the Socialist and Liberal families. Thus, Christian Democrats tend to be more egalitarian and less nationalistic than secular Conservative parties in Britain, Germany or France. Yet the differences between them seem to be diminishing.

8. Christian Union

The relatively liberal policies of the CDA disappointed and alienated some Christians. Attempts have failed to resuscitate a Catholic party with stricter morals, but Protestant alternatives to Christian Democracy have proved moderately successful. Apart from the rather isolated but very stable SGP there is the Christian Union (*ChristenUnie*), set up in 2000 by groups that had broken away earlier from the ARP for various reasons of their own. The Reformed Political Association (*Gereformeerd Politiek Verbond*, GPV) had split from the ARP mainly because of a conflict within the *Gereformeerde Kerken* (Harinck 2001). Practically all the members of the GPV belonged to the Free Reformed Church (*Vrijgemaakt Gereformeerde Kerk*). In 1975, three other Protestant groups who objected to the preparations for a Christian Democratic party founded the Reformed Political Federation (*Reformatorische Politieke Federatie*, RPF) (Bak 2001: 285–7). In 2000, the GPV and RPF began to merge. The Christian Union based its political programme (like the ARP, CHU and SGP) 'on the Bible, the inspired and authoritative Word of God' and the Three Forms of Unity which are considered the founding documents of Dutch Protestantism (ChristenUnie 2000a; see also Blei 2000: 25–7, 53). Their manifesto held that the government should recognize that Christ is our king and maintain God's commandments and, in particular, that it should protect human life from conception till (natural) death, and protect the family as well (ChristenUnie 2000b). As a consequence it should not recognize gay marriage, and prostitution and pornography should once again be banned. Thus one might say that the Christian Union campaigned for a morally more active state, one less liberal than the Christian Democratic state but not quite so strict as the SGP would like to see. Both Protestant parties co-operated in local government as well as in the European Parliament, even if they differed on issues like women's rights and social policies. Between 2007 and 2010, the Christian Union also participated at the national level in a coalition with the CDA and PvdA, which seems to have increased its distance from the SGP and encouraged development towards a mainstream party (Voerman 2010: 121–9; see also Vollaard 2010).

9. Concluding Comments

History may explain why there are still three religious parties represented in the Dutch parliament. Sociology may throw some light on this diversity, too: members and voters of the three parties generally belong to different denominations (Hippe and Lucardie 1998). But why are they still relatively successful in a rapidly secularizing society? The answer had already been implied in the preceding historical survey.

In the first place, the parties rely on support from 'pillarized' organizations, such as Christian trade unions, broadcasting networks, school boards and so on. Some of the organizations have disappeared or lost their religious character, but others survive and maintain loose, informal ties with the CDA, Christian Union or SGP.

In the second place, the rift between secular and religious parties has been politicized once more, mainly by the secular coalition of the PvdA, VVD and D66 which legalized euthanasia, prostitution and the gay marriage (1994–2002).

In the third place, the religious parties, and especially the CDA, have adapted to secularization and accepted liberal reforms. They seem to realize that they cannot halt secularization, let alone reverse it. At best, they can slow it down for a while, as they have done in the past—by protecting and promoting religious organizations such as churches and faith schools, by legislating for moral behaviour and by politicizing the rift between religious and secular sectors of the population. Even so, their future remains insecure in a secular society.

References

ARP (1911): 'Program van beginselen'. In: J.A. Jungmann and F.K. van Iterson (eds), *Parlement en kiezer*. The Hague, pp. 59–61.

Bak, P., Harinck, G., and Kuiper, R. (2001): 'Van ARP naar CDA 1973-1980'. In: G. Harinck, R. Kuiper and P. Bak (eds), *De Antirevolutionaire Partij, 1829-1980*, Hilversum: pp. 281–96.

Balkenende, J.P. (2002): *Anders en beter: Een pleidooi voor een andere aanpak in de politiek vanuit een christen-democratische visie op de samenleving, overheid en politiek*. Soesterberg.

Becker, J., and Hart, J. De (2006): *Godsdienstige veranderingen in Nederland. Verschuivingen in de binding met de kerken en de christelijke traditie*, The Hague.

Blei, K. (2000): *De Nederlands Hervormde Kerk: haar geschiedenis en identiteit*. Kampen: Kok.

CDA (1980): *Program van Uitgangspunten van het Christen Democratisch Appèl*. The Hague.

——— (1982): *Vernieuwing om behoud*. The Hague.

——— (1993): *Program van Uitgangspunten van het Christen Democratisch Appèl*. The Hague.

CDU (1994): 'Grundsatzprogramm der CDU Deutschlands', on-line: www.grundsatz programm.cdu.de/doc/grundsatzprogramm.pdf (4 November 2011).

ChristenUnie (2000a): 'Uniefundering', on-line: http://www.christenunie.nl/page/7254 (4 November 2011).

——— (2000b): *Kernprogramma*, Amersfoort.

CHU (1911): 'Program'. In: J.A. Jungmann and F.K. van Iterson (eds), *Parlement en kiezer*, The Hague, pp. 65–7.

Haan, I. De (1998): 'Het onderwijs in de Grondwet: van staatszorg tot vrijheidsrecht'. In: N.C.F. van Sas and H. te Velde (eds) *De eeuw van de grondwet: grondwet en politiek in Nederland, 1798–1917*. Deventer, pp. 182–217.

Jong, R. De (2000): 'De Algemeene Kiesvereeniging, 1868–1875. De eerste politieke partij van Nederland'. *Jaarboek 1999 DNPP*. Groningen, pp. 240–50.

Dölle, A. (2003): 'CDA behoeft ondertitel "sociaal conservatief"'. In: *Christen Democratische Verkenningen*, 23/2, 70–83.

Fieret, W. (1990): *De Staatkundig Gereformeerde Partij 1918—1948: een bibliocratisch ideal*. Houten.

Freeden, M. (1998): *Ideologies and Political Theory: A Conceptual Approach*. Oxford.

Harinck, G. (2001): 'Het ontstaan van het Gereformeerd Politiek Verbond 1945–1949'. In: G. Harinck, R. Kuiper and P. Bak (eds), *De Antirevolutionaire Partij, 1829–1980*. Hilversum, pp. 223–38.

Hippe, J., and Lucardie, A.P.M. (1998): 'Kanttekeningen bij de groei van de protestants-christelijke partijen in Nederland'. In: *Sociologische Gids*, 45/3, 153–65.

Holsteyn, J.J.M. van and Irwin, G.A. (2003): 'Never a Dull Moment: Pim Fortuyn and the Dutch Parliamentary Election of 2002'. In: *West European Politics*, 26/2, 41–66.

Houten, Maaike van (2003): 'De C van Conservatief'. In: *Trouw*, 24 July, p. 9.

Inglehart, R., Basañez, M. and Moreno, A. (1998): *Human Values and Beliefs: A Cross-Cultural Sourcebook*. Ann Arbor.

Janse, C.S.L. (1985): *Bewaar het pand: de spanning tussen assimilatie en persistentie bij de emancipatie van de bevindelijk gereformeerden*. Houten.

Janssens, R. (2001): 'Eenheid en verdeeldheid 1879–1894'. In: G. Harinck, R. Kuiper and P. Bak (eds), *De Antirevolutionaire Partij, 1829—1980*. Hilversum, pp. 73–92.

Kersbergen, K. Van (2011): 'De christendemocratische feniks en de moderne, niet-seculiere politiek'. In: G. Voerman (ed.), *De conjunctuur van de macht: het Christen Democratisch Appèl 1980—2010*. Amsterdam, pp. 197–216.

Koole, R., and Daalder, H. (2002): 'The Consociational Democracy Model and the Netherlands: Ambivalent Allies?' In: J. Steiner and T. Ertman (eds), *Consociationalism and Corporatism in Western Europe: Still the Politics of Accomodation?* Amsterdam, pp. 23–43 (special issue of *Acta Politica*, 37/1–2).

Kuyper, A. (1880): '*Ons Program*'. Second edition. Amsterdam.

KVP (1946): 'Algemeen Staatkundig Program'. In: F.K. van Iterson (ed.), *Parlement en kiezer*, The Hague, pp. 93–8.

Lijphart, A. (1969): 'Consociational Democracy'. In: *World Politics* 21/1, 207–25.

Lubbers, R.F.M. (1986): 'De voorsmaak van de hemelse gerechtigheid'. In: H. van Gerven and B. Rijpert (eds), *Geweten op het Binnenhof*. Amsterdam, pp. 13–30.

Napel, H.M.T.D. Ten (1992): '*Een eigen weg*': *de totstandkoming van het CDA (1952–1980)*. Kampen.

Pennings, P. (1997): 'The evolution of Dutch consociationalism, 1917–1997'. In: *The Netherlands Journal of Social Sciences*, 33, 9–26.

Schaepman, H.J.A.M. (1883): *Een katholieke partij: proeve van een program*. Utrecht.

Spanning, Hans van (2001): 'Van vrij-antirevolutionairen naar Christelijk Historische Unie'. In: G. Harinck, R. Kuiper and P. Bak (eds), *De Antirevolutionaire Partij, 1829—1980*. Hilversum, pp. 113–22.

——— (1998): *De Christelijk-Historische Unie (1908–1980): enige hoofdlijnen uit haar geschiedenis*. Ph.D. thesis University of Leiden.

Voerman, G. (2010): 'Van de marge naar de macht. De ChristenUnie (2000–2010)'. In: J. Hippe and G. Voerman (eds), *Van de marge naar de macht: de ChristenUnie 2000—2010*. Amsterdam, pp. 91–131.

Vollaard, H. (2010): 'Christelijke sporen in de Nederlandse politiek: de verhouding tussen ChristenUnie, SGP en CDA'. In: J. Hippe and G. Voerman (eds), *Van de marge naar de macht: de ChristenUnie 2000—2010*. Amsterdam, pp. 175–95.

Vries, B. De (2005): *Overmoed en onbehagen: het hervormingskabinet-Balkenende II*. Amsterdam.

Wetenschappelijk Instituut voor het CDA (1990): *Publieke gerechtigheid: een christendemocratische visie op de rol van de overheid*. Houten.

Wissen, G.J.M. Van (1982): *De christen-democratische visie op de rol van de staat in het sociaal-economische leven.* Amsterdam.

Woldring, H.E.S. (1996): *De Christen-democratie: een kritisch onderzoek naar haar politieke filosofie*. Utrecht.

——— (2003): 'CDA is niet conservatief'. In: *Trouw*, 8 August, p. 14.

——— (2010): 'Ik heb het niet bij twee kantjes gelaten'. In: *Trouw*, 18 November, pp. V28–9.

THE SGP—A NATURAL RELATIONSHIP BETWEEN POLITICS AND RELIGION

Evert-Jan Brouwer

In recent years, the role of religion in public and political life has become controversial. Religion features on the agenda of many conferences, research programmes and political debates. In the politics of the Netherlands it is frequently discussed topic, not least because of recent manifestations of militant Islam in Western societies. But it deserves our attention independently of discussions about the future of Islam in Western democracies. In this chapter, I want to present the position of the SGP (the *Staatkundig Gereformeerde Partij*, or in English the 'Reformed Political Party') on the issue. The SGP is a small Protestant party in the Netherlands. It takes a distinct view of the relationship between politics and religion. For SGP politicians, relating faith to politics is in a sense completely natural. It is habitual for them. For this reason, the chapter bears the challenging title that it does. While many participants in the debate on religion and politics advocate a separation of the two, the SGP pleads for a healthy symbiosis.

The chapter is divided into three sections. I begin by describing the SGP and what kind of party it is, and I explain how the SGP conceptualizes the relationship between religion and politics. I then discuss the question of women's participation in politics, a matter with which the SGP is often associated in the Dutch media. Finally, I address the rise of Islam in Dutch society, and the consequences for the place that religion might occupy in Dutch politics, from the perspective of the SGP.

1. The SGP and the Relationship between Religion and Politics

The SGP is the oldest political party in the Netherlands. It was founded in 1918 and has been represented in parliament since 1922. From the beginning, it has been a minority party. In eighty-eight years, the SGP never had more than three members in the House of Representatives. Since the general elections of September 2012, the SGP has again three seats out of 150 in the House of Representatives, one out of 75 in the Senate, and one out of 736 in the European Parliament. In addition, the party is represented on more than a hundred of the 430 municipal councils and in seven of the twelve provinces. Geographically, the party is best represented in the so-called 'Bible belt', which stretches from the Southwest to the Northeast of the country. Owing to the absence of a high voter threshold, the SGP is proportionally represented at all political levels. To summarize: the SGP is an old-established, stable, minority party.[1]

The SGP derives its principles and ideas ultimately from the Bible, the revealed Word of God. By contrast with the Christian Democrats, the SGP maintains that the Bible is not only a book that gives inspiration for daily life but also a universally authoritative book, the Word of the God whom all people should obey. Of course, the main importance of the Bible lies in its message about salvation through faith in Jesus Christ. This message is spread by the church. But the Bible also shows the practical consequences of the Christian faith for daily life, including politics.

What is the biblical message about politics, according to the SGP? First of all, it is that God has given powers or authority to make social life possible and to prevent anarchy. The most important biblical passage in this respect is Chapter 13 from St Paul's Epistle to the Romans, which provides the basis for the SGP's view of politics. The two main elements in Romans 13:1–7 are that God has ordained these powers and that they are given to human beings for their own good. This is a positive view of politics.

What Paul actually means by 'good' is clear from the context of Romans 13. It means that the government guarantees justice and maintains law and order. However, it would be wrong to limit the task of governments to the maintenance of law and order. The concept of justice is, biblically speaking, a broad one. When we look at other biblical passages about justice, we see that the concept has social dimensions as well, examples of which are protecting widows and orphans, helping down-and-outs to reintegrate into society, and fighting poverty.

Besides upholding justice, the government has to protect the true religion. Religious neutrality is impossible for governments, as it is for individual persons and communities. SGP representatives challenge others by proposing that those who disagree with the SGP on this issue should try to develop a plausible argument that strictly neutral politics is possible.

To summarize: the SGP's view of politics begins with the recognition that governments are God-given. It continues with the view that each authority, each government, should govern along the lines of God's commandments, which are the most compact operationalization of the concept of justice.[2] This view is firmly rooted in the tradition of the Reformation in sixteenth-century Europe (Calvin 1989: book 4, chapter 20.) and the so-called 'Nadere Reformatie', or 'Further Reformation', of the seventeenth and early eighteenth centuries in the Netherlands (Teellinck 1650).

These two fundamental assumptions need to be understood in any discussion of the concept of theocracy, with which the SGP is often associated.

---

[1] Up-to-date information about the SGP can be found on the party's website www.sgp.nl.

[2] The SGP's view is further elaborated in two important party publications, Massink 1993 and 1994.

In order to understand this concept, we have to see theocracy as one of the possible relationships between church and state. In the table below we find a continuum, stretching from a strictly theocratic regime to a strictly atheistic regime. On this continuum—strikingly enough—the SGP does not occupy an extreme position.

Table 1 *Five Possible Relationships between Church and State*

1	Theocracy as commonly understood: institutional conflation of church and state, as in Iran.
2	Church-state or ecclesiastical state, as in the Vatican.
3	Established or official church, as in the Anglican Church in the United Kingdom.
4	Separation of church and state. a *SGP view*: institutional separation of church and state, but the state should advance the church's cause and both should cooperate. b *Moderate view*: institutional separation but practical cooperation between the state and any of the religious organizations not prohibited, as is the political practice in the Netherlands. c *Extreme view*: absolute institutional separation and absolute state neutrality in religious affairs, as with 'laïcité' in France.
5	Atheistic state, as in communist countries such as North Korea.

1.1. The SGP and Theocracy

The SGP is said to be the only party in the Netherlands that advocates the introduction of a theocracy. In a report entitled *Dynamiek in islamitisch activisme*, the influential 'Wetenschappelijke Raad voor het Regeringsbeleid' (the Dutch Scientific Council for Government Policy), bluntly stated that 'The oldest party in Holland, the SGP, pursues a theocracy' (WRR 2006: 197).

In encyclopaedias, one reads that 'theocracy' entails a political system in which the divinity is regarded as the direct political authority, or a system in which the priests have the highest authority. In most encyclopaedia articles on theocracy, ancient Israel and Geneva during John Calvin's lifetime are cited as examples.

In the SGP's opinion, such descriptions of theocracy are confusing. In common parlance, theocracy is often tangled up with some kind of political system, as if there were a choice between autocracy, democracy, oligarchy and theocracy, or whatever system one could imagine. But such terminology is unhelpful. In the scientific literature on theocracy, we can broadly distinguish two perspectives:

(1.) The ruler is the direct representative of God on earth. He can justify his rule by referring to divine authority. According to this concept, the ruler is very powerful and he is also sovereign in religious affairs (e.g. able to reign over the church).

(2.) The ruler is bound by God's will, which limits his scope. The ruler is only a good ruler insofar as he rules according to God's laws. According to this concept, the ruler has limited powers and the church is allowed to criticize him if it sees fit (Jellinek 1920: 289–90).

The second perspective developed over the course of the fourth century, the time of St Ambrose and the Synod of Milan, when the emperor came to be seen as a member of the church, not as a ruler above the church. St Ambrose even ventured to criticize the emperor of the day. The political philosopher Eric Voegelin succinctly typified this development as follows: 'These are the beginnings of a theocratic conception of rulership in the strict sense, theocracy not meaning a rule by the priesthood but *the recognition by the ruler of the truth of God*' (Voegelin 1987: 85–6).

The second perspective on theocracy is the one to which the SGP adheres. For the SGP, theocracy has nothing to do with any political system; rather, theocracy means recognition by the rulers of the reality that God is King of the whole world and that He is entitled to our obedience. The SGP differentiates between the rule of God over the whole world (namely, theocracy or divine providence) and that which politicians do in accordance with God's revealed will in the Bible (namely, human obedience).

From this I draw three preliminary conclusions. The first is that the SGP does not call for the introduction of a theocracy, in the sense of direct rule by the priesthood or of rulers claiming to be God's exclusive representatives on earth. The SGP's view of theocracy approaches the second meaning of the concept as defined above, namely that the ruler is bound by God's will and is a good ruler only insofar as he rules according to God's laws. But because the second meaning of this term never entered common parlance, the SGP wants to use the term 'theocracy' simply to indicate the reality of God's rule over the world. Christian politics engaging with this reality could be dubbed 'theocratic politics', but why not simply call it 'Christian politics'? The word 'theocracy' points us so directly to God's rule over his creation that it is better not to use it to denote politics as practised by fallible Christians (Massink 1994: 20–1).

My second conclusion is that the recognition of this theocracy (namely, God's rule over the earth) by politicians implies—theologically speaking—that they should obey God's laws and apply them in their policies, irrespective of the political system in which they find themselves.

My third conclusion is that this perspective accommodates a distinction between church and state, as the SGP also clearly does. The distinction between the secular political realm and the spiritual realm of the church goes back to the teachings of Jesus, who said that we should pay to Caesar what belongs to Caesar and to God what belongs to God (Luke 20:20–6). The government should not involve itself in the appointment of the clergy, and synods should not take political decisions. Although God's laws are as important for politics as they are for the church, obedience to those laws is for both church and state a separate responsibility. The institutional separation between church and state was gradually accepted by the tradition of the Protestant Reformation.[3] It enables the church to be a healthy counterweight to the government, or a critical voice, whenever necessary. At the same time, the institutional separation protects the church from unwelcome state interference.

1.2. The SGP and Democracy

It is important to ask why the SGP favours constitutional democracy. Is not the SGP's exclusive preference for biblical values at odds with the pluralistic character of democracy? The SGP clearly favours representative democracy as the best political system. Those who accuse the SGP of anti-democratic sentiments have probably failed to understand that the SGP does not want to introduce a theocracy in the sense of a ruler who directly represents God on earth. On the other hand, the SGP does not idolize democracy as an end in itself, as some people do; instead, it favours democracy as the best form of government in which obedience to God's laws can be realized. What, then, are the SGP's arguments in favour of representative democracy?

(1.) In a democracy it is impossible to concentrate power in the hands of a single person or a few people. Protestants have always been wary of absolute power, because 'power corrupts and absolute power corrupts absolutely' in the hands of sinful people.

(2.) Democracy is a peaceful way of reaching political decisions by way of open debate, in which politicians with completely different convictions try to convince one another by argument. Such a system corresponds to the SGP's belief that religion is not just a matter of outward obedience but is first and foremost a matter of inner conviction. People are convinced not by force but by arguments and examples. The SGP's policy is never to enforce religious beliefs but always to promote them. In this way, democracy is the system that best fits the need for freedom of conscience and for political tolerance.

Of course, in any political system political decisions need to be enforced. Even in a democracy, when the majority have decided to do it *this* way, the minority cannot have it *that* way. The majority are entitled to execute decisions that have been taken in a democratic and legal way. The minority have no choice but to obey the majority decisions (otherwise, the majority would have to grant minorities their own rights), while always having the right to challenge

[3] Visser (1927) provides a good historical overview, with particular attention to the development of the relationship between church and state in the Netherlands.

majority decisions in the public debate. Therefore, democracy gives the best guarantee that political decisions, and decisions on religious matters, are taken in a peaceful way with the greatest possible legitimacy, thus minimizing the level of dissatisfaction among those who do not agree.

1.3. How to Relate Politics and Religion?

The last question I want to address in this section concerns the way in which the SGP relates politics and religion. Just as several relationships between church and state can be imagined, so it is with relationships between religion and politics.

Table 2 *Four Possible Relationships between Religion and Politics*

1	Conflation of religion and politics: theocracy as direct rule by the priests or politicians who see themselves as direct representatives of God, as in Iran.
2	Politics makes use of religion: religion is an instrument of the state to strengthen its position, as in present-day Turkey.
3	Religion makes use of politics: politics is an instrument of the church to strengthen its position or to promote its message, as in the Vatican.
4	Symbiosis of religion and politics, the position of the SGP: politicians and clergy submit themselves to God's will, but both have their own distinct responsibilities.

In some radical views, the separation of church and state is interpreted as a strict separation of religion and politics. Turkey and France are examples of countries in which the government wants to be completely neutral in religious affairs (WRR 2004). In France, this takes the form of an almost complete state indifference towards matters of religion, except for those aspects of religious life that might have consequences for public order and safety. This 100-year-old system is called 'laïcité'. While increasingly under discussion, it is still a constitutional principle. In Turkey, the strict separation takes the form of the state's allowing only a version of Islam that has renounced all political aspirations. The nominally secular Turkish state even uses this version of Islam to strengthen the social and political cohesion of the Turkish nation. In Turkey, too, the question of secularism has recently become a topic of public and political concern.

From more moderate perspectives, the separation of church and state does not automatically mean state indifference towards religion. Take the example of the Netherlands. Here—in theory, at least—any politician can put forward whatever religious arguments he or she chooses. In the Netherlands the separation of church and state means that, in addition to an institutional separation, the state will refrain from taking sides on religious questions. It will not favour Christians over Muslims, or the reverse. It will not favour religious people over secular people, or the reverse. It grants all religions the same rights and titles.[4]

In the opinion of the SGP, politics and religion have a natural relationship with each other, a 'healthy symbiosis'. So far as possible, SGP politicians will always try to translate biblical norms and values into practical politics, seeing it as their highest calling to promote biblical values in Dutch politics and society. So, while calling for an institutional separation of church and state, they plead for religion to be related to politics.

1.4. The Political Consequences of Hermeneutics

Of course, this raises the question of *what* biblical commandments are relevant to public life. It is an hermeneutical question. How does the SGP read the Bible, and how can it determine which biblical laws are binding and which ones are not?

In the Reformed theological tradition—within which the SGP places itself—it is held that the Ten Commandments handed down by God from Mount Sinai have universal force. These Commandments contain provisions for our relationship with God and with each other.[5]

However, the Bible contains many other laws and commandments. There are laws on religious offerings, agriculture, sexuality, public health, property, and so on. Most of them are found in the Old Testament. They were given to the people of Israel, God's only chosen people at that time. Reformed theology holds that the ceremonial and civil laws of ancient Israel have no direct validity for heathen nations since the death of Jesus Christ. We therefore need only to obey those biblical laws that are universal. The universality of a certain law can be determined by studying which Old Testament laws are dealt with by the New Testament and in what way. Generally speaking, all Ten Commandments are confirmed in the New Testament and therefore have universal validity.

The ceremonial and civil laws of Israel have a different status. A first example: although, for example, homosexuality is clearly condemned by the teaching of the apostle Paul, nowhere in the New Testament we can find that practising homosexuals should be put to death, as was the case in Israel during

---

4 The Dutch government's main position is outlined in two important publications: a memorandum of February 26, 1998, written by the Minister of Home Affairs (Kamerstukken II, 25 919, nos. 1-2) and a letter from the Minister of Integration and Urban Policy to the Dutch Parliament (December 10, 1999; Kamerstukken II, 26 333 no. 13).

5 Cf. the Heidelberg Catechism (1563), a Protestant document which is one of the Three Forms of Unity acknowledged by the main Protestant churches in the Netherlands. In the third part of this famous Catechism, the Ten Commandments are presented as a guideline for all believers how to conduct their lives.

the Old Testament. Another example: although the New Testament clearly commands us to take care of widows and poor people, nowhere can we find that we should do it in precisely the way it was determined by the laws of old Israel. A third example: strangers were always welcome in Israel, since the Israelites knew what it meant to be a stranger and to be taken in by others. Strangers could become normal citizens, provided they were circumcised and accepted all religious requirements that bind native Israelites. In the New Testament we read several exhortations to hospitality; however, these are issued without religious requirements such as circumcision.

In fact, the spirit behind the ceremonial and civil Old Testament laws remains the same, but the letter of those laws is not confirmed in the New Testament for heathen peoples. Generally speaking, what was evil remains evil, and what was good remains good. The literal provisions and punishments of the Old Testament laws do not apply, however, to our own society and present circumstances. We do not need to imitate ancient Israel.

To sum up: as far as the universality and applicability of the biblical laws are concerned, Reformed hermeneutics holds that the Ten Commandments still have universal validity. As concerns the other laws, we can learn much from the spirit behind them and we should try to translate that spirit into new laws in new circumstances.[6]

What does this mean for the SGP in everyday politics? Let me give some illustrations.

(1.) In January 2007, the scientific institute of the SGP finalized a report on European defence policy (De Haas 2007). In the report, ample attention is given to what the Bible says about the responsibility of the government for security, and about the way warfare should be conducted. Deuteronomy 20 is an important passage in this respect.

(2.) When the SGP formulates guidelines for policy on landed property, it derives its inspiration from the way property was protected in ancient Israel (Mulder 2003).

(3) When dealing with environmental problems caused by intensive farming, the SGP studies the Bible to see how the people of Israel had to deal respectfully with the natural resources that God gave them (Massink 1995).

---

[6] In article 25 of the Belgic Confession of Faith (1561), the second of the Three Forms of Unity (see note 12), the Protestant churches in Holland confess the following concerning 'The Fulfilment of the Law': 'We believe that the ceremonies and symbols of the [Old Testament] law have ended with the coming of Christ, and that all foreshadowings have come to an end, so that the use of them ought to be abolished among Christians. Yet the truth and substance of these things remain for us in Jesus Christ, in whom they have been fulfilled. Nevertheless, we continue to use the witnesses drawn from the law and prophets to confirm us in the gospel and to regulate our lives with full integrity for the glory of God, according to his will.'

(4.) When there is a debate about the protection of human foetuses, SGP politicians read in the Bible that life is gift from God and that we should therefore not take it into our own hands (Molenaar-Geurtsen 2000).

In this sense *the relationship between religion and politics is quite natural for SGP politicians*. For this party, the question is not *that* the Bible gives us commandments and guidelines for politics, but *how* we should interpret them and translate them in government.

2. Women and the SGP

In any account of the SGP, the position of women in the party calls for special attention. The SGP is widely known because of this issue. Even reports by the United Nations on the implementation of the CEDAW treaty have drawn attention to the (now-deleted) clause on women in the SGP statutes, which made it impossible for them to become members, and consequently impossible for them to be elected as SGP representatives.

The position of women has always been an issue in the history of the SGP. One of the reasons for the formation of the SGP was that many Reformed people rejected the introduction of universal suffrage in the Netherlands. Their view can be summarized as follows. The Bible teaches us that 'the head of the woman is the man'. He has the final say in the family, the church, society, and politics. Women have a primary calling in the household and in childcare. Politics is a job for men. It follows that, as casting a vote at the ballot box is the exercise of political power, women should abstain from voting (Fieret 1990: 42–5).

Later, there were internal party discussions about the question: should voting really be regarded as the exercise of authority? The outcome of these discussions was a change in the SGP Declaration of Principles: women's suffrage was no longer rejected as contrary to women's calling.[7]

In the nineteen-eighties and nineties some women became members of local SGP associations, in a way that was contrary to the party's culture. Formally, women members had never been excluded from the SGP. The statutes did not say anything about them. But it was so obvious that women should not become party members that no woman had ever attempted to join. The admission of these women thus prompted fierce debate. The outcome was to amend the statutes on the issue of women's membership and so, in 1996, female membership was explicitly excluded.

But that did not mean that the internal troubles were over. There was continuing dissatisfaction within the party. Besides, the UN's annual reports on

---

[7] However, in article 8 of the Programme of Principles, the SGP affirms a preference for 'organic' suffrage over universal suffrage. Organic suffrage means that every family has one vote, which—under normal circumstances—is cast by the head of the family, the husband.

the implementation of the Treaty on the Rights of Women have criticized both the SGP and the Dutch state for not taking measures against the SGP (United Nations, CEDAW 2005: 47–8). The Clara Wichmann Institute, a Dutch organization campaigning for women's emancipation, filed a lawsuit against the State for not taking measures against the SGP, and in September 2005 the court decided in favour of the Institute. Its ruling was that the SGP should no longer receive state subsidies because of its discrimination against women. After 1 January 2006, the SGP received no State subsidies. However, the State challenged the judge's decision and lodged an appeal, leading to the temporary repeal of this measure. The internal frictions and the external pressures led to renewed discussion within the party. After profound reflection by theologians and jurists, the board proposed to delete the contested clause from the statutes. The arguments for the proposal were as follows. Of course, the head of the woman is the man. That will never change, because the Bible will not change. But, as with women's suffrage, it is open to question whether women's party membership and attendance at meetings should be regarded as an exercise of political authority. The board decided to allow women to become party members, but not to allow them to stand for election. So, according to the new proposal, women were still not permitted to become SGP representatives at any political level. This is necessarily the case because being a representative is clearly a form of exercising authority, and this conflicts with the biblical calling of women (SGP Hoofdbestuur 2006). On June 24, 2006, the party congress supported the proposal with an overwhelming majority. On December 5, 2007, the Council of State, the highest administrative court in the Netherlands declared in a judgment that the public subsidy to the SGP should be reinstalled.[8]

This was however not the end of the legal battle. After a quite complicated judicial procedure, in which the Dutch state, the successor to the Clara Wichmann Institute (Proefprocessenfonds Clara Wichmann) and the SGP were parties, the Supreme Court (to be distinguished from the Council of State) issued a final judgement on 9 April 2010, against which no appeal in the Netherlands is possible.[9] According to this judgement, the State is obliged to take effective measures against the SGP in order to enforce full rights for women in the party. Because the government was under resignation when the judgment was published, it decided to leave a response to this judgment to the next government, that would be sworn in after the elections, half a year later. However, because the SGP observed a fundamental conflict between the positive 2007 judgment of the Council of State, and the negative 2010 judgment of the Supreme Council, it decided to appeal to the European Court for Human Rights in Strasbourg. The Dutch judicial system does not provide for a solution for cases in which the Supreme Court and the Council of State have conflicting opinions. According to the SGP, earlier judgments of the European Court showed that the internal freedom of political parties should be respected. It is

[8] 200609224/1, Council of State, December 5, 2007.

[9] BK4549, Supreme Court, 08/01394.

likely that the legal procedure with the European Court will last for years. At the moment nothing can be said about its outcome.

From an outsider's perspective, all this might seem to be an aberration of a religious party that has lost sight of political reality. Is not the unequal treatment of women a thing of the past? From an insider's perspective, the SGP's position on women's involvement in politics is not an aberration but part of its worldview. As with everything else, the SGP seeks to base its view of the male-female relationship on the Bible. The biblical perspective is that men and women are equal in worth and dignity before God, but that they differ in both role and status in the family and in society. The man is the head of the woman and of the family. He has the last word. The woman's primary task is to care for the children (if there are any) and to manage the household. This division of roles leads to a harmonious society composed of healthy families. The SGP's view that women should not become political representatives is simply a logical consequence of this wider perspective. It has nothing to do with discrimination or with male desire for power. It has more to do with healthy complementarity (Piper and Grudem 1991).

3. The Rise of Islam and the Future of Dutch Democracy

My final topic is the rise of Islam and its consequences for the relationship between religion and our democratic system. I want to discuss it because, more often than not, opinion-formers have suggested that there are similarities between fundamentalist (or even extremist) Muslims and the SGP. I acknowledge that this is a very sensitive issue. It is almost impossible not to tread on anybody's toes when taking a position on this question. But part of the democratic spirit is that we fully respect each other even when we detest one another's opinions.[10]

First of all, it is important to specify the level that we have in mind. Do we mean Muslims and democracy, or do we mean Islam and democracy? I propose to discuss Islam and democracy. We need to study the concept of democracy and the central tenets of Islam, following which we can formulate a careful answer to the question as to whether the two are compatible. A prerequisite for this is to reject the relativist view that it is impossible to talk about Islam and that Islam has as many faces as there are Muslims. Just as Christianity is characterized by belief in the Trinity, in the Holy Scriptures, in creation, the Fall, redemption, resurrection, heaven and hell, so Islam is characterized by belief in

[10] The view that I present in this paragraph is based on Brouwer 2005. With this publication, the SGP was the first political party in Holland to develop an integrated perspective on the political aspects of Islam. Some important publications from which I derive the insights in this paragraph and in Brouwer 2005 are: Caner and Caner 2002, Douwes 2003, Kellerhals 1945, Lewis 1996, Ruthven 1997 and 2000.

one god (Allah), the angels, the holy Qur'an, the prophets (especially Muhammad), the last day and predestination.

I have previously discussed the relationships between church and state and between religion and politics in Protestant Christianity. Similarly, I now focus on these relationships within Islam. I derive my description of these relationships from traditional Islam, which means from mainstream Islam before the closure of the gates of *ijtihad* (interpretation of Qur'an and Sunna) in the tenth century. It is my conviction that since that time, notwithstanding the work of several Islamic philosophers up to the present day, the ancient concepts that dominated Islamic theology have not been fundamentally altered.[11]

The relationship between religion and politics is very close in traditional Islam. Muhammad, the religious mystic from Mecca, became the militant ruler of Medina after successes on the battlefield (Jansen 2005 and 2007). The spread of Islam in the first century of its existence was mainly attributable to military conquests. Islam was clearly promoted by political means. By contrast with Christian theology, in which 'Caesar' has his own domain since Jesus' teaching on that point, Islam teaches that the reign of Allah in people's lives must be promoted *directly* by the rulers. So, in terms of possible relationships between religion and politics, Islam does not preclude a conflation of religion and politics and is thus the mirror image of the atheistic state.

The relationship between church and state, or rather between mosque and state, in Islamic theology is not easy to determine. Islam originated in the context of a tribal society lacking clear institutional arrangements. The tribes each had their own leaders, but it would be anachronistic to allot them to the political domain as we understand it. When Islam took root in the tribal culture on the Arabian peninsula, it did not erect an elaborate religious infrastructure, as was the case in the Protestant and Roman Catholic traditions. Each mosque was independent, there were no 'synods', and nobody had the final say in religious affairs. Islam is a religion without clear institutional concepts, without clear boundaries between the mosque and the state. Islam therefore does not preclude a conflation of mosque affairs and state affairs. It opens the way for a theocracy in the sense of direct rule by religious leaders.

Lastly, I ask whether Islam can be related to democracy in a harmonious way. Earlier on, I developed some arguments to explain why the SGP favours democracy as the best political system. Democracy offers a peaceful way to reach political decisions with broad legitimacy. Democracy offers a procedure for reaching decisions by an exchange of arguments. Inherent to democracy is a certain degree of tolerance, giving others room to disagree fundamentally and to take time to convince one another.

---

[11] Even the WRR, which is quite positive about the possibilities for democratization of Muslim countries (WRR 2006), has to acknowledge that the reawakening of the tradition of *ijtihad* in the nineteenth century has encountered fierce opposition (WRR 2006: 112).

On the theoretical level, the relationship between Islam and democracy is problematic, as I now argue. Traditional Islam does not exclude the use of violent means to defend or even to advance the faith and to extend the *Dar al Islam*, i.e. the territory where Islam is dominant (Spencer 2003, Yeor 1996 and Bostom 2005). And when Islam has become dominant in a particular territory, followers of other religions will be 'rewarded' with second class citizenship (Yeor 2002, Spuler-Stegemann 2004). It is true that traditional Islam has the concept of *shura* or consultation, but this concept is too weak to provide a strong Islamic argument for democracy. There are modern Muslim theologians who have developed a *fiqh* (jurisprudence, or set of rules) for Muslim minorities in modern democracies. Others have developed the concept of *Dar al Sulh*, a temporary agreement between Muslims and non-Muslims (Ruthven 1997: 118, Douwes 2003: 23). But these theological developments have not taken root in mainstream Islamic theology. I think it is only by way of re-reading the Qur'an and the Hadith, or by way of practical secularization and increasing pragmatism among many Muslims in the Western world, that Muslims have come increasingly to accept democracy.

To summarize, at the theological (or theoretical) level the relationship between religion and politics, between mosque and state, and between Islam and democracy, is problematic.

But even if mainstream Islamic theology would come to terms with democracy and the separation between church and state, not every problem would be solved. Imagine that Islamic theologians would be able to provide for a solid reconciliation between Islam and democracy. Imagine that consequently Muslims would wholeheartedly take part in the democratic process. The question would then arise about which goals they want to achieve and which laws they want to introduce. Unlike Protestant Christianity, traditional Islam lacks a hermeneutics which mitigates the drastic provision for corporal punishment for thieves, adulterers and homosexuals, or the death penalty for apostates. Moreover, here the only 'solution' lies in taking the Qur'an and the Hadith less literally.

I reach a conclusion regarding the relationship between Islam and democracy. I have substantiated the proposition that a harmonious relationship between traditional Islam and democracy is difficult to imagine. In this respect, there is a qualitative difference between Protestant Christianity, the theology of which can to a large extent be harmonized with democracy and a separation between church and state, and traditional Islam, the theology of which does not preclude conflicts both with democracy and also over the separation of church and state. A harmonization can take place only when Muslim theologians become able to introduce a new reading of the holy sources, both regarding the acceptability of our political system and also regarding the validity and applicability of the sharia. The only alternative for a new hermeneutics would be—politically speaking—a practical secularization.[12] Anyway, I hope I have shown that any suggestion of a parallel between Islamic fundamentalism and 'SGP fundamentalism' cannot be justified.

Final remarks

In this chapter I have presented a portrait of the SGP and its position in Dutch politics. With ninety years experience of democracy, and with as many years experience in relating the Reformed faith to practical politics, I repeat that for the SGP there is a natural relationship between religion and the state, and more specifically between religion and democratic politics. But I make one important proviso: there is not a natural relationship between *any* religion and democracy. There are religions which *might* overturn democracy, when practised literally. Islam is the most important present-day example. The SGP does not want to introduce a theocracy in the sense this concept is normally understood. The SGP wants to promote biblical values in a committed, democratic way, trying to convince others that Jesus Christ is King, that his written revelation, the Bible, is the only way to temporal well-being and eternal salvation, and that all citizens owe Him their service and honour. Simply labelling the SGP 'fundamentalist' or 'theocratic', as these words are commonly understood, is therefore unjustified.

References

Bostom, A. (2005) (ed.): *The Legacy of Jihad: Islamic Holy War and the Fate of Non-Muslims*. New York.

Brouwer, E.J. (2005): *De islam in huis: Een politieke positiebepaling* [Islam at home: A political position]. The Hague.

Calvin, J. (1989): *Institutes of the Christian Religion*. Transl. by H. Beveridge. Grand Rapids.

Caner, E.M., and Caner, E.F. (2002): *Unveiling Islam: An Insider's Look at Muslim Life and Beliefs*. Grand Rapids.

Douwes, D. (2003): *De islam in een notendop: Wat iedereen over de islam moet weten* [Islam in a nutshell: What everybody should know about Islam], Amsterdam.

Ercomer/Sociaal en Cultureel Planbureau (2004): *Moslim in Nederland* [Muslim in the Netherlands]. The Hague.

Fieret, W. (1990): *De Staatkundig Gereformeerde Partij 1918-1948: Een bibliocratisch ideaal* [The SGP 1918-1948: A bibliocratic ideal], Houten.

---

[12] Parallel with trends towards radicalization among Muslim youth, new empirical research shows that there is a trend towards practical secularization among large numbers of Muslims in the Netherlands (Ercomer/Sociaal en Cultureel Planbureau 2004). However, this practical secularization does not mean that Muslims no longer identify themselves as Muslims. Their religious affiliation is not in dispute; the key issue is that they become less strict in fulfilling their religious duties.

Haas, M. de (ed.): *Geeft acht: Europees veiligheidsbeleid in een onzekere wereld* [Attention! A perspective on European security policy in an insecure world], SGP, Gouda.

Jansen, H. (2005): *De historische Mohammed: De Mekkaanse verhalen* [The historical Muhammad: The Meccan stories], Amsterdam/Antwerp.

——— (2007): *De historische Mohammed: De verhalen uit Medina* [The historical Muhammad: The stories from Madina], Amsterdam/Antwerp.

Jellinek, G. (1920): *Allgemeine Staatslehre*. Vol. II. Berlin 1920.

Kellerhals, E. (1945): *Der Islam: Seine Geschichte, seine Lehre, sein Wesen*, Basel.

Lewis, B. (1996): *Het Midden-Oosten: 2000 jaar politieke en culturele geschiedenis* [The Middle East: 2000 years of political and cultural history], Amsterdam.

Massink, H.F. (1993) (ed.): *Dienstbaar tot gerechtigheid: SGP-visie op over aard en omvang van de overheidstaak* [Serving for justice: An SGP-perspective on the character and extent of political authority]. Houten.

——— (1994) (ed.): *Theocratische politiek: Principes, geschiedenis en praktijk* [Theocratic politics: principles, history and practice], Houten.

——— (1995) (ed.): *Met zorg boeren: SGP-visie op landbouw* [Responsible farming: An SGP-perspective on agriculture]. Houten.

Molenaar-Geurtsen, H.G. (2000) (ed.): *Op de grens van leven en dood: Over euthanasie en ander levensbeëindigend handelen* [On the verge of life and death: About euthanasia and other forms of life-termination]. Houten.

Mulder, J. (2003) (ed.): *Grondig bekeken: Over grondbeleid* [Thorougly examined: About land policy], The Hague.

Piper, J. and Grudem, W. (1991) (eds): *Recovering Biblical Manhood and Womanhood: A Response to Evangelical Feminism*, Wheaton, Ill.

Ruthven, M. (1997): *Islam: A Very Short Introduction*. New York.

——— (2000): *Islam in the World*. New York.

SGP Hoofdbestuur (2006): *Man en vrouw schiep Hij hen: Politieke participatie in bijbels perspectief* [Male and female He created them: Political participation from a biblical perspective]. The Hague.

Spencer, R. (2003): *Onward Muslim Soldiers: How Jihad Still Threatens America and the West*. Washington.

Spuler-Stegeman, U. (2004) (ed.): *Feindbild Christentum im Islam: Eine Bestandsaufnahme*, Freiburg.

Teellinck, W. (1650): *Den politycken christen, ofte instructie voor alle hooge en leege staetspersoonen: wijsselijck voorghestelt door den conincklijcken prophete David inden 101. psalm, tot destructie vande hedendaegsche Machiavelsche wijsheydt om op een recht compas den hemel wel te bezeylen [The Political Christian ...]*. Middelburg.

United Nations, CEDAW (2005): *Fourth Periodic Report of States Parties: Netherlands*. New York.

Visser, J.Th. De (1927): *Kerk en staat* [Church and State]. 3 vols. Leiden.

Voegelin, E. (1987): *The New Science of Politics: An Introduction*, Chicago/London.

WRR (2004): *De Europese Unie, Turkije en de islam* [The European Union, Turkey and Islam]. Amsterdam.

——— (2006): *Dynamiek in islamitisch activisme* [Dynamics in Islamic Activism]. Amsterdam.

Yeor, B. (1996): *The Decline of Eastern Christianity under Islam: From Jihad to Dhimmitude*. New Jersey.

——— (2002) *Islam and Dhimmitude: Where Civilizations Collide*. New Jersey.

HISTORY AND BASIC IDEAS OF THE CHRISTIAN DEMOCRATIC PARTY IN THE NETHERLANDS

Henk E.S. Woldring

The central purpose of this chapter is to explain why there is a Christian democratic party in the Netherlands and what the party stands for. First, I shall outline the political history of the Netherlands in the nineteenth and twentieth centuries. Second, I shall explore the religious or worldview ideas that underpin the Dutch Christian Democratic Party (the official name of which could be translated as 'Christian Democratic Appeal'). Third, I shall ask what these ideas mean for the task of government, for the nature of civil society, and for the relationship between civil society and the state.

1. Political History

Political development in the Netherlands at the end of the nineteenth century and the beginning of the twentieth century can be illustrated by a combination of various socio-political problems, and by the two great political leaders who responded to those problems. With respect to the socio-political problems, these leaders were confronted by groups of Protestant and Catholic citizens who criticized the public (or state) school system; they were struggling for a legal right to start their own Protestant and Catholic schools because they considered schooling to be part of their family education. Another difficulty at the time was finding a solution to the 'social question', or the problem posed by workers on low wages and others who lived in economically disadvantaged conditions. Had the government the right to make social laws and, if so, what social laws were necessary? In addition, universal suffrage was an urgent question. It is noteworthy that the political leaders in the Dutch parliament were not only representative of various social classes and religious denominations but that they were also extremely strong personalities and, moreover, that some of them were excellent scholars.

In the mid-nineteenth century, Johan Rudolf Thorbecke (1798–1872) was the capable leader of the liberals. He was prime minister twice, from 1849 until 1853 and from 1862 until 1866. Since the new constitution that he introduced was a product of liberal thought, influenced by the Enlightenment, his critics struggled against it and also against other laws. These critics inaugurated their own political movements and founded their own political parties. One such critic was Pieter Jelles Troelstra (1860–1930), who was one of the principal leaders of the Social Democratic Party of Workers. Other critics were Abraham Kuyper (1837–1920), the founder of the protestant Antirevolutionary Party, and Herman Schaepman (1844–1903), who founded the Roman Catholic State Party. By virtue of their cooperation, Kuyper and Schaepman were able to win the 'school struggle'. The result of their struggle was an article in the Dutch constitution acknowledging the right to found and to organize denominational schools. Kuyper and Schaepman also secured state funding for denominational schools on a par with funding for state schools. Through cooperation with the socialist party, and with occasional support from the liberals, the Protestant and Catholic parties also contributed to the development of a system of social laws.

In 1980 the Protestant Antirevolutionary Party (and another small Protestant party, the Christian Historic Union) and the Roman Catholic State Party decided to unify into a single Christian Democratic Appeal, with about fifty seats in parliament or one-third of the total number of 150 seats. The Social Democratic Party had about the same number of seats then, while the liberals had between twenty and thirty seats. The political landscape has since changed. As a consequence of increasing secularization and declining church attendance, the Christian Democratic Appeal has lost much of its electoral support. For more than hundred years the Protestant and Catholic party, later the Christian Democratic Appeal, took part in government (and they provided the prime minister on many occasions). It was seen as exceptional when, from 1994 until 2002, the Netherlands had a government coalition of social democrats and liberals without any involvement from the Christian Democratic Appeal. As of 2010, the Christian Democratic Appeal is only the fourth-largest political party in the Netherlands, with twenty-one seats in parliament (2012: fifteen seats), lagging behind the largest, liberal party (VVD), the social democrats (PvdA), and the right-wing Party for Freedom (PVV). Moreover, there are several smaller parties: a green party, a radical socialist party, and two orthodox Christian parties.[1]

Next, I would like to explain what worldview or religious ideas underpin the Christian Democratic Appeal. Since the party is a coalition between Protestants and Catholics, both Protestant and Catholic ideas will be discussed.

2. Catholic Ideas of Solidarity and Subsidiarity

Like Thomas Aquinas, the Catholic Church teaches that human beings are by nature social beings; they are created to live alongside each other. In the Catholic social philosophy there is a logical and a historical order: first individual human beings, then social associations, and then the state as the supreme and most perfect secular community. Although the state comprises private

[1] On the party-political landscape in the Netherlands, see the chapter by Paul Lucardie in this volume. The chapter by Evert-Jan Brouwer discusses the SGP, one of the two small orthodox Protestant parties in the Dutch parliament.

associations, human beings have existed longer than the state, and thus families and other associations are ontologically and historically prior to the state. This implies a rejection of any individualist-liberal view of society because, according to their social nature, human beings should demonstrate solidarity and cooperation within both their associations and the state.

Solidarity is an important principle of Catholic social philosophy. It should be understood from the metaphysical (or Thomist) background to this philosophy that our world has been created not as chaos but as a cosmos: a designed and therefore well-ordered reality in which all things are connected and have their meaning and value in relationship to the whole. This idea of creation implies that solidarity has an ontological foundation. It is not based primarily upon personal sympathy or upon an exhortation to brotherly love; rather, it implies that such sympathy and such love should bear witness to the ontological order. Thus, solidarity is a precondition for cooperation. Several papal encyclicals acknowledge, for instance, that capital cannot exist without labour, and that labour cannot exist without capital. Moreover, one social class cannot exist without the other. All classes should cooperate, and thus the socialist class struggle must be rejected.

Closely connected to solidarity is the idea of subsidiarity, which is often associated with a corporate social structure. Industries, occupational groups, trade unions and employers' organizations, like other private associations, should assert their rights and acknowledge their responsibilities (encyclical *Quadragesimo Anno*, § 83). However, if a private association cannot successfully assert its own rights and perform its duties the state should have a right to intervene based upon the principle of subsidiarity (to assist, to accomplish or to substitute: *Quadragesimo Anno*, §§ 79, 80). The Catholic worldview is reflected in this idea of subsidiarity because, from the Catholic perspective, the well-ordered reality is characterized by a hierarchic order. The Catholic church is, in religious and moral affairs, superior to the state, while the state as an all-embracing whole is superior to other social associations. However, notwithstanding this hierarchic order, the responsibility of individual human beings and their associations has primacy. Human beings are members of these associations, which in their turn constitute society at large; and society is organized from bottom to top. Only as a last resort should the state intervene at lower levels of the hierarchy.

One exponent of contemporary neo-Thomist philosophy is the French philosopher Jacques Maritain (1882–1973), who exerted a powerful influence upon Catholic political thought in the Netherlands. He argued that the state is the most perfect society endowed with the task of maintaining the rule of law and promoting the common good. However, in Maritain's opinion, within the hierarchic social order the state should acknowledge the autonomy of its associations; every association is self-governing, enjoying its rights and discharging its duties in addition to acknowledging its responsibilities. However, if those associations cannot achieve full autonomy, the state should provide assistance so that they can manage their own affairs (Maritain 1951: 9–13). Thus, subsidiarity means primarily that the state should create conditions to preserve the integrity of its component parts so that citizens and their private associations can enjoy their rights and discharge their responsibilities. If those conditions are inadequate, the state should take over the role of the private associations for the common good.

After corporatism had been introduced in the Fascist Italy of Mussolini, the word 'corporatism' became suspect. In the Fascist system, corporations were regarded as subordinate to the state, which restricted their freedom according to its dictatorial policy. However, the Catholic idea of corporatism has nothing to do with state corporatism of that kind because it begins by acknowledging that the rights and responsibilities of private associations are not alienable to the state. In contemporary Catholic thought, the hierarchic social order is organized from bottom to top.

3. The Calvinist Idea of Sphere Sovereignty and Social Structure

At the end of the nineteenth century Calvinism was revived in the Netherlands, in a movement inaugurated by Abraham Kuyper, the founding father of Dutch neo-Calvinism. He was the founder of the Antirevolutionary Party (1879), the first Christian political party in the Netherlands. He was the inspiration in the struggle for free denominational schools, and he established the Reformed Vrije Universiteit (Free University, 1880) in Amsterdam.

'Sphere sovereignty' is the title of Kuyper's inaugural address at the Free University, founded because the policy for state universities in the Netherlands, particularly the appointment of professors, was at that time dominated by the government. Kuyper's proposal was that his Free University should be free from interference, whether from the state or from any church. It was to enjoy the right to organize its own teaching and research activity. Moreover, all private associations were to be be invested with their own rights and responsebilities.

Kuyper derived his defence of the concept of 'sphere sovereignty' from neither the liberal nor the socialist tradition. He referred explicitly to the ideals of liberty which had been developed and implemented in sixteenth- and seventeenth-century European Calvinism. The Huguenots in France, the nonconformists in the United Kingdom, and the founding fathers in North America had elaborated upon those ideals. Unlike many liberals, they defended not only the fundamental right to individual freedom but also the right to freedom of association. Unlike socialists, they did not believe that it was for the state to grant freedom of association; instead, they held that the government was obliged to acknowledge the right of association (as a reality *sui generis*). Kuyper argued that early Calvinism was the cradle of Western democracy.

According to Kuyper, sphere-sovereignty is based on the idea that God is the Creator of a world that is a well-ordered reality and that differentiated social associations are a part of this ordered reality, or 'creation order'. Further to that, 'sphere sovereignty' is founded on a recognition that God is the absolute sovereign to whom all other forms of authority are subordinate. Unlike the Thomist philosophers, Calvinists do not believe that any church is superior to the state nor do they believe that the state is superior to other associations. Although churches and other social institutions and associations function within the state domain and must obey the state's laws, the government must concede as a matter of law the rights and liberties of those institutions and associations. All have their unique rights and responsibilities. No association is self-sufficient, neither does it have power over other associations, so that society should be characterized by a non-hierarchical social order. In Kuyper's opinion, society is a unity that preserves the integrity of the parts. This Calvinist view of social reality in reflected is Kuyper's defence of the concept of 'sphere sovereignty':

> In a Calvinistic sense we understand hereby that the family, business, science, art, and so forth are all social spheres, which do not owe their existence to the state, and which do not derive the law of their life from the superiority of the state, but obey a high authority within their own bosom; an authority which rules by the grace of God, just as the sovereignty of the state does. (Kuyper 1899: 116; see also 123–7)

Kuyper acknowledged that his idea of 'sphere sovereignty' involves a sharp distinction between the state and civil society. Private associations belonging to each of those social spheres have their own sovereignty, authority and freedom which are not derived from the competence of the state. These private associations should assert their proper authorities and freedoms to promote their private interests. The state should acknowledge these authorities and liberties and not intrude. On the other hand, private associations contribute to the development of public policy. Private associations are often perceived as special-interest groups. Kuyper argued, however, that from their special interest they also should contribute to the public interest.

According to Kuyper, the law must acknowledge the rights and liberties of citizens and their private associations against the abuse of power by the government and other institutions. Although he wrote about the concept of 'sphere sovereignty' in relation to civic associations, which are characterized by their own authority, he also wrote of these spheres as a 'palladium of our liberties' (1899: 141).

Kuyper's neo-Calvinist political philosophy is powerfully anti-liberal, because he rejected the (Lockean) liberal idea of society as a collective of individuals. His political philosophy was also powerfully anti-socialist, because he rejected centralizing social policy on the part of government. However, he was deeply committed to ameliorating the deplorable situation of the working class and to addressing the social injustice (the 'social question'). On this issue, he wrote:

> Whenever one uses the phrase 'social question,' one recognizes, in the most general sense, that serious doubt has arisen about the soundness of the social structure in which we live. (...) This [social] question does not exist for you until you exercise an architectonic critique of human society, which leads to the desire for a different arrangement of the social order. (Kuyper 1991: 50–1)

While Kuyper argued that the state should reorganize society by introducing just laws, he acknowledged that the government was not the only agent in society. On the contrary, all citizens and communities were to be treated as agents in civil society in order to renew its structure. He phrased this appeal to all citizens as the principle of 'sphere sovereignty'. And now, since I have used the term 'civil society' on two occasions, I ought to explain it.

4. The Idea of Civil Society

The fall of the Berlin Wall in 1989 symbolizes the end of the era of communist rule over Central and Eastern Europe. Generally, it is seen as a victory for Western democracy and the capitalist economy. Many people in the West are easily satisfied with the superficial view that communism crumbled and that Central and Eastern European countries are now copying the Western democratic model and the capitalist economy. However, the revolution of 1989 signifies something more profound.

For many former dissidents in Central and Eastern Europe, the concept of civil society served as a model for social and moral reform. It related to social reform in that it created spheres of life in which people could reclaim responsibility for their social and physical environment. It also related to moral reform in the sense it restored moral values, so as to enable citizens to live with dignity. Thanks mainly to the initiatives taken by those former dissidents, democratic institutions could be installed in several Central and Eastern European countries. These institutions represent the idea of civil society.

According to the communist ideology, the economy was the foundation of society. All other sectors of society were dependent on the economy. Because of this, all means of production were placed in the hands of the state. The state wanted to give people what they needed, and it was argued that people could not achieve freedom and responsibility by themselves.

Since 1989, the governments of the Central and Eastern European countries have been searching for alternatives to state-run economies. The neo-capitalist ideology looks attractive because governments and inhabitants of the former Eastern Block countries are longing to achieve material progress. Some governments have introduced rapid economic reform. Their unadjusted application of the capitalist model is consistent in some respects with the communist ideology: the capitalist economic model is introduced by a government assuming that once the economic foundation is in place, the rest of society should follow more or less automatically.

Critics oppose this view of society and the economy. In the long run, they argue, the unadjusted application of the capitalist model and the functioning of the market will seriously affect the quality of society, since it lacks social cohesion and the moral values of civil responsibility and care, or indeed anything beyond self-interest. Critics argue that democracy cannot survive, and the economy cannot flourish, without the growth of civil society.

For the time being, readers can take the concept of civil society as a characterization of the 'architecture' of society: within national boundaries there are pluralist communities having their own rights, freedoms and responsibilities which differ from the state's own institutions. However, civil society is inadequately characterized by this pluralist structure. The essence of civil society is to do justice to dignity, freedom and individual responsibility, and as such it embodies a strategy for moral reform so as to promote a moral attitude to revitalize the rights, freedoms and responsibilities of pluralist communities (Research Institute of the Christian Democratic Party 1996: 11–32, 62–65, 95).

The origins of the idea of civil society can be traced back to more than one tradition in European civilization. In any case, civil society is not a product of liberal thought alone. Civil society is a result of the cultural development of Western Europe and Northern America, not over recent decades but over many centuries. It began at the time of the Reformation, and it has been influenced by the philosophers of the Enlightenment, by the French revolution, the industrial revolution, liberal and Marxian philosophers, and also by religious movements such as Protestantism and Catholicism. Nineteenth- and twentieth-century neo-Thomist and neo-Calvinist philosophers gave an account of the pluralism of civil society that they considered an adequate answer to the question about what kind of society we need.

However, it has been disputed that civil society has origins in religion. Hannah Arendt, for instance, argued that 'Christianity, with its belief in a hereafter whose joys announce themselves in the delights of contemplation, conferred a religious sanction upon the abasement of the vita activa to its derivative, a secondary position'. She also critically discussed the 'otherworldliness of Christianity' (1958: 16, 74). However, she overlooked the fact that both Luther and Calvin had introduced the concept of 'occupation'. They not only wrote about labour but they also had in mind differentiated occupations and responsibilities characterized by what Max Weber later dubbed 'innerworldly asceticism'. That is to say, they already had a concept of civil society.

Consequently, we can claim that the Catholic idea of subsidiarity and the Calvinist idea of sphere sovereignty give accounts of a diversity of responsibility in civil society. These Catholic and Calvinist ideas provide the rationale according to which we distinguish the rights and responsibilities of the state from the rights and responsibilities of private associations. They characterize the nature of the relationship between the state and private associations. However, we must ask how it is possible to prevent differentiated communities from precipitating social disintegration. In other words, we ask what makes a civil society a *society*, or what constitutes social cohesion.

5. The Catholic Idea of Social Cohesion

Maritain acknowledged that the concept of civil society is characterized by democracy. However, he argued that the word 'democracy' has a wider meaning than that which is found in many treatises on government. First and foremost, it refers to a general philosophy of human and political life and to a state of mind. Following Abraham Lincoln, Maritain defined democracy as a 'government of the people, by the people, for the people' (1951: 24). However, he knew from history that many of the theories of democracy that employ this device embody conflicting implications.

Maritain rejected Rousseau's idea of the sovereignty of the people. Although like Rousseau he resisted despotism and defended the people's rights and liberties, he rejected Rousseau's theory because it leans towards the totalitarian state. Rousseau had refused to recognize a deeper ground of political life than what was found in the people as a collective of individual human beings (Maritain 1951: 45–9). In addition, Maritain rejected the idea the state was sovereign, an idea implying that everything must bow before the will and the aim of the almighty state. He argued that there is no other right but the immanent right that is written down in law. The law is right not because its content is in harmony with principles of right but because it is the law. In Maritain's opinion, the sovereignty of the state entails the risk of centralization of power by the government at the cost of individual rights and liberties. In this case, the government becomes totalitarian, taking over many of the responsibilities of individual citizens, and thus it saps the vitality of society (Maritain 1986: 61).

In his own philosophy of democracy, Maritain discussed a pluralist type of democracy. Citizens who belong to a variety of autonomous social groups and associations participate in this type of democracy. However, it does not admit that the state is a superpower incorporating all authority and is able to impose its authority upon human life. It sustains the idea of a civil society requiring autonomous groups in possession of authority commensurate with their function to be invested with their proper rights and responsibilities. Moreover, citizens who belong to very different philosophical and religious creeds participate in a pluralist democratic state, and it is expected that they cooperate towards the common good (Maritain 1951: 11–12, 1986: 58–9). Maritain argued that a genuine democracy implies a consensus with respect to the public arena: '[I]t must bear within itself a common human creed, the creed of freedom' (1951: 109, 1952: 165–71), and this creed is not religious but secular or civic. Maritain criticized liberal theories that conceptualize democratic society as an arena in which all private conceptions of communal life are met without any shared conception of society.

This secular creed deals with practical principles or with a practical charter containing a legal structure, articles, and formal rules and procedures that together induce citizens to converge toward the political organization of a democratic state. After that, citizens can try to justify this practical charter from very different philosophical or religious outlooks. Moreover, Maritain argued that notwithstanding the diversity of worldviews the democratic sense should be kept alive by the allegiance of minds, no matter how various, to a moral charter. This moral charter or code of social and political morality deals, for instance, with the following items: people's social and political rights and liberties and their corresponding responsibilities; the rights and liberties of people who are members of a family or of associations, and the liberties and obligations of associations to the body politic; the government of the people, by the people and for the people; human equality, fraternity, mutual tolerance and respect, and the obligations of each person and the state towards the common good (Maritain 1951: 111–13). Moreover, Maritain also discussed a common ethos: the inner drive of both the secular democratic faith and the socio-political moral impulse to revivify the practical charter (1951: 145).

In short, Maritain discussed a practical charter for democracy and its theoretical justification, but argued that democracy should be consolidated by the secular faith in a common democratic concept and a moral charter, both of which are strengthened by an inner energy or common ethos.

When reviewing the theoretical justification for the practical charter, Maritain acknowledged that people maintain very different fundamental theoretical conceptions of democracy. He also acknowledged that neither the state nor any political party was able to impose a philosophical or religious creed. He therefore argued that these justifications 'must cling only to the common practical recognition of the merely practical principles upon which the people have agreed to live together, despite their diversity or the conflict between their spiritual traditions and schools of thought' (1951: 120–1).

These practical principles of agreement—the practical charter—are reduced to a mere series of abstract or formal formulas, Maritain thought, if they do not originate and derive their support from the citizens' philosophical or religious worldviews and moral motives. Therefore democracy have need of education: citizens should learn to make theoretical justification for those practical principles from their philosophical or religious convictions. By this justification, citizens also contribute to the implementation of the moral charter (1951: 121–2). This implementation of the practical and the moral charter will promote social and moral cohesion in a pluralist democracy. Otherwise, a pluralist democracy runs the risk of disintegration. The state should encourage citizens to develop their own diverse justifications of the practical charter in order to strengthen it, and to revitalize both the secular faith and the moral charter of democracy.

6. The Calvinist Idea of Public Social Justice

Kuyper argued that, no matter what form government takes, every government ought to be considered as 'God's servant' with an obligation to maintain social justice (1899: 105–6). Because of this religious calling, Kuyper rejected the Enlightenment idea of sovereignty of the people that underpinned the French Revolution. The revolutionaries opposed divine authority, and they refused to recognize any deeper ground of political life than that which is found in the people as a collective of individual human beings. Consequently, Kuyper rejected any individualist view of society (1899: 109–12).

Like Maritain, Kuyper also rejected the idea of the unrestricted sovereignty of the state. This idea means that everything is subordinate to the will and the goal of the all-powerful state and that there is no other right but what is enshrined in law. For Kuyper, the law was right, not because its content was in harmony with any principles of justice but simply because it was the law. This idea of the sovereignty of the state entails the risk of centralizing the power of the government at the cost of individual rights and liberties. In this case, the government would take over the citizens' responsibilities and would compromise the vitality of society (1899: 113–14).

As an alternative both to the idea of popular sovereignty and also to the idea of unrestricted state sovereignty, Kuyper presented his organic view of society. He argued that a nation is an organic whole comprising both individual citizens and also civic associations. Citizens should not only stand up for their individual rights and liberties but also for the rights and liberties of their civic associations. The government would be tasked with intervening if there were conflicts between the rights and liberties of individual citizens and those of civic associations.

In the 1930s, Kuyper's idea of 'sphere sovereignty' was extended philosophically by Herman Dooyeweerd,[2] who made a clear distinction between the state and civil society. On the one hand, he held that the state should always be guided by the idea of public social justice; on the other hand, he believed that there are differentiated associations within the domain of the state—namely families, schools, industries and churches—which should be distinguished according to their own nature, with their own rights, freedoms and responsibilities

[2] Dooyeweerd (1953–8). Like Kuyper, Dooyeweerd held that 'sphere sovereignty' has it basis in God's 'creation order'. This word was not used by Protestants in the sixteenth and seventeenth century, but it was introduced in the nineteenth century by the Lutheran theologian Adolf G.C. von Harlesz, who called marriage, family, and the state 'divine institutions'. Kuyper and Dooyeweerd did not restrict the 'creation order' to those institutions, but they had in mind a dynamic world order created by God which could be investigated through scientific and philosophical research. Like Augustine and Thomas Aquinas, Kuyper and Dooyeweerd admitted that the creation was governed by the *lex aeterna*. This eternal law should be understood as a dynamic force of divine wisdom that is effective in all things, actions and processes, and that concentrates everything in the Creator.

(Dooyeweerd 1953–8: 3.446). Dooyeweerd, *pace* Maritain, did not consider the structure of civil society as an hierarchic one in which the state is the highest level and private associations are the lower levels but, like Kuyper, he thought of it as non-hierarchical.

Dooyeweerd was apprehensive of the idea of subsidiarity because he interpreted the principle in accordance with the classic Thomist model, in which the state is regarded as the superior or all-inclusive secular community and private associations are regarded as its subservient parts. Dooyeweerd acknowledged another interpretation of subsidiarity, namely one that refers to the social order as organized from bottom to top, as Maritain had argued. However, Dooyeweerd maintained that in the Thomist view society is organized ultimately from the top downwards. He therefore concluded that subsidiarity would have no fundamental defence against state totalitarianism which continues to threaten society (Dooyeweerd 1979: 122–9).

Dooyeweerd's interpretation of subsidiarity was strongly influenced by an outdated Thomist view. He did not give an adequate account of the interpretation of subsidiarity in contemporary Catholic thought which interprets society from bottom to top and intends to circumscribe the power of the state for the sake of autonomous associations.

Dooyeweerd argued—and, I believe, rightly so—that the state should create conditions to promote the interests of science and the fine arts, education, public health, trade, agriculture and industry, popular morality, and so on (1953–8: 3.445–6). He acknowledged that the leading concept of a state promoting 'public social justice' requires government to take an active role in civil society. According to Dooyeweerd, this implies that the government should create conditions so that citizens and their private associations can assert their rights, discharge their duties, and acknowledge their responsibilities. If private associations cannot perform their tasks, he acknowledged that the state should ultimately do so for the sake of social justice. Thus, he acknowledged the gist of the idea of subsidiarity. Although we can point to the influence of different philosophical traditions in contemporary Catholic and neo-Calvinist thought in the idea of civil society, the differences between subsidiarity and 'sphere sovereignty' are only marginal. In practical politics, as in the Dutch Christian Democratic Appeal, in which Catholics and Protestants have combined, this difference is non-existent.

Kuyper's and Dooyeweerd's ideas on freedom and authority are compatible with those of Maritain. Maritain's idea of autonomy in differentiated social communities and Kuyper's idea of 'sphere sovereignty' are not compatible with either individualist or totalitarian social theories. Maritain (1971: 46) and Kuyper (1899: 141) characterized their theories of freedom as both communal and personal.

7. Conclusion

One of the questions posed at the beginning of this chapter, about the characteristics of pluralistic responsibility in civil society, can be answered in brief by the principles of subsidiarity and 'sphere sovereignty' that are embraced by the Dutch Christian democratic party as a template for the structure of society. Society consists of many different spheres of human involvement, each with its own specific quality, and each in need of its own autonomy and authority. Subsidiarity means that responsibility should be handed over to those most concerned, in order to meet the demands of solidarity and concern for the integrity of the earth.[3]

As an equivalent of subsidiarity and sphere sovereignty I want to introduce the modern sociological term 'functional plurality', which generally means that civil society contains multiform communities that are interrelated. The term 'functional plurality' has two specific meanings: (1) Membership of, and participation in, multiform communities mediates people's participation in society in general and specifically in politics. These activities inform, channel and mobilize people's opinions of public life, and as such they underpin it. People are not too divided to be able to sustain a coherent society. This coherence may be strengthened by a common ethos that underlies civic faith and democratic morality, which are the basis of a constitutional democratic state. (2) The state's attitude towards the revitalization of civil society and social cohesion should be characterized by its requirement to achieve public social justice in political practice. This means:

> The state should actively support citizens, their communities and organizations, by the rule of law, security and an international legal order, by upholding basic social standards, by providing infrastructural networks, energy, water supply, basic environmental standards, by creating preconditions for health-care, education, and by actively defending the interests of the poorest and most vulnerable groups in society. (Research Institute of the Christian Democratic Party 1996: 114–15)

I have now answered all but one of the questions posed at the beginning of this chapter. There is, however, one remaining question that I would like to discuss, namely what surplus value may the idea of multiform responsibility have above liberal and centralistic ideas of society? I have already briefly discussed liberal ideas about the structure of society. Liberalism, together with its neo-liberal variants, adheres to the individual human being as its 'ultimate value' and to the capitalist market model for the economic foundation of all sectors of society, including education and health care. Although liberalism aims to revitalize economic activities, in the long run the application of the capitalist model and

[3] See the Basic Programme of the Christian Democratic *European People's Party*, articles 142–151, in: Research Institute of the Christian Democratic Party 1996: 88–9.

the operation of the market will seriously impair the quality of society. In this model we recognize the potential for arbitrary authority, human exploitation, consumer fraud and environmental pollution, which are undermining social cohesion and the moral values of civil responsibility and care. That is, it will compromise the vitality of civil society.

On the other hand, the centralizing state is characterized by a 'hierarchical structure in which power is, for ultimate purposes, collected at a single centre' (Laski 1975: 149–50). Defenders of the centralizing state also argue for the priority of the state over individuals and their associations. In this model, the state does not have an adequate account of its rights and of the responsibilities of individuals and private associations; instrumentalism prevails, and the subordinate units are fully deployable, manipulable and expendable. According to the policy of a centralizing government, the subordinate units can be compelled to fulfil externally determined purposes. Laski adds that a centralizing state is 'both administratively incomplete and ethically inadequate'. According to him, the remedy is to acknowledge the empirical phenomenon of a socially differentiated society, of which this chapter has given a political-philosophical account.

References

Arendt, H. (1958): *The Human Condition*. Chicago and London.

Dooyeweerd, H. (1953–8): *A New Critique of Theoretical Thought*. 4 vols. Amsterdam, Paris, and Philadelphia.

——— (1979): *Roots of Western Culture: Pagan, Secular, and Christian Options*. Toronto.

Kuyper, A. (1899): *Calvinism: Six Stone-lectures*. Amsterdam and Pretoria.

——— (1991): *The Problem of Poverty*. Ed. J.W. Skillen. Washington, DC and Grand Rapids, MI.

Laski, H.J. (1975): 'The Pluralist State' (1921). In: D. Nicholls, *The Pluralist State*. London.

Maritain, J. (1951): *Man and the State*. Chicago.

——— (1952): *The Range of Reason*. New York.

——— (1971): *Freedom in the Modern World*. New York.

——— (1986): *Christianity and Democracy*. San Francisco.

Research Institute of the Christian Democratic Party (1996): *Dignity and Truth: Civil Society and European Cooperation*. The Hague.

Wolfgang Huber
Christian Responsibility and Communicative Freedom
A challenge for the future of pluralistic societies. Collected essays, edited by Willem Fourie
The public role of religion continues to be a complex and controversial topic. In a career spanning nearly five decades, Wolfgang Huber has written extensively on the role of Christian ethics in societies across the globe. This collection of essays provides an introduction to his thought and access to some of his most important and thought-provoking essays. He continues to engage issues of both local and global importance at institutions in a number of countries, currently as Guest Professor at the University of Stellenbosch in South Africa.
Theology in the Public Square – Theologie in der Öffentlichkeit, vol. 5, 2012, 216 pp., 29,90 €, br., ISBN-CH 978-3-643-90239-9

LIT Verlag Berlin – Münster – Wien – Zürich – London
Auslieferung Deutschland / Österreich / Schweiz: siehe Impressumsseite

Janez Juhant, Bojan Žalec (Eds.)
Reconciliation
The Way of Healing and Growth
The book considers reconciliation from various points of view: biblical foundations of reconciliation, philosophical aspects, Girardian and Bonhoefferian reflections on reconciliation, intellectual and (post)totalitarian history, psychotherapeutic approaches ... The authors consider reconciliation also in very concrete (historical) contexts (Hungary, Russia, Slovenia, Islam and Christianity). Despite some disagreements, their common message is clear: human history and present times are covered with blood, suffering (of innocent victims) and negative emotions. Hence the only acceptable way is cultivation of the culture of reconciliation. Read the book to find out how.
Theologie Ost – West, vol. 16, 2012, 304 pp., 19,90 €, br., ISBN-CH 978-3-643-90202-3

LIT Verlag Berlin – Münster – Wien – Zürich – London
Auslieferung Deutschland / Österreich / Schweiz: siehe Impressumsseite